S0-DTI-452

Paving the Way

Paving the Way

Contributions of Interactive Conflict Resolution to Peacemaking

Edited by Ronald J. Fisher

JZ
6045
·C66
2005
West

LEXINGTON BOOKS
Lanham • Boulder • New York • Toronto • Oxford

LEXINGTON BOOKS

Published in the United States of America
by Lexington Books
An imprint of The Rowman & Littlefield Publishing Group, Inc.
4501 Forbes Boulevard, Suite 200, Lanham, Maryland 20706

PO Box 317
Oxford
OX2 9RU, UK

Copyright © 2005 by Lexington Books

All rights reserved. No part of this publication may be reproduced,
stored in a retrieval system, or transmitted in any form or by any
means, electronic, mechanical, photocopying, recording, or otherwise,
without the prior permission of the publisher.

British Library Cataloguing in Publication Information Available

Library of Congress Cataloging-in-Publication Data

Contributions of interactive conflict resolution to peacemaking / edited by Ronald J.
Fisher.
    p. cm.
  Includes bibliographical references and index.
  ISBN 0-7391-0674-0 (cloth : alk. paper)
  1. Mediation, International—Case studies. 2. Conflict management—Case studies. 3.
Pacific settlement of international disputes—Case studies. I. Fisher, Ronald J.
JZ6045.C66 2005
327.1'72—dc22   2004020885

Printed in the United States of America

∞™ The paper used in this publication meets the minimum requirements of American
National Standard for Information Sciences—Permanence of Paper for Printed Library
Materials, ANSI/NISO Z39.48–1992.

To the pioneers of unofficial peacemaking,
whose insight and courage have shown the way forward

Contents

Preface

The idea to produce an edited collection of successful cases of Interactive Conflict Resolution has been in my head for some time, more distinctly since writing my 1997 book on the method, and thereby finding that documentation and assessment has been both limited and scattered. There was clearly a need to pull together a study of well-executed interventions in ICR, and to attempt to distill out the characteristics of successful practice.

Another agenda behind this book is political—to continue the educative and persuasive processes required to impress upon realist academics and practitioners the point that unofficial, relationship-oriented methods have much to offer international conflict management, even in this era of the continuing use of violence. Realist academics have studied traditional methods of intervention (through interviews, memoirs, and other accounts), and have declared that approaches such as power mediation have considerable efficacy—a not-too-surprising conclusion, given that these methods and the use of force that backs them up define the very world in which they operate—a self-fulfilling prophecy that continues to create a dangerous reality. Therefore, as a counterbalance, unofficial methods also require their academic champions, who analyze successful work that makes a contribution to achieving a more peaceful world.

This collection brings together in one analysis the strongest available evidence of successful transfer effects from unofficial third-party work to official peacemaking. The enterprise is based on a premise of complementarity between unofficial and official approaches, working independently but in a coordinated and respectful manner toward peaceful, sustainable outcomes. The cases are drawn from different time periods in the brief history of ICR, from the first pioneering and seemingly audacious effort of John Burton and his colleagues to address the Malaysia-Indonesia conflict of the 1960s, to the successful track-two contributions of Edy Kaufman, Saúl Sosnowski, and others, to the official processes that brought peace between Peru and Ecuador in the late 1990s. In between these two interstate anchors, there are seven cases that address a variety of internal conflicts, which range from Lebanon to Tajikistan, and from Mozambique to Moldova. These conflicts share a protracted, violent nature and resistance to traditional methods of conflict management. In each case, unofficial interventions made contributions that helped pave the way, in varying degrees, to successful peacemaking, not all of which have reached full fruition.

Success, it is said, has a thousand fathers, while failure is a bastard. Thus, many actors claim some credit for the accomplishments toward peace described in the nine cases. The actual degree to which unofficial efforts contributed to successful outcomes is unknowable in a complex field of multiple influences. Nonetheless, the analysis herein should be compelling in terms of its argument that ICR has arrived on the world scene in a serious manner and deserves increased recognition and support in order to make its unique contributions to international conflict resolution.

An undertaking of this magnitude requires the acknowledgment and expression of appreciation to many contributors, not the least of whom are the chapter authors. They are very busy people, typically stretching their professional agendas to work toward the integration of theory, research, and practice in the field of conflict resolution. I want to acknowledge their willingness to set aside precious hours and complete the chapters contained in this volume. The diversity and depth of their contributions is a testament to the strength and potential of the field. Permission to reprint figure I.1 from Ronald J. Fisher, *Interactive Conflict Resolution*, Syracuse University Press, 1997 is also gratefully acknowledged.

I also want to acknowledge the influence of Alexander George on this volume, although he played no direct role in its creation. I served with Alex on a study committee on International Conflict Resolution at the National Research Council in the mid-1990s, and I was struck by his commitment to bring the best of social scientific thinking to bear on the very practical challenge of improving policy and practice in international affairs. Moreover, his lucid articulation of the method of structured, focused comparison served as my primary guide in completing the analysis on which the book's conclusions are based.

The completion of any major scholarly work, it has been said, requires 1 percent inspiration and 99 percent perspiration. In completing this task, I want to thank Serena Krombach, Editorial Director at Lexington Books, for her support and guidance through the entire process of bringing this work to fruition. I believe that Lexington Books is serving a rare and valuable role in publishing scholarly work, while many houses are now only interested in textbooks that bring a significant commercial return. Turning a rough manuscript into a polished presentation is a formidable task, and I express much appreciation to Deanna Bearden, my editorial assistant, for a diligent and conscientious effort that was always performed in an expeditious and cheerful manner. And lastly, I express my deep appreciation to my wife Carol, who understands that some of us are driven to efforts like this in hopes of a more peaceful world.

Washington, DC, July, 2004   Ron Fisher

Introduction

Analyzing Successful Transfer Effects in Interactive Conflict Resolution [1]

Ronald J. Fisher

Definition of Interactive Conflict Resolution

Increasing attention in the field of international conflict resolution is directed toward a variety of unofficial, facilitated interactions between antagonists in violent and protracted conflicts of both an intrastate, often ethnopolitical, nature and an interstate character. Such interventions are increasingly being directed toward all levels of such conflicts, involving high-level influentials who have the ear of the leaderships, mid-level influentials from a variety of sectors, who can influence policy making and/or public opinion, and grassroots leaders, who are essential in shaping public attitudes and peacebuilding initiatives on the ground. While it is now close to impossible to track and describe this profusion of unofficial activity, various strands of it can be separated out and focused on for purposes of description and evaluation.

One of the initial interactive approaches to understanding and resolving international conflict was pioneered by John Burton and his colleagues in the mid-1960s through his method of "controlled communication," later referred to as "problem solving conflict resolution" (Burton, 1969, 1990). Herbert Kelman soon followed in Burton's footsteps and fashioned a related theory of practice, initially with his colleague Stephen Cohen under the rubric of "interactive problem solving" (Kelman and Cohen, 1976; Kelman, 1986). Fisher (1972, 1983) proposes a generic model of "third party consultation," which captures the essential elements of the method through a number of components including the identity and role of the third party and the objectives of the method. These and other similar approaches have been more recently identified as "interactive conflict resolution" by Fisher (1997a), who reviews work from 1965 to 1995, and

1

provides definitions that capture both the seminal ideas of Burton, Kelman, and others, as well as some of the proliferation of related interventions that have followed.

A focused definition of Interactive Conflict Resolution (ICR), along the lines offered by Burton and Kelman, sees the method as comprising "small group, problem-solving discussions between unofficial representatives of identity groups or states engaged in destructive conflict that are facilitated by an impartial third-party panel of social scientist-practitioners" (Fisher, 1997a, p. 8). This variant is characterized by the high or mid-level of the unofficial yet very influential participants and by the identity of the third-party facilitators, who are scholar-practitioners able to bring knowledge about social conflict and expertise in small group processes to the interaction. Thus, the third-party panel is able to contribute to as well as lead the participants toward a shared analysis of the conflict, and is able to effectively facilitate the often intense and difficult interactions within the group. Theorists vary on the degree of knowledge about the specific conflict that the facilitators should possess, but the most common opinion is that they should have a good working knowledge of that situation and its context.

A broader definition of ICR casts it as "facilitated face-to-face activities in communication, training, education, or consultation that promotes collaborative conflict analysis, problem solving, and reconciliation among parties engaged in protracted conflict in a manner that addresses basic human needs and promotes the building of peace, justice, and equality" (Fisher, 1997a, p. 8). This wider net includes interactions between antagonists from all levels of society, from the grassroots to the leadership, and provides a wider set of identities and roles for the third-party interveners. It would encompass, for example, dialogue at the community level with neighborhood residents from conflicting groups facilitated by skilled practitioners who have little formal knowledge about conflict etiology and dynamics. It could include training workshops in the concepts and skills of conflict analysis and resolution, which bring together participants from contending collectivities in interactions that may only at times focus on the relations between their groups. In this case, the third-party facilitators may have generic knowledge of conflict, but limited knowledge of the conflict from which the participants come. As another example, third parties may organize intergroup educational activities, more structured and information-laden, with the intent of broadening and informing the attitudes that members of the groups hold toward each other. And, as a final example, third parties may consult with members of the groups separately, conveying perceptions and options between them, and offering potential avenues for further analysis or problem solving that the parties might find useful. All of these variants can be considered as forms of ICR broadly defined, and many of them as currently operationalized are in need of detailed documentation, which preserves the sanctity and confidentiality of the intervention process, but which allows the broader field of conflict resolution and its various stakeholders to appreciate and evaluate the profusion of work that is being carried out.

The focused approach to ICR carries a number of other characteristics that are essential to its understanding and successful implementation, and germane to the question of transferring effects from the unofficial to official domains. First, it is a quiet yet not a secret back-channel approach, which does not seek publicity, but is quick to explain its purpose as an analytical exercise designed to increase mutual understanding of the conflict among unofficial influentials that might assist in charting broad directions toward peaceful outcomes. It offers to the leaderships of the parties, an informal, low-risk, neutral, and noncommittal forum, where people they trust can engage in an exploratory analysis geared to joint problem solving, which just might create some ideas that could point the way out of their mutually destructive mess, while assuring that their basic needs are addressed. Thus, the method can be cast as potentially serving useful prenegotiation, paranegotiation, or post-settlement functions, depending on the stage of official interactions. In other words, the initial rationale behind ICR was to develop alternative forms of interaction, which could be complementary to official negotiation and settlement implementation. The question is therefore immediately raised about the transfer process—that is, how effects (e.g., attitudinal changes, new realizations) and outcomes (frameworks for negotiation, principles for resolution) are moved from the unofficial interventions to the official domain of decision and policy making.

Intentions and Rationale for Transfer

The pioneering contributors to the field of ICR expressed definite, albeit differing, ideas about the transfer process, particularly as it involved contributions to official negotiations. Burton (1969) considered controlled communication to appropriately occur at a stage prior to negotiations and to focus on an exploration of the relationship between the parties with a view to revealing the underlying causes of the conflict. He was at pains to point out, as with all theorists of the method, that the interactions did not involve bargaining over positions and issues, even though preconditions for agreement might be established. Once the outcomes of problem solving had accrued, Burton's approach downplayed the role of negotiations, seeing these simply as a discussion of administrative details and planning required to act on and implement the analysis and options produced in the unofficial interactions. For this purpose, discussions would be transferred to the official level (Burton, 1987). With the advent of needs analysis into Burton's theorizing, he became even more dismissive of official negotiations, in the sense that "deep-rooted conflicts" based in the frustration and denial of basic human needs are not negotiable and cannot be satisfied through compromise, thus rendering negotiation irrelevant (Burton, 1990). At the same time, it is expected that the satisfiers of basic needs are open to negotiation, in that various forms and combinations of satisfiers would be included in agreements between the parties in a manner that would satisfactorily address their basic needs.

Kelman, in contrast to Burton, has always acknowledged the essential role of negotiations in resolving ethnopolitical and other conflicts, and has stressed the complementarity of unofficial interactions to the official domain. Kelman and Cohen (1976) clearly stated that the problem-solving workshop was not intended as a substitute for negotiations, but could be complementary to the official track at all stages of the settlement process. Kelman (1992a) particularly stressed that the communication process of interactive problem solving could help the parties (through transfer from participants) to overcome the common barriers to entering negotiations, to reaching agreement, and to changing their relationship in the post-agreement phase. From his long experience in applying problem solving to the Israeli-Palestinian conflict, Kelman is able to identify a range of specific learnings that participants have acquired and communicated to their publics or leaderships—for example, insights into the other's priorities, rock-bottom requirements and areas of flexibility. On a broader scale, Kelman (1995) identifies three ways that his work on the Israeli-Palestinian conflict contributed to the 1993 breakthrough captured in the Oslo agreement: 1) the development of cadres of past participants who were prepared to negotiate productively, and did so, through their subsequent involvement as negotiators or advisors, 2) the provision of substantive inputs to negotiations through the sharing of information and the formulation of new ideas, and 3) the development of a political atmosphere favorable to negotiations and to a new relationship between the parties. The fact that subsequent policies and actions on both sides of this conflict have squandered the opportunities provided by Kelman's work and the Oslo agreement should not discount the contributions that were made up to that point in time.

Embedded in the positive intentions for transfer articulated by Kelman and other scholar-practitioners is a logical and psychological rationale explaining why the activities and effects of ICR workshops should help pave the way toward constructive negotiations. Building on the work of Kelman as a prime example, Fisher (1989) articulated a rationale for how ICR can enhance the potential for successful negotiations in situations of protracted ethnopolitical conflict. The typical processes and outcomes of workshops are deemed to include more open and accurate communication, more accurate and differentiated perceptions and images, increased trust, and a cooperative orientation, all of which may be transferable to official interactions. Such changes in attitudes and orientations are seen to underlie the "perceptual shift" that has to occur for parties to consider entering into negotiations. In addition, positive changes in attitudinal and relationship variables should encourage parties to sustain the negotiation process through its many impasses and turning points. The design requirement that participants be influentials who have the potential to influence the leadership's thinking and policy making is essential to the rationale that such participants can persuade decision makers that a shift in perceptions of the adversary and in policy regarding negotiations is necessary to move toward resolution. As Fisher (1997a) points out, this also requires a shift in group norms among influentials and decision makers in the direction of sanctioning mutuality, reciprocity and cooperation with the adversary in order to move toward negotiation. In line with this rationale, it must be emphasized that a continuing series of workshops over time is necessary to induce and sustain such a perceptual shift, and that corresponding activities toward rapprochement at other levels of society are necessary to support the related shift in policy favoring negotiation. Furthermore, it is realized that the potential effects of transfer from a successful series of workshops are further affected by a multitude of variables and dynamics, which influence policy making, and thereby render prediction and evaluation extremely difficult. Nonetheless, it is essential for the field of ICR to bring forward a rationale for transfer and a conceptualization of how it may occur in order to support the claims that scholar-practitioners in the field have made.

A Model of Transfer

The question of transfer was handled in a straightforward fashion by Burton (1969), who maintained that the realizations and options generated in workshop sessions would simply move into negotiations on implementation details, partly because participants were very close to decision makers and partly because the solutions would be obvious. Kelman (1972) was the first to identify the ultimate goal of ICR as affecting policy making and also to acknowledge that the transfer process was complicated and difficult. He noted that transfer involved two basic elements: the changes in individual perceptions, attitudes and so on that participants experience, and the effect of these changes on the policy-making process. Similarly, Mitchell (1981) distinguished internal effectiveness, in terms of changes experienced by participants, from external effectiveness, by which the nature and course of the conflict are influenced. Between these two forms of effectiveness lie the thorny challenges of reentry, wherein participants returning from workshops are subjected to multiple forms of pressure to drop their new realizations and orientations, and the many difficulties of transfer, wherein a small number of influentials attempt to persuade decision makers that a sea change in modal thinking is required.

In spite of the complexity and difficulty of the transfer process, it is important to attempt to conceptualize, at least in general terms, how the outcomes of workshops might be fed into policy making. Fisher (1997a) has made an initial attempt to develop a schematic model of transfer within the context of the major constituencies and interactions that influence foreign policy in a situation of international (or intergroup) conflict (see figure I.1). The figure distinguishes be-

tween international politics—that is, government-to-government interactions—
and intersocietal relations—that is, interactions among all manner of transnational organizations and individuals, including the unofficial ones that occur
through ICR interventions.

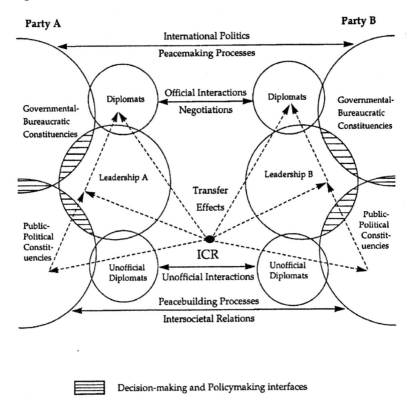

Figure I.1. A Model of Transfer Effects

The lines of transfer effects from ICR workshops run in three directions to
constituencies and groups that have input into policy making. Influential participants (writers, academics, political activists, etc.) can influence the thinking of
public-political constituencies through disseminating ideas and options, both to
the public at large and to think tanks, research institutes, study groups, and so
on. Participants who are informal advisors or representatives can influence the
leadership more directly to consider the perceptual shift required to initiate or
sustain negotiations. Some participants may be connected to the actual negotiation process itself, either as advisors or as members of negotiating teams. In this

case, the transfer is direct to the analysis and option generation that is integral to negotiations. These types of influences have occurred in cases of ICR that are regarded as making important contributions to the negotiation process, most notably in the work of Herbert Kelman and Nadim Rouhana (Israeli-Palestinian), Harold Saunders and Randa Slim (Tajikistan), John (A.J.R.) Groom and Andrew Williams and Irene Sage (Moldova), and Vamik Volkan and Joyce Neu (Baltic Republics and Russia) and their colleagues. The challenge is to adopt a method that draws on and at the same time transcends these individual case studies, and that identifies the commonalities in interventions and in the contexts of the conflicts that appear to be related to positive transfer effects. It appears that the method of comparative case analysis provides such a vehicle.

The Method of Comparative Case Analysis Applied to the Transfer Question

The comparative method of research has received considerable attention in the discipline of political science, particularly in the field of comparative politics, where it has been contrasted with the experimental and statistical methods (Liphart, 1971). However, the field of conflict resolution has made limited use of comparative analyses in comparison to experimental research and individual case studies. Rare examples include the Crocker, Hampson, and Aall (1999) analysis of multi-party mediation, Fisher's (1997b) treatment of commonalities across a variety of training interventions in ICR, Nan's (1999) comprehensive analysis of the coordination of conflict resolution efforts in three recent cases of ethnopolitical conflict, and Lewicki et al's (2003) content analysis of the frames that parties adopt in intractable environmental conflicts.

Essentially, comparative case analysis involves examining comparable cases to identify relationships among variables (George, 1979). Thus, it is necessary to identify what are considered to be independent, intervening (or contextual) and dependent variables, and to develop values or categories of variation for these. According to George (1979), the categories are not determined beforehand, but are developed inductively from the examination of how the variables vary in the different cases. This interpretation thus sees the method as an inductive approach to theorizing, in a manner consistent with Liphart's initial description of the comparative method as a means of "discovering" empirical relationships among variables. However, Liphart (1975) later tightened his interpretation to define the method as a means of "testing" relationships among variables, that is, hypotheses, and thus placed it on a plane of using the same logic as the statistical method. In a more recent discussion of the method, Faure (1994) contends that the comparative case strategy is really a small *n* version of the statistical (i.e., correlational) method, and that the basic logic is the same as that of experimentation. However, both the small number of cases and the inability to manipulate the independent variable render comparative case analysis much less powerful in determining causality. It is therefore best to see the present analysis as one of hypothesis formation rather than one of hypothesis testing.

The tack taken here is to see the approach as an inductive one, and to more or less follow the steps identified by George (1979) in the implementation of the method of structured and focused comparison. Thus, the class of events of interest are cases of successful transfer, which has to be prejudged, as opposed to cases of ICR regardless of outcome, that is, successful, unsuccessful, or indeterminate effects. Characteristics of the intervention, including differences in the interventions, are regarded as independent variables, while intervening or contextual variables are selected characteristics of the conflict deemed important by previous theorizing, for example, the stage of escalation. The dependent variables are different aspects of intervention success, that is, positive transfer effects. The comparative case analysis is therefore an attempt to discover relationships among these variables so as to identify what aspects of intervention under what conditions of conflict lead to successful outcomes in terms of transfer effects to official peacemaking. Thus, the exercise is designed to help develop explanatory theory that will account for constructive outcomes from ICR interventions. As such, the analysis is guided somewhat in the selection of variables and values by the existing theory of practice on what constitutes effective interventions (e.g., Azar, 1990; Burton, 1987; Fisher, 1997a; Kelman, 1992a; Mitchell, 1981).

In line with George's (1979) definitions, the analysis is both structured, in that general questions are used to guide the data analysis, and focused, in that it deals with only certain aspects of each case as represented in the questions. The task is to draw on an historical description and explanation for success in each case and to translate it into the variables that are assessed across all cases, thus inducing a theoretical formulation that generally accounts for positive outcomes. The challenge is to develop a theoretical framework that is adequately comprehensive to capture the main elements of the explanations of the different cases, and which thereby represents a causal explanation of the outcomes (George, 1979). However, in contrast to this optimistic, positivistic point of view, it must be acknowledged that ICR interventions are complex operations, taking place in an even more complex field of conflict affected by countless conditions, dynamics, and other forces that determine outcomes, all of which are subject to varying interpretations. Thus, it is difficult if not impossible to ascertain the effects of particular interventions (Keashly and Fisher, 1996). Nonetheless, by carefully studying selected cases, it should be possible to identify some of the characteristics and conditions that appear related to success, and thereby provide some guidance within a developing theory of practice.

To reflect the theoretical framework that will initially be applied to the cases, the researcher develops a set of general questions that express the "data requirements" to be satisfied in the analysis of the cases (George, 1979). These general questions should relate to the sets of independent, intervening, and dependent variables of interest, in this case, the nature of the intervention, the nature of the conflict, and the nature of the transfer process and outcomes. Table I.1 presents a list of general questions that were used to guide the case descriptions, direct the comparative case analysis, and to initially identify variables in the three sets that seemed to be relevant to the analysis.

Table I.1. General Questions for the Comparative Case Analysis

A. What was the nature of the conflict?

1. Who were the parties, including significant factions?
2. What were the parties' goals?
3. What is a brief history of the conflict?
4. What were the issues, positions, interests, and underlying needs of the parties?
5. What were the power relations and predominant form of interaction between the parties?
6. What was the stage of escalation of the conflict?
7. What indicators of intractability existed in the conflict?
8. What indicators of stalemate or impending catastrophe existed in the conflict?
9. What other elements of the conflict affected the appropriateness of the intervention?
10. What cultural differences existed among the parties and the third party?
11. What were the attitudes of the parties toward de-escalation and unofficial intervention?
12. In terms of timing, why did it seem to be an appropriate time to intervene?
13. What changes or events in the conflict affected the implementation of the intervention?

B. What was the nature of the intervention?

1. Who were the participants in identity, number, and connection to the official domain and to public-political constituencies?
2. What meetings were held in terms of number, duration, and frequency?
3. What was the setting in terms of neutrality, informality?
4. What was the agenda/topics for the meetings?
5. Who was the third party in terms of identity, knowledge, and skills?
6. What were the third party's role, primary functions, and relationship with the parties and the participants?

Continued on next page

Table I.1—Continued

7. What were the objectives of the intervention as seen by the third party and the parties?
8. What was the process of the meetings in terms of the nature of the discussions in establishing the necessary conditions of interaction (analytical focus)?
9. What were the perceived outcomes of the meetings in terms of effects on participants?

C. What was the nature of transfer?

---

1. What was the third party's rationale for transfer?
2. Who were the targets of transfer?
3. What were the mechanisms or lines of transfer?
4. What were the objectives of transfer?
5. How was the intervention complementary to official processes?
6. What was the nature of the transfer effects/products:
    a. New or innovative analyses, attitudes, interpretations or language?
    b. Creative ideas, directions or options?
    c. Concepts or documents, such as principles, plans, proposals, or frameworks?
    d. Connections through participants taking other roles such as advisor or negotiator?
7. How were the transfer mechanisms and effects evaluated?
8. What conclusions did the third party draw about transfer effects?

The general questions were translated into a list of variables for each of the three sets of variables (see conclusion). The development of the variables was a means of operationalizing the questions to provide for a more explicit and detailed analysis of the cases. In forming the questions and elaborating them through the specification of variables, I was guided by existing theories of understanding relevant to conflict analysis and by existing theories of practice relevant to conflict interventions. For example, stages of escalation (question A.6) were drawn from the composite model of conflict escalation developed by Fisher and Keashly, based in part on the work of other theorists including Quincy Wright, Morton Deutsch, and Friedrich Glasl. Indicators of intractability (question A.7) were drawn from the thinking of Peter Coleman, while indicators of stalemate and impending catastrophe (question A.8) were based on the ideas of William Zartman and Saadia Touval. Questions and variables relating to the nature of the intervention (questions B.1 to B.9) were drawn largely from my work on a model of third party consultation. On the nature of transfer, the development of variables was informed by my theorizing on ICR (questions C.1 to C.5), and was elaborated by drawing on the work of other scholar-practitioners, including Herbert Kelman, Nadim Rouhana, and Tamra Pearson d'Estree (questions C.6 and C.7) Thus, the comparative case analysis is well connected to the existing literature in the field of conflict analysis and resolution.

The plan for the book is to complete a comparative case analysis using the same set of variables for all nine cases described in the ensuing chapters, and to then draw conclusions based on the commonalities that emerge. Whether this analysis will add significantly to current knowledge represented in existing theories of practice remains to be seen, but at a minimum it will provide the first piece of detailed, analytical support for transfer effects connected to a wide range of cases in a systematic manner. It is also possible that the analysis will identify gaps or weaknesses in existing theories of practice, particularly around the nature of transfer. Based on the analysis of the nine cases and the commonalities of successful interventions identified, it is expected that a picture will emerge of what characteristics of ICR interventions tend to be associated with positive transfer effects. The hope is that these aspects can then be taken into account in the design and implementation of future interventions.

The Cases for Analysis

The cases of intervention described in the following chapters evidence variation on a number of dimensions, although all fit the focused definition of ICR, that is, where an external, unofficial third party facilitated conflict analysis and problem-solving discussions between influential yet unofficial representatives of the conflicting leaderships. The intention of the third party in every case was to make a contribution to the de-escalation and resolution of the conflict as well as to the improvement of the wider ongoing relationship between the parties.

The cases come from different time periods, from 1965 to 2000, and cover many regions of the world, including Asia, Africa, South America, the Middle East, the Caucuses, and Eastern Europe. Thus, the cases include a range of cultures in conflicts that have cultural, ethnic, racial, religious and/or ideological overtones, that is, which are identity-based. In contrast, the third parties are typically from modernized, Western cultures with nationalities mainly based in Europe or North America. Two of the cases are clearly interstate disputes (Indonesia-Malaysia-Singapore and Peru-Ecuador), both related to territory, while a third (Israeli-Palestinian) may continue to evolve toward an interstate conflict over time, although it is clearly based in identity and existential concerns. Six of the cases are internal conflict, either over the control of the government (Lebanon, Mozambique, South Africa, and Tajikistan) or the issue of the secession of a constituent part (Moldova-Transdniestria and Georgia-South Ossetia). All would be regarded as serious armed conflicts deserving of international attention.

Although the cases are varied and thereby illustrative of a wide range of applications, they cannot be considered as a representative sample of violent, protracted conflicts in general. Nonetheless, they do evidence common themes of intractability and apparent resistance to traditional methods of management, and this in part occasioned the use of innovative approaches to conflict resolution. Although the approaches implemented also vary on several dimensions, on this score, the cases provide a relatively good representation of ICR interventions, and thus a short history on the development of the method.

In chapter 1, Christopher Mitchell describes what appears to be the first documented case of the use of ICR, as applied to the mid-1960s conflict between Indonesia and Malaysia/Singapore, the latter entity becoming an independent state partway through the conflict. In this instance, a largely academic panel of social scientists led by John Burton, with national identities not entirely neutral in the dispute, created an approach as they facilitated a series of informal, seminar-style discussions with mid-level diplomatic representatives functioning in unofficial capacity. The conflict revolved around disputed territories that were incorporated into the creation of the Malaysian federation in 1963, much to the chagrin of Indonesian authorities, who supported local insurgencies and engaged in hostilities that continued through a U.S.-brokered cease-fire in 1964. The unofficial intervention thus occurred during a time of high tension, armed incursions, and the failure of traditional means of management, largely mediation by the U.K. and other actors. Although meeting in unofficial capacity, the representatives were in constant touch with their leaderships, and hesitatingly moved into the mutual analysis encouraged by the third-party panel. This process resulted in the correction of misperceptions, the reassessment of the motives of the enemy and the costs of the conflict, and the development of policy options directed toward resolution. It appears over a series of meetings and ongoing consultations with the decision makers, that the framework of a solution was developed in terms of broad understandings and the major heads of agreement. Along with elements of a changing context, including a coup in Indonesia, these innovative workshops are seen as contributing to the Peace Accord in 1966.

The Israeli-Palestinian conflict is an ongoing tragedy of major proportions, and has understandably garnered the attention of many official and unofficial actors. The genesis, escalation and continuation of this dispute provide one of the most dramatic and frustrating instances of violent, intractable conflict between different identity groups. The conflict has a long history, but became crystallized in 1948 with the establishment of the state of Israel and the expulsion and flight of hundreds of thousands of Palestinian refugees. A series of wars between Israel and its Arab neighbors have culminated in Israeli military dominance and continuing tension between Israelis and Palestinians, expressed in part through two Palestinian *Intifadas* or uprisings in the territories occupied by

Israel. Herbert Kelman, the author of chapter 2, and his colleagues have labored for over thirty years in addressing this conflict through his method of interactive problem solving, organizing and facilitating numerous small group workshops with increasingly influential Israelis and Palestinians. Kelman focuses on the most impactful period of his work in the 1980s and 1990s leading up to the Oslo accord, and notes in particular a continuing workshop with most of the same participants, which overlapped with the start of official negotiations in 1991 and had transfer effects to both these talks and the back-channel Oslo process. At the same time, the contributions to the realizations and principles incorporated into the Oslo accord drew from the entire flow of Kelman's workshops and from the resulting policy analyses by both participants and by Kelman as an engaged third party.

The long civil war that debilitated Lebanon serves as the backdrop for chapter 3, in which George Irani presents an illuminating analysis of the focus and the context of two problem-solving forums organized by the late Edward Azar, who founded the Center for International Development and Conflict Management at the University of Maryland. Azar and his colleagues organized two four-day workshops in 1984, which brought together several influential individuals representing the various religious/political factions (along a generic Christian/Muslim divide). The analysis of the workshops, which have been previously described in Azar's own writings, indicates how the intervention was situated in the overall political context, wherein Azar worked to maintain a relatively neutral stance on the ground in both Lebanon and in the U.S. capital. Irani's assessment presents a mixed picture. On the one hand, the workshops pointed the way to the general nature of an acceptable resolution and generated some elements that found their way into the eventual settlement. On the other, the workshop outcomes were five years removed from the Taif Accord, and dealt only superficially and in principle with the complex constitutional arrangements necessary to resolve the conflict. Thus, both in magnitude and in extent of transfer, this intervention has clear limitations, but it stands nonetheless as a courageous and instructive illustration of ICR.

In chapter 4, Andrea Bartoli of the Community of Sant'Egidio provides a fascinating account of how this little-known Italian religious NGO developed a sensitive and caring approach to fostering human relations and then used this approach to play a central role in bringing peace to the war-torn African country of Mozambique. Bartoli describes how the Community slowly built relationships with major players on each of the two sides, and then how it was able to provide a critical third-party role in bringing them together when conditions on the ground were propitious. The respectful and empowering attitude of the Community was essential in building a working trust (to use Herbert Kelman's phrase) with the parties, and in encouraging them to overcome the hostility and hatred engendered by a vicious, protracted conflict. A series of meetings with influential members and leaders of Frelimo and Renamo were necessary in order to build a base on which to launch a face-to-face dialogue process, which produced a joint communiqué demonstrating a commitment to the peace process. These dialogue sessions then "morphed" into the full-blown negotiations that produced a viable agreement. While the actions of numerous other players contributed to the peaceful and sustainable outcome, the role of Sant'Egidio appears to have been essential. Thus, Bartoli presents a unique case, which develops new elements within the theory of practice of ICR and thereby extends and enriches our thinking, while at the same time providing a successful instance of positive transfer effects.

The longstanding interracial conflict in South Africa, represented primarily by the African National Congress and Afrikaner-dominated governments, gave rise to fears of an eventual bloodbath that would add significantly to the world's list of ethnopolitical tragedies. The achievement of conflict resolution in South Africa is almost entirely due to the humanity and wisdom of the South Africans themselves, but there were some important roles played by outside parties. One such instance of positive intervention is described by Daniel Lieberfeld in chapter 5, who meticulously documents a little-known process initiated by a British mining company, Consolidated Goldfields (Consgold). With careful organizing and limited facilitation, the third party provided for a series of dialogue meetings between high-level ANC representatives in supposedly unofficial capacity and influential Afrikaners with direct links to the National Party government and its security apparatus. At considerable expense, Consgold hosted a dozen meetings in England from 1987 to 1990 at which ANC representatives and the Afrikaners explored each other's intentions, aspirations and preconditions for negotiation. In that context, the discussions developed the broad framework for a future settlement on matters such as the legalization of the ANC and constitutional protections for Afrikaner culture, education and economic activities. Thus, the sessions comprehensively explored and clarified each side's major concerns and positions as well as almost every issue that later became a focus of negotiations. Concurrently, the dialogue process increased mutual understanding, provided reassurances, built trust and enabled the visioning of a common future. Lieberfeld traces the networks of transfer in considerable detail, based on interviews and writings of the major actors, and makes a clear case that these semi-official interactions played a central role in preparing the way for successful negotiations.

One of the longest running and most impressive interventions in ICR is that of Harold Saunders and his colleagues in the former Soviet republic of Tajikistan. The author of chapter 6, Saunders followed a distinguished career in public service, including a key role in the peace treaty between Israel and Egypt, with a continuing involvement in unofficial peace work. After decades of engagement on U.S./Soviet (then Russian) relations through the Dartmouth Conference, Saunders along with American and Russian colleagues turned his attention to the struggling country of Tajikistan, which was ravaged by a civil war in 1992-1993 after the break up of the Soviet Union. Following a carefully constructed theory of practice, expressed in part as five stages of sustained dialogue, the third-party moderators have organized and facilitated from 1993 to the present a continuing series of sessions with high-level influentials from the government and opposition sides of the conflict. Saunders uses the concept of a multilevel peace process as a framework for assessing the transfer effects from the unofficial dialogue to the official peace negotiations and the subsequent reconciliation process. Significant transfer mechanisms included a number of documents that stimulated and supported official developments, the involvement of dialogue participants in later official interactions, and the development of NGOs to build civil society in Tajikistan. Thus, the Inter-Tajik Dialogue stands as a most compelling example of the utility of long-term, well-crafted ICR interventions.

In chapter 7, Andrew Williams provides a firsthand account of a series of problem-solving workshops focusing on the conflict between the former Soviet republic of Moldova and the breakaway region of Transdniestria. Working with a team of mainly academic third-party consultants from the University of Kent in Canterbury and the Foundation for International Security in London, Williams helped to facilitate a series of unofficial meetings between high-level officials and others, which moved from analyzing the conflict to producing constitutional options for the reunification of the country. Split by parallel declarations of independence and a brief civil war in 1992, the two sides remain at odds, even though there has been effective complementarity between the unofficial intervention and the official mediation effort led by the Organization for Security and Cooperation in Europe (OSCE). Williams describes three stages of contact from 1993 to 2000, focusing on the status of Transdniestria within a reconstituted Moldova and the various arrangements between the two entities, and culminating in a common state document, which is reproduced in its entirety in the chapter annex. Thus, the informal process not only instituted communication and built understanding and cooperation between the two sides, it also culminated in a creative solution to the conflict that may yet be implemented in some form when contextual factors, such as economic realities, are favorable to a resolution.

Another former Soviet republic that has experienced significant internal conflict is Georgia, with aspirations for independence being expressed by South Ossetia, Abkhazia and more recently Ajaria. In 1990, South Ossetia declared itself an independent republic, and armed conflict with Georgia broke out briefly before being controlled by Soviet forces in 1991 and a formal cease-fire in 1992. Susan Allen Nan in chapter 8 describes how a high-level conflict resolution initiative by the Conflict Management Group, with assistance from the Norwegian Refugee Council, contributed to the negotiation process between Georgian and South Ossetian officials. Through interviews with participants, third parties and others, Nan traces the effects of the workshops held from 1996 to 1998 (a mix of dialogue, conflict analysis, option generation and negotiation skills training) to the official negotiations mediated by the OSCE and Russia. The workshops began at a point when the official talks were stalled, and contributed to a resumption of negotiations and to their quality. Following four workshops, the two sides formed a joint Steering Committee in order to meet more frequently to reflect on and assess the ongoing negotiations. This initiative ended in 2000 due to a lack of funding and the two parties have yet to reach an agreement on the status of South Ossetia. Nonetheless, Nan concludes that the intervention made a number of contributions to the peace process in terms of improved relationships, a more effective negotiating process and the introduction of substantive ideas to help resolve the conflict. Hopefully, these effects will come to full fruition with the conclusion of a future peace agreement.

In the final chapter, Edy Kaufman and Saúl Sosnowski elucidate the significant contributions of an ICR intervention in the form of Innovative Problem Solving Workshops (IPSW) to the peace process that ended the border dispute between Peru and Ecuador. This longstanding conflict erupted in armed hostilities in 1995, stimulating intense diplomatic activity by the two parties and third parties involved through international agreements. Following the design rationale of the IPSW, influentials from the same sectors (academia, human rights, media) in the two countries were invited to what became a series of four workshops over a three-year period. Generally following the ARIA process developed by Jay Rothman, the third-party facilitators engaged the participants in conflict analysis activities and the generation of ideas in working groups to address the different elements of the conflict at both the official and the societal levels. The authors provide a detailed description of the workshop activities and how these were linked to negotiations and public initiatives in both countries that helped to build support for the momentum toward peace. Furthermore, the track-two process concentrated on peacebuilding activities to support the formal peace agreement in 1998 and to consolidate the peace through strategies such as joint economic ventures in the border region. Thus, this case stands as a broad effort directed toward multiple levels and sectors with the intention of facilitating an overall peace process that can be implemented and sustained.

In developing their case descriptions, the authors were encouraged to provide information relevant to the questions for analysis, and generally did so with some variation. In addition, authors were provided the freedom to describe each case in their own way, using section headings they preferred and drawing on various sources of information (written reports, interviews, direct experience) as appropriate. Thus, there is considerable variation in the style of presentation, and somewhat less so in the breadth and depth of information provided. In all cases, what follows is a rich and valuable portrayal of ICR at work on some of the world's most perplexing and costly conflicts.

Notes

1. Portions of this chapter were presented in papers at the Annual Convention of the International Studies Association, New Orleans, March, 2002 and at the Annual Meeting of the International Society of Political Psychology, Boston, July, 2003.

1

Ending Confrontation Between Indonesia and Malaysia

A Pioneering Contribution To International Problem Solving [1]

Christopher Mitchell

Introduction: The Background

There is no certainty about when or where the first application of problem-solving processes to the resolution of an intractable international or intercommunal conflict occurred. However, there can be little doubt that the series of meetings that took place in London during the winter of 1965-1966 represents at least one of the very first such initiatives—and a successful one at that. This pioneering effort was carried out by John Burton and his colleagues from University College, London, together with members of the Tavistock Institute's Human Resources Centre and colleagues from the University of Edinburgh and the London School of Economics. The focus of the series, which lasted from December 1965 to the early summer of 1966, was on the interstate dispute initially involving the governments of Malaysia and Indonesia, a bilateral conflict that became a trilateral one once Singapore broke away from Malaysia and became a separate and independent state in its own right.

Apart from its effects on the actual conflict itself, this series of workshops has an intrinsic importance in that it was, in many ways, the precursor of the whole range of informal and unofficial conflict resolution initiatives that gradually began to be employed on intractable, usually violent conflicts during the 1970s, 1980s and 1990s—initiatives variously labeled "interactive conflict resolution," "collaborative, analytical problem solving," "facilitated negotiations," "cross party dialogues," "interactive problem solving"—or, simply, "Track Two." The workshops were seminal in many ways. Together with a subsequent problem-solving workshop dealing with the conflict on Cyprus held in London in the autumn of 1966, the series offered a model of innovative procedures that could be used to contribute significantly to the resolution of conflicts previously deemed thoroughly intractable, or at best amenable only to temporary and fragile compromise, often backed up by the threat of Great Power coercion or large side payments from international institutions. This first initiative, by focusing with apparent success on the triangular conflict between Malaysia, Indonesia, and Singapore, provided both an initial success and a subsequent inspiration for all those who later struggled to have what became known as "Track Two" approaches to conflict resolution accepted as useful and legitimate adjuncts to formal and official "Track One" efforts to bring international conflicts to an end. For these reasons alone it is worthwhile to put on record a description of the workshops and to attempt to evaluate their impact on the conflict that was the subject of these early, exploratory efforts at problem solving.

There were a number of reasons why this pioneering initiative took place when and as it did, and for the choice of the particular South East Asian conflict as the focus of the efforts undertaken by what subsequently became known as "the London Group." Chief among them was John Burton's background as a senior Australian diplomat during the 1940s and 1950s, which partly accounted for his interest in the conflict that had arisen between Indonesia on the one hand and the new federation of Malaysia and Singapore on the other. The conflict, then known by its Indonesian title of "Konfrontasi," had involved low-level guerrilla violence, the imposition of rival economic sanctions, Indonesian withdrawal from the UN and a number of fruitless attempts to mediate the conflict using traditional diplomatic procedures.

The conflict seemed to be ripe for an informal intervention, and its attractiveness as a possible test case was enhanced by the fact that Burton knew personally many of the leaders involved. This personal knowledge dated from the time when he had been permanent head of the fledgling Australian Diplomatic Service. At that time, between 1945 and 1948, Australia had championed Sukarno's government as the legitimate representatives of a new state of Indonesia, during the anticolonial struggle against the Dutch.[2] Thus, Burton's regional credibility was high, and what was to become known in later years as "the entry problem" was considerably eased in this pioneering case.

Burton first floated the idea of addressing this confrontation as some kind of a test case to his colleague, Tony de Reuck, at a conference on *Conflict in Society* held at the CIBA Foundation in June 1965, characterizing it as an initiative to try out ideas from "the sociology of conflict" on a real-world case. In the autumn of 1965, the London Group, with Burton at its head, decided to try to organize an informal, low-key, and unofficial small group meeting of Indonesian, Malaysian, and Singaporean officials, together with a panel of social scientists, to try to help find a resolution for "Konfrontasi" by injecting some recent insights on the nature and dynamics of conflict into what were likely to be hostile, acrimonious, and difficult discussions. What sort of a conflict did they confront?

The Nature of the Conflict: "Konfrontasi" Examined

At first sight, Burton and his colleagues seemed to have chosen an elusive conflict on which to try out their new approach. Initially, Konfrontasi appeared to be a straightforward, if intractable, mixture of territorial rivalries over former British possessions in the Far East, arising from Britain's decision to establish a lower profile "East of Suez"; plus strong ideological differences arising mainly from Indonesian President Sukarno's stridently neutralist stance in the Cold War, together with his regime's sensitivity to possible remnants of imperialism in the region.[3]

The origins of Konfrontasi go back to June 1961, when the prime minister of the Malayan federation, Tunku Abdul Rahman, first suggested extending the federation by including Singapore, Sarawak, and Sabah in an enlarged federal association on their achievement of independence from British rule.

In Britain, reaction to the idea was positive, as it solved a problem about how the three British possessions might be decolonized in a viable form, yet with some British influence in the area retained. Hence, the British were happy with the joint Malayan-British announcement of the intention to form a new federation made in November 1961. For the Malayan government, the scheme offered a way by which the valuable *entrepot* of Singapore might become part of Malaya without creating a Chinese majority that would have challenged existing Malay political primacy.

However, the proposal was thoroughly inimical to the government of Indonesia, the leaders of which clearly regarded the territories in northern Borneo, "North Kalimantan" to Indonesians, as territory necessary to round out the boundaries of Indonesia, as well as being rightfully theirs. Furthermore, they saw the proposed Malaysian federation as little more than a screen for continued imperialist domination of the region. (This last impression was reinforced when arrangements for independence and British withdrawal clearly involved the retention of a British base in Singapore and a defense agreement between Britain and Malaysia.) The situation was further complicated by the fact that the government of the Philippines maintained a territorial claim to Sabah on the grounds that its original sovereign, the Sultan of Sulu, had only *leased* the territory to the British in 1878.

However, the main opposition to the establishment of the new federation came from Indonesia and particularly from President Sukarno, Foreign Minister Subandrio, and the minister of defense, General Nasution. The intensity of Indonesian opposition became evident at the end of 1962, when both Indonesian political leaders issued strong statements, which both condemned the proposed federation and supported an abortive rebellion in Brunei. The latter had started on December 8, 1962 but was suppressed with much loss of life by the intervention of British troops, planes and ships. Indonesian statements and warnings were matched by

military moves in the region bordering "British Borneo," all of which were preludes
to a sustained Indonesian political and diplomatic campaign, lasting from January
1962 to September 1963, aimed at preventing the enlargement of Malaya and the
incorporation of the northern Borneo territories into any new federation. The political phase of Konfrontasi had begun.

In spite of both Indonesian opposition and consequent regional efforts to find a
solution to the conflict, negotiations for the establishment of the new federation
proceeded in Singapore, London and Kuala Lumpur, although hardly at a rapid
pace. The last tricky financial obstacles to a merger between Malaya and Singapore
were finally cleared up by July 7, 1963 and the final agreement for the establishment of the new federation of Malaysia signed in London two days later. August
31st was set for the formal establishment of the federation.

In the event, "Malaysia Day" did not occur until September 16th, the delay being due to a subsequent agreement concluded at one of the peace conferences that
had been set up to try to reach an accommodation between Malaysia and Indonesia
and avoid an escalation of the conflict. Under the sponsorship of the Philippine
government, a preparatory foreign ministers' round table had been held in Manila
in June 1963, partly to try to reduce tensions between Malaya and Indonesia over
the new federation, and partly to begin discussions of Philippine President Macapagal's scheme for an even larger regional community, to be known as "Maphilindo."
Unfortunately, one tension-increasing result of these meetings was a clear mis-
apprehension between Malaya and Indonesia about whether it had or had not been
agreed there that Malaya would delay the creation of Malaysia until the people of
Sarawak and Sabah had been given a chance to "express their views" on the federation. Two days after the signing of the Federation Agreement in London on July 9,
1963, Sukarno sent a strongly worded protest to Kuala Lumpur, accusing the
Malayan leader of reneging on an agreement. At an emotional anti-Malaysia mass
rally in Jakarta sixteen days later he announced Indonesia's intention to "crush Malaysia," which he characterized simply as "a British project." In a last attempt to
prevent the whole conflict from becoming militarized, President Macapagal sponsored another summit conference between July 31 and August 5, 1963, again in
Manila, at which it was agreed that Malaysia Day would be postponed until the UN
Secretary General had had an opportunity to "ascertain" peoples' wishes in Sarawak and Sabah, Indonesia accepting that this need not involve a referendum.

Some six weeks later, the three agreements concluded on this occasion and
known collectively as "The Manila Accords" disintegrated in acrimony. UN Secretary General U Thant duly arranged to carry out his "ascertaining" mission to Sabah
and Sarawak and the resultant report, published on September 14th, stated that previous elections held there in 1962 and 1963 had been properly conducted in a free
atmosphere, and that a majority of electors had clearly expressed their desire to become part of the proposed Malaysian federation. With the publication of the UN
Mission's Report, and given the pressures for rapid progress on federation emanating especially from Singapore—ironic in view of Singapore's rapid exit from the

federation two years later—the new federation of Malaysia officially came into being on September 16, 1963.

Analytically, then, the structure of the conflict was basically one involving three primary parties—the governments of Malaya and Singapore joined initially as the federation of Malaysia (and at this time excluding any representatives from the territories in dispute); and the government of Indonesia. Secondary parties included the government of the Philippines and—more importantly—the government of the United Kingdom as the primary supporter of the Malaysians and the somewhat reluctant supplier of military assistance in defense of the federation. On the surface, the major issues appeared to be simply the possession of disputed territory, together with Indonesian fears about retention of imperialist domination of the region.

Conflict Dynamics and Timing the Intervention

From this point forward, Konfrontasi escalated rapidly and coercion and counter-coercion became the chief feature of ensuing interactions over the following months, although there were also a number of traditional diplomatic efforts to mediate between the adversaries.

Escalation and Enlargement

The formal establishment of "Malaysia" led to immediate Indonesian reactions. The inauguration was denounced by Indonesian leaders and anti-British and anti-Malaysian riots took place throughout Indonesia, with the British embassy in Jakarta being sacked and British residents threatened by indignant mobs. The Indonesian government announced trade and economic sanctions against Malaysia and the seizure of Malaysian property. Hit-and-run raids into Brunei and northern Borneo, which had not stopped throughout 1962 and 1963, now increased in numbers and extent. It became clear that most of the infiltrators had secure bases in Indonesia, were trained by the Indonesian army, and increasingly involved Indonesian "volunteers." Such attacks across the border continued in spite of a "cease-fire" announced by Indonesia on January 23, 1964 following a mediatory visit by U.S. Attorney General Robert Kennedy.

Following the September 1963 riots in Jakarta and the intensification of Konfrontasi, Malaysia broke off diplomatic relations with both Indonesia and the Philippines, and Britain began a process of reinforcing troops in northern Borneo to stem the increasing number of Indonesian incursions. In March 1964 the United States cut off aid to Indonesia, while in the same month the Malaysian Cabinet, alarmed by the increasing incidence of sabotage apparently by Indonesian agents or supporters, decided to call up all able-bodied male citizens between 20 and 28 for military service or civilian defense. President Sukarno's response was to proclaim a nationwide mobilization and to order Indonesian youth to register as "volunteers" to help crush Malaysia. It was reported in Jakarta that 21 million did so (Keesings Contemporary Archives, 1964).

The conflict escalated further in August 1964 when Malaysia took the dispute to the UN Security Council over Indonesian seaborne and paratroop landings in southern Malaya. The Council spent some time attempting to find common ground on which a settlement could be built, but they were unsuccessful in this as well as in their efforts to pass a resolution calling on the adversaries to refrain from the use of force. This was vetoed by the Soviet Union. In January 1995, however, President Sukarno withdrew Indonesia from the United Nations, and Konfrontasi continued into the summer and autumn of that year, with Malaysian-Indonesian relations at their worst possible level, with continuing if sporadic violence in Sarawak and Sabah, with an increasing toll on the resources of both countries and with no solution in sight.

Formal Peacemaking Efforts

This was the situation in the summer of 1965 when the London Group began to consider the possibility of a problem-solving initiative in respect of Konfrontasi. At the time, the chances of this new kind of process having any positive effect on the conflict must have seemed remote, no matter how innovative the attempt might prove. A considerable amount of traditional diplomatic effort had already gone into unsuccessful official, track-one attempts to mediate a compromise settlement. In total, four governments attempted traditional government-to-government mediation during the period 1963-1965. Curiously, the most active was the Philippine government of President Macagapal, which itself had a direct interest in Konfrontasi through its claim to Sabah and which had hardly rendered itself acceptable to Malaysia because of its refusal to recognize the new federation. However, these gaps in its credibility did not seem to deter decision makers in Manila and, quite apart from the three Manila meetings in 1963, the following year saw strenuous efforts by Dr. Lopez, the Philippine foreign minister, to arrange further joint discussions of the problem. These culminated in another tripartite meeting in Tokyo when Konfrontasi was at its height—unfortunately to no effect.

Other initiatives were launched by the U.S. government, in the person of Attorney General Robert Kennedy who undertook a round of talks in January 1964 to little avail; and the Thai government, which was relatively the most successful official mediator through the efforts of its foreign minister, Thanat Khoman. In November 1963, Thai efforts at a Colombo Plan ministerial meeting in Bangkok were abortive, but Khoman managed to arrange a tripartite meeting in Bangkok in February 1964 at the end of which Indonesia and Malaysia agreed to a cease-fire in northern Borneo and to its supervision by Thai monitors—which proved a frustrating and thankless task, even when a Thai-supervised, token withdrawal of Indonesian forces was agreed in June 1964—perhaps the sole positive result of the Tokyo Summit.

Finally, the Japanese government not only managed to maintain cordial relations with both Kuala Lumpur and Jakarta throughout Konfrontasi, but also played a major role in arranging and hosting the preliminary direct talks between Tunku Abdul Rahman and President Sukarno held in Tokyo in June 1963. Apart from hosting the tripartite talks a year later, however, Japan played little part in the conflict until April 1965, when Premier Sato dispatched a special envoy to Malaysia and Indonesia to seek both sides' agreement to attend, without any preconditions, a summit conference in Tokyo. In spite of initial acceptance by President Sukarno and a more cautious agreement by Tunku Abdul Rahman, the proposal broke down when Sukarno finally declined to attend, apparently because of strong pressure from the Indonesian Communist Party (PKI). This was to be the last formal diplomatic effort to mediate an end to Konfrontasi before the dramatic events within Indonesia from October 1965 onwards, and the efforts of the London Group to arrange an alternative approach to resolving the conflict.

The London Initiative

Efforts to interest the governments concerned in the possibility of a new and basically experimental approach to seeking a solution to their conflict took place during the autumn of 1965, a period which saw official efforts by British prime minister, Harold Wilson, to start formal negotiations in London rebuffed and official efforts to end Konfrontasi deadlocked. Burton and his colleagues then approached the British prime minister with a proposal that an informal initiative might succeed where official efforts had failed. Probably without much expectation of success Mr. Wilson agreed and three invitations were sent to the three conflicting heads of government, asking them to take part by nominating three close colleagues or friends as informal participants in quiet, non-publicized discussions.[4]

Clearly, approval was forthcoming and by the end of November the initiative had progressed to the point where participants had been agreed on (some from the local embassies and High Commissions in London), a date in mid-December set for the discussions and, largely through the good offices of its Deputy Director, Tony de Reuck, a site chosen at the London offices of the CIBA Foundation. The participants who eventually arrived at the CIBA offices on December 13th were assigned to the task by the central governments in each capital, through the formal invitations sent directly to President Sukarno, Premier Lee Kuan Yew and Prime Minister Tunku Abdul Rahman, who had all responded favorably to the requests. The Malaysian High Commission was represented by the Acting High Commissioner, Mr. Lim Taik Choon, although it seems probable that his duties only enabled him to attend these initial meetings sporadically and the Malaysian lead was taken by Mr. Mohammed Sopiee. The latter was a former journalist who held the post of information minister at the High Commission, but who was also a personal friend of Tunku Abdul Rahman. The Indonesian participants were Mr. Rachmat Sukartiko, First Secretary at the Indonesian embassy, and the Press Attache, Mr. R. Sukarno, a distant relative of the president. Finally, the Singapore High Commission also supplied a representative, Mr. K. C. Wan, who, in the event, turned out to be a close friend of Premier Lee Kuan Yew. As it transpired, the participants were hardly traditional diplomats, perhaps partly because of the recency of the establishment of diplomatic services in two of the countries. Reflecting later on this factor, one of the panelists commented on the ". . . unconventional backgrounds and trainings of the three principal government representatives . . ." going on to say that each of them ". . . had previous experience in revolutionary or political activities and also in some branch of social science or journalism or both . . ." and arguing that this produced a combination of ". . . deep practical insights with a keenly intellectual approach . . ." which very much aided the development of a common intellectual framework and exchange of ideas (De Reuck, 1966, p. 5).

The fact that Singapore was represented separately draws attention to one of the two major political events that had taken place in the conflict since the idea of discussions had first been considered. The first of these occurred in early August when, for reasons that go beyond the scope of this chapter, Singapore left the federation and established itself as an independent sovereign state, a move which had the effect of turning Konfrontasi, formally at least, into a three-party conflict. This structural change was, however, overshadowed by events in Indonesia during October and subsequently. On October 1st an attempted military coup in Jakarta was put down by troops who remained loyal to the Sukarno regime, and this was used as occasion for the army and the Indonesian population at large to turn on the PKI and virtually destroy it. Accounts of these events vary, but it has been estimated that over 500,000 people were killed throughout Indonesia (mainly Chinese and PKI members). It is certainly the case that Communist influence in the country ceased to be even a minor political factor, and to a large degree this also destroyed a significant part of President Sukarno's domestic support base. At the government level, Sukarno remained in power, but his position had been seriously weakened, especially vis-à-vis the Indonesian army. In the months that followed he became increasingly a figurehead with diminishing ability to influence events, except perhaps to delay them. I return briefly to the significance of these events for Konfrontasi below.

For the London Group, the immediate issue in early December was how many and which social scientists should sit with the participants as the "panel" supplying ideas from the "sociology of conflict" to help in an analysis of the issues at stake and possible solutions. In terms to be used later about such discussions, who would be the "facilitators" and what would be their specific "roles"? Again, it is necessary to emphasize the lack of any real precedent for such a meeting. All the London Group had to draw upon as models were the experiences of study groups and human resource interventions at the Tavistock Institute, the use of T-Groups (sensitivity training), mainly in the USA, some studies of unstructured group dynamics carried out by the CIBA Foundation, and some examples from the industrial relations literature about "problem solving" as opposed to "bargaining" groups.

In the end it was decided to construct a large and varied panel in the hope of covering a wide range of contingencies.[5] Apart from John Burton, Tony de Reuck as host clearly would take a major role and had also had useful experience in analyzing the structure and process of small group discussions. Two members of the Human Resources Centre at the Tavistock Institute were panelists, Dr. Fred Emery and Mr. David Barkla. Two social psychologists from the London School of Economics, Dr. Bram Oppenheim and Dr. Roger Holmes, participated, as did Dr. Roger Fisher from Harvard, who was on sabbatical leave at the LSE.[6] The panel was completed by two regional experts on Southeast Asia, Dr. Peter Lyon from the LSE and Dr. H. M. Lo from Australian National University, and by Mr. Jeff Newnham from University College. (Professor of Sociology, Tom Burns, from the University of Edinburgh also attended the discussions for one of the sessions.)

It is worth commenting on the composition of the panel in the light of the subsequently developed guidelines for workshop panels that they should not only be small and cohesive, but that they should not contain any individuals who might not be deemed disinterested or impartial. On this occasion, the panel of "facilitators" initially contained three Australians, whose government had sent troops to defend Malaysia in 1963; four from Britain, then supplying most of the military forces involved in Konfrontasi; one American, whose government had put pressure on Indonesia by cutting off aid and investment; and one panelist with a Dutch colonial background that might easily have become a source of unease and contention to some of the participants. To say the least, this was hardly a "disinterested" panel and it says much for Burton's personal credibility that the workshop took place at all, and for the attitudes and behavior of the panelists that the issue of impartiality seems never to have been raised.

Developing a Process

The next practical problem for the members of the London Group was what procedure ought to be used so that "social science analysis" might usefully be applied to this real-world conflict. In other words, what guidelines should be followed once the discussions had commenced. The members of the Group were more than aware that they were venturing into unknown country with few maps to help them. Looking back, de Reuck uses the phrase "hastily improvised, *ad hoc* techniques and procedures" to describe the processes that were adopted for the initial meetings that took place between December 13th and 17th (de Reuck 1966, p. 7) and subsequent accounts and recollections bear this out.

One contradiction between principles of seeking or imposing a structure on the one hand, and on the other of allowing the discussions to flow freely in directions that seemed fruitful arose and remained strong throughout the week. On the first morning of the week's discussions, Burton still wished to present a list of twelve points or questions to focus discussion for the participants. Tony de Reuck argued strongly that they should adopt some of the principles developed at CIBA for conducting unstructured or semi-structured meetings, in which roles are uncertain, norms of behavior and procedures unspecified, and even the eventual goals of the meeting somewhat nebulous. He felt that avoiding formalized procedures and even mildly authoritarian leadership would lead eventually to a stage of attentive listening, the development of shared perceptions and a common vocabulary, and the attainment of a degree of trust among the participants that would enable some subsequent creative thinking to take place; and that this would be worthwhile even if the initial stages were likely to follow a pattern involving the challenging assertion of positions and argumentation about differences.[7]

Burton agreed that this should be the initial procedure adopted and, on the morning of the 13th, following personal introductions, de Reuck as last minute chairman suggested to the participants and the panel that the basic rule of the meeting should be to have no rules, in the sense that anyone should feel free to say anything. Moreover, the discussions should take any direction that participants felt appropriate. In this opening stage there appeared to have been a general feeling of puzzlement among the diplomatic participants, even about what they were doing there, and a number of comments indicated that they were prepared to give "the process"—whatever it was—one day and if no progress was apparent they would not return the following day. However, they were willing to present their views of the conflict to the panel, the Indonesians volunteering to present first.[8]

What then followed was the beginning of a subsequently familiar first stage in many workshops, with both sides presenting their case, telling their stories and to some degree venting, although recollections are that levels of tension and hostility were not as high as in some later workshops, where participants had direct experience of loss, damage and death caused by their adversaries. The first days were thus devoted to the participants presenting their own historical account of Konfrontasi and its origins, with much emphasis on interaction, and explanations couched in terms of responses to the actions and initiatives of the other. One of the panelists also had the strong impression that the participants were, to some degree, covering themselves against subsequent official questions about whether they had taken care to present their government's case forcefully and in detail, when they returned to their respective embassies or capitals.[9] Hence, in these first two days and even later in the week, there was a great deal of what a third panelist described as acting or playing to the gallery.[10]

By the end of the first day another subsequently familiar aspect of such workshops was evident. The participants were becoming frustrated with what they perceived as a lack of substantive progress, and they announced that they would not be returning the following day. The panel responded with encouragement and said that they intended to be at the CIBA center at 9:30 the following day and they hoped to see the Indonesian, Malaysian and Singaporean guests there. In the event, everyone arrived on the following morning and the discussion proceeded with the completion of the Malaysian and Singaporean accounts of the sources and nature of the dispute.[11]

The ending of the second day and much of the subsequent week were taken up with the panel asking questions of the participants and commenting on aspects of the conflict that seemed to them to link to theoretical or conceptual formulations from appropriate social sciences. One surprising feature of this process for the panel was the beneficial effects of their not knowing too much of the historical background to the conflict. With a few exceptions, the panel could convincingly only claim "expertise" that did not directly arise from knowledge of the region or the conflict. This enabled them to ask penetrating, if basic questions about underlying sources of the conflict and its dynamics without the participants feeling that answering these would involve the springing of some clever trap. What de Reuck later described as the panel's "innocence" enabled the panel to ask "naively penetrating questions" and to "view hypotheses and explanations . . . with direct and innocent vision" (de Reuck, 1966, p. 5) that increased participants' trust that the panel was not being manipulative, and helped to produce a less superficial analysis than might otherwise have been the case. This unexpected benefit clearly underlies the familiar rule of thumb that workshop panels should not be steeped in the details of the conflict they are dealing with, and also the principle that only the parties involved *really* know what the conflict is all about.

As far as these initial workshops are concerned, most panelists recollect that a central focus for the discussions in the latter part of the workshop was on ideas of misperceptions and misapprehensions, concepts which the participants rapidly adopted as tools for explaining why the other party had assigned inaccurate meanings or motivations to actions and statements of their own leaders. (It was, apparently, only "the other side" that failed to understand accurately one's own positions, goals, perceptions and motivations. "Our own side" was blessed with immaculate perception.) They appeared particularly interested in the others' perception of their own motivations and images and the mistakes that had been made in the past because initially incorrect interpretations underlay many reactions. The importance of these ideas was particularly revealed in discussions of Indonesian fears of being "encircled," which had been generally dismissed as ill-founded or simply used for propaganda purposes during Konfrontasi. However, the perception of British imperialism surviving through Australia, of U.S. imperial control via the Philippines, and of the threat of Chinese ambitions to the north meant that the close ties which Britain maintained with Malaysia effectively completed this perceived encirclement and confirmed Indonesians in their strong beliefs about efforts to maintain imperial control over their region. Further discussion revealed that all three countries shared concerns about nation building and the difficulties of maintaining minimal unity over such widely dispersed territories and about the dangers of separatist tendencies within their diverse populations. This shared set of concerns and misapprehensions led one of the panelists to write later that one fruitful way of understanding the conflict was to abandon any approach which focused on traditional International Relations concepts such as "power" or "territorial aggression" and instead to substitute a "fear-framework," in which motivations are sought in feelings of insecurity and instability. Substantive issues might be only "an expression of underlying insecurity and anxiety" that arise so frequently because "it is only too easy to find other objects to fear" (Oppenheim, 1966, p. 3). Linked to this analysis is also the element of symbolism, in that certain actions, quite irrespective of their substantive effects, can take on larger and even different meanings through what they represent to others. Thus, Indonesians' *feelings* of encirclement emerged from the discussions as having been intensified by Malaysia's continuing links with an imperial Britain—that is the *kind* of federation that emerged, symbolized by the British base retained in Singapore.

Apart from this major theme, others that emerged from the interactive discussion in the workshop mainly arose, according to one panelist, from the process of the participants exploring each other's motivations for past actions, beliefs on the other side about these motivations, and mis-reactions based on these assumed motivations.[12] Much attention was devoted to actions seen as themselves reactive, but perceived as new threats by the other, while the theme of fears regarding outside intervention provided another common interest within all three parties.

Equally, there was some discussion of the "functionality" of the conflict for elements on both sides, undoubtedly arising from panel members' familiarity with the then very influential theories of Lewis Coser (1956). While apparently not embracing the theories wholeheartedly, participants indicated that there had been clear payoffs from being in conflict and that these were rather reluctantly acknowledged as being of considerable value. For example, both Malaysian and Indonesian participants agreed that before Konfrontasi there had been considerable doubt about the rationality of having two states, given the ethnic similarity of Malays and Indonesians, but that now there was no question about the separateness of the two countries; conflict had clearly drawn and reinforced boundaries, as suggested by Coser.[13]

Toward the very end of the week's work, panelists recall that participants began to float what might be called *what if* ideas into the discussions, which is conventionally a way of exploring likely reactions to possible moves and statements without making any firm commitment that these would be made. Many of these ideas involved possible actions by other relevant parties—mainly the British—who were not represented among the participants. Hence, a feeling began to grow that, if there were to be a follow-up meeting, then additional parties would have to be represented at the table. However, most panelists recollect that the week ended somewhat ambiguously, with the participants simply saying that they would need to report back to their governments, although it was implied that the discussions would soon need to be resumed, possibly some time in January.

Part of the procedure worked out at the start of the meeting had been that no written record of the exchanges would be made, nobody would list agreements—or disagreements—over whatever points were discussed, and that there would be no formal report of the workshop proceedings. All of the panel and most of the participants had kept personal notes, and it was understood that these would form the basis of the participants' reports to their individual governments. On December 17th the discussions came to what Tony de Reuck recalls as a "natural break point"[14] and the initial workshop came to an end.

In the recollection of many of the panelists, it had clearly been an interesting but somewhat unstructured event. For one thing, the idea of a formal agenda had been rejected. For another, it was difficult to maintain continuity of panel members throughout the week. Roger Holmes recalls that people "came and went," and that some attended only infrequently.[15] However, the process was clearly held together by a core group of Burton, de Reuck, Oppenheim and Emery.

The team convened briefly to review progress and consider future possibilities on December 18th or 19th, but at that stage the next move clearly lay with the three governments and it seems probable that little firm planning could be undertaken. At this point there seems to have been a recognition that something unusual had taken place over the previous week, but nobody was yet quite certain what this was, nor how the very open and flexible procedures that had developed—almost of their own accord—had contributed to such a result. These matters might clarify in the New Year.

The Process of Peacemaking

The New Year saw the beginnings of a number of important structural changes within Indonesia that significantly affected the context for the London meetings. Some of these had clearly began in late 1965, when some behind-the-scenes efforts to modify the policy of Konfrontasi became evident. For example, in the middle of December Dr. Sudandrio had approached the Dutch ambassador in Jakarta to suggest the possibility of a "dialogue" between Indonesia and the United Kingdom, to be brokered by Dr. Josef Luns, the foreign minister of the Netherlands, but nothing came of this tentative "feeler" although it was sent to London from Jakarta a few days later.[16]

In summary, the structural changes within Indonesia involved a gradual shifting of power from those in Indonesian political and military circles who favored continuing Konfrontasi to those who saw the whole policy as an irrelevance to Indonesia's real needs, or simply as damaging other important Indonesian goals, particularly those involved in economic development. At an individual level, this meant a gradual lessening of the power of President Sukarno—although he retained the role of "spoiler" right up to the end of the formal peace process that terminated in the Bangkok/Jakarta Agreement signed on August 11, 1966. This slow change was signaled by an increased number of contradictory statements about continuing or ending Konfrontasi emanating from different ministries and ministers in the Indonesian government, but more especially by a number of "reshuffles" in the country's inner Cabinet which involved the gradual replacement of key ministers who had supported Konfrontasi. In March 1966, while the killing of PKI members was

still continuing, a further major shift in real power took place, with Lt. General Suharto and other military chiefs finally taking control of the government from the
hands of President Sukarno, who was also forced to remove his minister of defense,
General Nasution, from office. Shortly afterward, following anti-leftist demonstrations by students and others in Jakarta, First Deputy Premier and Foreign Minister
Subandrio was sacked and arrested a few days later. Other former ministers, such as
the minister of information, Major Achmadi, were placed in "protective arrest."

Thus, over the first six months of 1966, anti-Konfrontasi individuals led by Lt.
General Suharto for the army and by the new foreign minister, Adam Malik, began
to shape new Indonesian attitudes and policies towards the Malaysian federation
and Singapore and, in spite of continued opposition from the president, to signal
this change to their adversaries and the world at large. As early as the beginning of
March, Jakarta Radio was reporting even Mr. Subandrio as saying that the president
would agree to talks with Tunku Abdul Rahman and President Marcos. In mid-
March, a private emissary from General Suharto contacted British Ambassador
Gilchrist in Jakarta with the information that Suharto wished to renew good relations with Britain; that there was an urgent need to wind up Konfrontasi, although
this would have to be done "bit by bit"; and that Suharto and his group would
emerge into public power very soon. The suggestion was also made that the Australian government might be asked to provide good offices.[17] Almost a month later the
official Indonesian news agency, *Antara*, was reporting publicly that the new foreign minister, Adam Malik, was prepared to discuss peace with Malaysian leaders,
by which time another of Suharto's emissaries, Colonel Ali Moertop, had already
had informal and confidential discussions lasting two days in Bangkok with Tan Sri
Ghazali, the Malaysian Permanent Secretary for External Affairs.[18]

In May the pace of events quickened. On the 15th, after what was undoubtedly
a difficult, four-hour meeting of Indonesian leaders at the presidential palace at Bo-
gor, the Indonesian government actually proposed direct peace talks at the foreign
minister level, although a few days later President Sukarno was trying to prevent
such talks taking place by forbidding his foreign minister to travel abroad. However, on May 27th a delegation of senior Indonesian military officers arrived in Malaysia for talks, later described as "cordial" and two days later Malik and Tun Abdul Razak opened peace talks in Bangkok.

The London Meetings Resume

It was against this background of change that the workshops continued in London. The steering group from the panel held a planning meeting shortly after the
opening of the New Year on January 4th. Clearly there had been some encouragement from the three governments to continue because the next full workshop took
place only six days later on January 10th. It was probably at this latter meeting that
it became clear to the participants something that had already been considered by
members of the panel: that it would beneficial to have some input to the discussions

from both the British and Australian governments. Hence, the diplomatic participants made a specific request that a British and Australian presence should be arranged subsequently, and this was agreed.

Subsequent one-day, follow-up workshops took place at the CIBA Foundation
on February 4th and 16th and on March 14th, while the London Group's steering
committee also met formally on January 19th and later on April 22nd, although the
"inner circle" kept in close touch with one another during the intervening periods.
Tony de Reuck recalls that these later workshops became gradually more characteristic of "direct, bilateral negotiations," with informal bargaining taking place and
heads of agreement being drafted. In essence, the diplomatic participants "took over
the running" with the panel helping with ideas and suggestions when necessary.

At the meeting held on February 16th, two new diplomatic participants attended, namely Mr. Tam Dalyell, who was Under-Secretary of State at the Foreign
Office; and Mr. Tom Critchley, who was then Australian High Commissioner in
London and who had been a colleague of John Burton's for many years. Both new
participants were brought into the discussions to provide some information about
British and Australian aims and intentions in the region, and it appears that they did
so in a manner which defused many of the medium and long-term concerns of the
other participants, particularly those from Indonesia. At this time the labor government in London was reviewing the whole of British policy "East of Suez"—as well
as Britain's overall defense posture—particularly the cost of maintaining a strong
military presence in the region, and Dalyell was probably able to inform the workshop of possible future directions of British policy and the likelihood of a major
diminution of the British presence in the region—or the British "threat," as it had
initially been defined in Jakarta.[19] Panel members clearly regarded this intervention
as very useful in removing some of the remaining obstacles to finding a solution to
Konfrontasi and opening up possibilities for the regional governments.[20]

By mid-March the discussions had progressed to a point at which the participants had thrashed out some heads of agreement and some detailed terms, at least at
an acceptable draft level although, again, no formal records of discussions or points
of agreement were kept by the panel and each of the participants was responsible
for making his record of what might have been said and tentatively agreed. Panelists recall that participants gave clear indications that they were reporting regularly
on progress to their embassies in London and that information about the workshops
was reaching the foreign ministries in Singapore, Jakarta and Kuala Lumpur. Thus,
the workshops' penultimate meeting on March 14th occurred at roughly the same
time as the transfer of power in Jakarta to General Suharto and the appointment of
Mr. Malik as foreign minister. Both of these changes clearly led to the revival of
official, track-one peacemaking efforts and eventually to the meetings in Bangkok
in late May.

These official meetings became the occasion for the final workshop which occurred on June 6, 1966, when some of the panel and most of the participants (less
Mr. Wan who had left for Singapore but with Mr. Critchley representing Australia)

attended to discuss their work in the light of the Bangkok meetings and the agreement to end confrontation.[21] There seems to have been a general feeling that the workshops had made a contribution to the approaching peace, and that the meetings had been unusual but worthwhile. As a follow up, the steering committee and the panel decided that visits should be made, as soon as possible, to the three capitals, in order to ascertain what had been achieved and what further might be done.

Contemplating a New Process

During the summer of 1966, the academics of the London Group who had become, somewhat to their surprise, involved in an initiative aimed at helping to resolve a rather low-key but nonetheless intractable international conflict, had a little time to take stock of what their initial experiment in "social scientific intervention" had achieved. Leaving aside the issue of how the workshops had helped institution building,[22] the two obvious questions to be addressed were, firstly, what contribution (if any) had the workshop series made to the search for a solution to the conflict between Indonesia, Malaysia and Singapore; and secondly, what lessons could be learned from the initiative about how to analyze complex conflicts (if one could do this *with* the participation of those intimately involved) and about how to develop mutually acceptable and self-supporting solutions in such conflicts.

Only the first of these questions will be considered in any depth in this chapter. Those who had helped to organize the London workshops and most of those who had sat on the panel facilitating the discussions were positive that they had, indeed, made a contribution to the final resolution of the conflict via the Bangkok and Jakarta agreements. One word of caution was sounded by Peter Lyon, who remarked later on the relatively low status of the participants in their respective diplomatic hierarchies, and questioned how seriously the three governments were taking the initiative and what level of attention would be given to reports emanating from such a low-key event.[23] On the other hand if, as John Burton had requested, these were individuals with personal links to very top decision makers—to Sukarno, to Tunku Abdul Razak and to Lee Kuan Yew—then their formally low status would have not prevented their insights being transmitted to top decision-making circles in their respective capitals.

Moreover, many panelists felt that, in spite of the fact that—by agreement—no formal record of the points discussed or tentative agreements suggested had been kept, nonetheless the diplomatic participants had made their own records of possible de-escalatory moves, of issues that could be sidelined or ignored because of previous misperceptions and misunderstandings, of areas of mutual interest and mutual concern, and of points that might possibly be included in any final settlement. Everyone on the panel had been struck by the fact that the diplomatic participants had, on several occasions, announced that they would need to consult their own governments back home before proceeding any further. They had all—apparently—been keeping in regular touch through their embassies with their own foreign ministries and probably beyond. It was also very likely that they had been given some high-level permission to explore the position of the other side, the possibly bizarre insights made available by the social scientists, and the room available for various solutions, even, after the December meeting, those involving compromise of publicly stated goals.

However, the most that the facilitators would actually claim about the impact of the workshop series on the actual conflict—particularly those that committed their thoughts to paper—was that it seemed to have helped to arrive at a solution, although the precise form this help had taken and how it had operated remained vague. Tony de Reuck, for example, wrote shortly after the ending of the series that the meetings "at the very least must have contributed to the favourable climate surrounding the present detente" (de Reuck, 1966, p. 9). Much later on, he continued to feel that the meetings enabled the participants to discuss—and later to actually negotiate—in a way that would never have been possible if they had remained within the normal bargaining framework.[24]

The impression of the London Group that what took place at the meetings had an impact on the official level of negotiating and peacemaking was later reinforced when the text of the Jakarta Agreement appeared, and members of the panel were struck by the fact that the heads of agreement and general outline resembled drafts that were being discussed in London at the February and March meetings, while some phrases and expressions seemed to be echoes of those heard at the London meetings or were even the same, word for word. Tony de Reuck's point that, had Suharto or Malik been searching for a ready-made way of ending confrontation that was reasonably sure of acceptance by the other side, then a draft was "there, ready for use on the shelves of the Foreign Office in Jakarta."[25]

Less speculatively, British records indicate that some informal intermediary activity, at the least, had a direct impact on the accord. Shortly after the official Bangkok meetings Tan Sri Ghazali, the leading Malaysian diplomat, in conversation with the British ambassador in Kuala Lumpur, commented that, in fact, it had been Adam Malik and he, rather than Tun Razak, who had worked out the agreement late on the evening of May 31st. Moreover, consensus had finally been reached "on the basis of a formula which Ghazali had previously agreed in principle with Suharto during the course of their private contacts through intermediaries and had confirmed during the last week's visit of the Indonesian goodwill mission."[26]

Only the diplomatic participants and their political chiefs can confirm beyond doubt the existence and the effects of such linkages, of course, but some positive indications were gained during the follow-up visit to Kuala Lumpur and Jakarta undertaken by John Burton in the summer of 1966. Burton recalls being impressed by the welcome he received "at top levels" and by the assurances that, with all parties in good communication, there would be no need for further meetings in London.

On the matter of what impact the workshops might have had on the development of this approach for future use we are on rather more certain ground, as some of the core members of the panel and steering group put their thoughts on paper for discussion at the June 3rd meeting. Fred Emery's account, for example, was focused mostly on the lessons to be learned for future exercises, although he did conclude that what he termed "participative case studies" would be "the most hopeful way of testing and extending our knowledge and . . . the ability of social scientists to be even more helpful" (Emery, 1966, p. 7). Most interestingly, Emery's paper did extract some general lessons from the workshops which later became standard guidelines for this type of initiative.[27] Some were obvious, even at the time, such as the argument for "protection from public perusal" for the participants' freedom of exploration; and the point stressing the advantage of the participants not being present in any final decision-making capacity, which would restrict discussion "to those matters . . . seen to have a significantly probable contribution to the decision" (Emery, 1966, p. 6). Exploring "mere possibilities" would free participants so that they could follow a discussion down whatever paths appeared, however ostensibly irrelevant.

On the other hand, the workshops on Konfrontasi appeared to have revealed a number of counterintuitive guidelines, which often emerged at points during the first week's discussions when disagreements about process arose. The first was that a major contribution from the social scientists—apart from their independence from the conflict itself—was their ability to assist participants both to begin a *joint* analysis or search and sustain it in the face of the inevitable hostility which would accompany even the most urbane diplomat to such discussions. Emery argued strongly that this involved facilitators in allowing the participants to guide the direction and content of the meeting, in not trying to contain outbursts of anger or avoid hostile confrontations during the exchanges, and in not trying to force participants to explore what they seemed to want to avoid—for example, concerns about the overseas Chinese—or make them become involved in processes—anything resembling formal negotiation—about which they were clearly uneasy.

The second major role for the panel was to help develop what Emery called "a 'theory' of the conflict" which was not only accurate and objective, but was accepted as such by the participants. This "theory" needed to be articulated to the conflict under consideration so that it guided discussion toward the next stage in the process, that of searching for possible solutions, in which the facilitators played a third important role. Here, Emery first articulated the principle that, to find an outcome that was acceptable to all parties—the famous *win-win* solution—it was often necessary for the facilitators to help participants redefine the nature of the conflict by examining their more general values and needs and then seeking solutions at that level rather than at the level of publicly expressed positions and interests. Emery discusses this idea as that of "recentering"—finding a relevant issue linked to the ostensibly "prime" conflict, which provides an opportunity to engage in "some creative thinking and to effectively restructure the way the contestants looked at the prime conflict" (Emery, 1966, p. 5). In the case of Konfrontasi, Emery argued that shifting the focus from the "prime" conflict over Sabah and Sarawak to the problems caused by the British Strategic Reserve Base at Singapore "recentered" the problem and led toward a possible resolution, and this does seem likely to have been the case.

John Burton's paper was also written in January 1966, in the light of the first week's discussions of Konfrontasi and, being intended for delivery at the annual British International Studies Association Conference, is of a far more general nature than any of the others. Much of the paper is taken up with a discussion of the nature of "testing" and Burton's argument that the only really valid form of theory testing is to see whether any theory or theories about a particular conflict situation seem relevant, insightful and applicable to those actually involved in that situation. On the other hand, reading between the lines, Burton seems to have concluded, even at that early stage in the workshop series that, quite apart from its theory-testing potentialities, the Konfrontasi initiative had shown that one major revelation was the manner in which the process could restore sophisticated and non-threatening communication. At the same time, it introduced the representatives of conflicting parties to useful ideas and concepts that helped in analyzing their mutual problem as well as suggesting exits.

Conclusion

Whether the ideas, the principles and the theories that had been used in the workshop series had, in fact, helped the governments of Singapore, Malaysia and Indonesia to find that exit still remains something of an open question, although the strong indications are that it did play a major role in the overall peacemaking process. All the evidence seems to show that the discussions certainly played a part in altering the views and ideas of the diplomats who participated in the series of meetings in London over the winter of 1965 and the spring of 1966—not least because the panelists most of the time seem to have instinctively avoided the trap of forcing their own analysis on the participants. Fred Emery recalls the warning provided by Kurt Lewin over a decade before: "the direct assault of new ideas provokes a stubborn resistance, thus intensifying the difficulty of producing a change of outlook. Conversion is achieved more easily by unsuspected infiltration of a different idea" (Lewin, 1950, p. viii). The lesson that the panel does not necessarily know best was an important one for future initiatives.

Could the new technique be used in other cases? In the summer of 1966 the London Group was cautiously optimistic. A second workshop series was planned for the autumn. Burton's new Centre at University College was recruiting researchers and associates, and one of its major purposes was to continue using the new approach until a body of experience had been accumulated about what did and what did not work, plus (hopefully) some theoretical ideas about why. It was left to de Reuck to express a necessary note of written caution about assuming that ideas from the CIBA workshops could be transferred, lock, stock and barrel, to other types of conflict, involving parties from other cultures[28] with long histories of emnity and mistrust. Tony de Reuck made the crucial point that it should not be forgotten that Konfrontasi was, as international conflicts go, somewhat extraordinary even if not unique. He noted that, in many ways, it was an unreal conflict in terms of its causes and its conduct; relatively few people had been killed or injured, and relatively few had even been directly affected by it. He referred to it as a "phoney war," which echoed the term used later by another observer of Konfrontasi, who called it a "quasi-war" (Ott, 1972, p. 599). For de Reuck, the main problem seemed, by the start of 1966, to have become one of finding a peaceful exit for all concerned, given that the workshop series revealed that there existed no objective conflicts of interest between two very similar emergent nations, and a powerful ambivalence on all sides regarding what had become an increasingly unrewarding dispute.

Rhetorically, at the end of his paper written in May 1966, de Reuck asked whether the new approach would be equally successful in conflicts that involved deep ideological or cultural differences, in disputes over the sharing of political power, in differences over how to treat national minorities, or in conflicts over possession of or access to valuable raw materials. He might have added to that list conflicts that were long-lasting, violent, destructive, or cyclical, or that seemed to involve real conflict of interest, perhaps central to survival. The next thirty years were to see a variety of social scientists using problem-solving workshops to try to answer those questions.

Notes

1. My thanks to Julie Marcus, Scott Grummon, and Susan Allen Nan for their work in helping to carry out background research for this paper and to all of the participants and panel at the CIBA Workshops who allowed me to interview them at inordinate length about past events in which they had been involved.

2. Australia had been one of the two members that brought the Indonesian issue to the Security Council in 1946 (the other was India); and when in 1947 the UN sent a Good Offices Committee to try to mediate between the Dutch and the Indonesian nationalists, the latter chose Australia to represent them on the three-man committee (Coast, 1952, p. 58).

3. The most detailed English-language account of confrontation between the three countries is by J. A. C. Mackie in *Konfrontasi* (London, Oxford University Press: 1974).

4. See the account in Burton, "Negotiation to Prevent Escalation and Violence," pp.13-14.

5. A number of other social scientists acted as an informal support or steering group, attending planning meetings, offering comments and suggestions, and contributing to the analysis of the process and its effects. These included Mr. Michael Banks (International Relations, LSE); Mr. John Groom (International Relations, University College); Mr. Ian Hamnett (Sociology, University of Edinburgh); Dr. Michael Nicholson and Mr. Charles Raab (Peace

Research, University of Lancaster); and Mr. Andrew Wilson (Defence Correspondent of the "Observer").

6. Oppenheim also possessed local knowledge and experience of Indonesian society as his family came from a Dutch colonial background and he had served in the Dutch forces in Indonesia after World War II.

7. Anthony de Reuck. interview; London; November 20, 1987.

8. De Reuck, interview.

9. Bram Oppenheim, interview; London; January 4, 1983.

10. David Barkla, interview; London; July 16, 1985.

11. De Reuck, interview.

12. Oppenheim, interview.

13. De Reuck, interview.

14. De Reuck, interview.

15. Roger Holmes, interview; London; June 10, 1984.

16. Public Record Office, London. File #FO 371 181501/IM 1042/141.

17. Public Record Office, London. File #FO 371 187562/IM 1042/30. The emissary Mr. Van Tjong also indicated to Ambassador Gilchrist that the new regime was desperate to make arrangements for new food supplies for Indonesia, and unless this could be arranged (and continuing Konfrontasi prevented this) the whole Indonesian reform movement would lose its impetus.

18. Public Record Office, London. File #FO 371 187562/IM 2042/51.

19. At this point in time it seemed clear that the Indonesian perceptions of the British base were also shifting, at least among the new group of power holders led by Suharto. Whereas to Sukarno, Nasution, and Subandrio the base had seemed to represent a colonialist's effort to retain control of the region, for Suharto and his group it was likely to represent a bulwark against any renewed communist threat to their hold on power and part of a deterrent against Chinese expansionism into Southeast Asia.

20. De Reuck, interview.

21. Three days previously, on June 3, 1966, a meeting of the social scientists involved had taken place at CIBA to review progress from an academic perspective and the four papers mentioned in the bibliography by Burton, de Reuck, Emery and Oppenheim had been read and discussed.

22. Partly as a result of this first exercise, John Burton was able to establish the Centre for the Analysis of Conflict, at University College London, with a major focus on the exploration and development of this approach to conflict analysis and its resolution—what became known three years later as "controlled communication" (Burton, 1969).

23. Peter Lyon, interview; London; July 21, 1985.

24. De Reuck, interview.

25. De Reuck, interview.

26. Public Record Office, London File # FO/187565/IM1042/108/G. Report from Sir M. Waller, British ambassador to Kuala Lumpur on meeting with Tan Ghazali on June 3, 1966.

27. Emery begins his paper with an interesting discussion about the values and objectivity of the facilitating panel, and of the conflicting pressures to which panelists from countries party to the conflict might be subjected. Both of these are topics on which debate still continues.

28. De Reuck acknowledges that the informal process adopted at CIBA may have worked well there because it resembled the Malay concept of *Musharawah*, that is, continu-

ing to talk a subject "into the ground" until consensus is achieved, rather than arbitrating it or voting on it or adjudicating it according to some abstract principles as in the Western tradition. However, subsequent experience with open-ended and flexibly conducted workshops seems to show that this approach does not work only with people from non-Western, consensus-based cultures.

2

Interactive Problem Solving in the Israeli-Palestinian Case

Past Contributions and Present Challenges

Herbert C. Kelman

Since the early 1970s, my colleagues and I have been actively engaged in track-two efforts designed to contribute to the resolution of the Israeli-Palestinian conflict. Our work has primarily involved the intensive application to this conflict of the concepts and methods of *interactive problem solving* (Kelman, 1998b, 2003), which is my particular variant of Interactive Conflict Resolution. Interactive problem solving is an unofficial, third-party approach to the resolution of international and intercommunal conflicts, derived from the work of John Burton (1969, 1979, 1984, 1987) and anchored in social-psychological principles (Kelman, 1997a).

Our first problem-solving workshop with Israelis and Palestinians took place in 1971 (Cohen, Kelman, Miller, and Smith, 1977). The work continued with a series of workshops in the 1970s and 1980s (see Kelman, 1979, 1986, 1992a), culminating in a continuing workshop with highly influential Israeli and Palestinian participants that met over a three-year period, between 1990 and 1993 (Rouhana and Kelman, 1994; Kelman, 1998a). The last session of the continuing workshop took place just prior to the announcement of the Oslo agreement in 1993. Our efforts have continued and taken new directions in the years following the Oslo agreement. The focus of the present chapter, however, is on the pre-Oslo period: on the contributions of our work to laying the groundwork for the Oslo agreement—which I still regard as a major breakthrough in the Israeli-Palestinian conflict, despite its inherent flaws and despite the failure of the

Camp David talks in the summer of 2000, the onset of the second *Intifada* later that year, and the breakdown in "the Oslo process" in 2001.

Historical Background[1]

The Israeli-Palestinian conflict is now more than a century old (see Tessler, 1994, for a comprehensive account of the history of the conflict, or Mendelsohn, 1989, and Gerner, 1991, for shorter accounts). Its origins go back to the birth of political Zionism at the end of the nineteenth century (see Halpern, 1969, and Hertzberg, 1975). The early decades of the twentieth century brought to Palestine waves of Jewish immigrants who purchased land, built settlements and social institutions, and clearly signaled their intention to establish a Jewish homeland and ultimately a Jewish state in Palestine. The growing Jewish presence was soon perceived as a threat by the Arab population of the land, which was itself influenced by the development of Arab nationalism and the construction of a specifically Palestinian identity (see Muslih, 1988, and R. Khalidi, 1997). Violence first erupted in the 1920s and has continued to mark the relationship between the two peoples ever since.

During the period of the British mandate, which was established after World War I, various formulas for the political future of Palestine were explored—including partition and establishment of a federal state—but none was found to be acceptable to both the Arab and the Jewish populations (or indeed to either one of them). In November 1947—in the wake of World War II and the decimation of European Jewry—the United Nations General Assembly voted to end the British mandate over Palestine (on May 15, 1948) and to partition the land into a Jewish and an Arab state. The Zionist leadership accepted the partition plan, with reservations. The Arab leadership, both within Palestine and in the neighboring states, rejected it. Fighting between the two sides broke out immediately after adoption of the UN resolution and turned into all-out war after May 15, 1948, when the British forces withdrew, the Jewish leadership in Palestine declared the independent state of Israel, and regular armies from the neighboring Arab states joined the fray. Fighting continued until early 1949.

In July of 1949, Israel and the Arab states signed armistice agreements (though the state of war continued). The armistice lines became the official borders of the State of Israel. These borders included a larger portion of Palestine than the UN partition plan had allotted to the Jewish state. The Arab state envisioned by the partition plan did not come into being. Two parts of mandatory Palestine remained under Arab control: the West Bank, which was eventually annexed by Jordan, and the Gaza Strip, which came under Egyptian administration. The establishment of Israel and the war of 1948-1949 also created a massive refugee problem, with the flight or expulsion of hundreds of thousands of Palestinian Arabs from their homes in the part of Palestine that became the State of Israel.

The map changed radically as a result of the Arab-Israeli war of June 1967, and along with it, the political atmosphere in the Middle East. By the end of the Six-Day War, as Israelis called it, Israel occupied the West Bank and the Gaza Strip—thus extending its control over the entire territory of mandatory Palestine. It also occupied the Sinai Peninsula and the Golan Heights—Egyptian and Syrian territories, respectively. The new geopolitical and strategic situation created by the 1967 War led to the Palestinianization of the Arab-Israeli conflict, bringing it back to its origin as a conflict between two peoples over—and increasingly within—the land they both claimed (Kelman, 1988).

The Palestinianization (or re-Palestinianization) of the conflict has manifested itself in the actions of the Arab states, of the Palestinian community itself, and of Israel. Israel's neighboring Arab states gradually withdrew from the military struggle against Israel—though not before another major war in 1973—leaving it, essentially, to the Palestinians themselves. The disengagement of the Arab states became dramatically clear with the 1977 visit to Jerusalem of President Anwar Sadat of Egypt, the largest and most powerful Arab state, an initiative that led to the Camp David accords of 1978 and the Egyptian-Israeli peace treaty of 1979. The Palestinians took repossession of their struggle, which in the years between 1949 and 1967 had been mostly in the hands of the Arab states. Fatah, under the leadership of Yasser Arafat, and other Palestinian guerrilla organizations grew in strength and eventually took over the Palestine Liberation Organization (PLO), which was originally a creature of the Arab League. Between the 1960s and the 1980s, the Palestinian movement gradually shifted its emphasis from the liberation of all of Palestine through armed struggle against Israel to the establishment of an independent Palestinian state in the West Bank and Gaza through largely political means. The end of the occupation became the immediate goal of the movement and, with the onset of the *Intifada*—the uprising in the West Bank and Gaza—in December 1987, the occupied territories became the focal point of its struggle.

On the Israeli side, the *Intifada* further underlined the Palestinianization of the conflict in the wake of the 1967 War. What had been largely an interstate conflict between 1948 and 1967 had now been internalized by Israel, that is, transformed into a continuous confrontation with a resentful Palestinian population, living under occupation within Israel's post-1967 borders. Many Israelis were persuaded by the *Intifada* that continuing occupation was not tenable and that the Palestinians were indeed a people, whose national movement had to find some political expression if there was to be a peaceful accommodation between the two sides (Kelman, 1997b).

By the end of the 1980s, there was a strong interest on all sides in finding a peaceful accommodation and an increasing recognition that some version of a two-state solution would provide the best formula for a broadly acceptable historic compromise. The political obstacles to such a solution, however, remained severe. A number of strategic and micropolitical considerations—traceable, in particular, to the end of the Cold War and the aftermath of the Gulf War—eventually brought the leaderships on both sides to the negotiating table at the Madrid Conference in 1991 and the subsequent talks in Washington. These talks, however, never developed momentum. It was only after Prime Minister Yitzhak Rabin came into power in Israel in 1992, at the head of a government led by the Labor Party, and gradually (and reluctantly) concluded that Israel would have to deal directly with the PLO leadership in order to make progress in the negotiations, that a breakthrough was finally achieved. This breakthrough occurred in the secret Oslo talks, which culminated in the exchange of letters of mutual recognition between the PLO and the State of Israel (which, in my view, was the most significant achievement of the Oslo process) and the Declaration of Principles signed in Washington in September 1993 (see Kelman, 1997b, for further details).

I shall return to a discussion of the conditions that made the Oslo agreement possible—and of our contribution to the wide array of activities that helped bring these conditions about—after a brief description of our problem-solving workshops with influential Israelis and Palestinians and related activities.

Problem-Solving Workshops

The primary (though not the sole) instrument of interactive problem solving is the problem-solving workshop. A workshop is a specially constructed, private space in which politically involved and often politically influential (but generally unofficial) members of conflicting communities can interact in a nonbinding, confidential way. The microprocess of the workshop provides them the opportunity to penetrate each other's perspective; to explore both sides' needs, fears, priorities, and constraints; and to engage in joint thinking about solutions to the conflict that would be responsive to the fundamental concerns of both sides.

Our Israeli-Palestinian workshops prior to the Madrid Conference in 1991 (which opened an official Israeli-Palestinian peace process) clearly took place in the prenegotiation phase of the conflict. Their primary purpose was to help create a political atmosphere that would encourage the parties to move to the negotiating table. Moreover, until 1990, all of our workshops were one-time, self-contained events. Some of the Israelis and Palestinians, as individuals, participated in more than one workshop and the workshops we held over the years had a cumulative effect within the two societies. But, because of financial, political, and logistical constraints, we did not attempt, before 1990, to bring the same group of participants together for more than one occasion.

Workshops take place under academic auspices and are facilitated by a panel of social scientists knowledgeable about international conflict, group process, and the Middle East. A typical one-time workshop would begin with two pre-workshop sessions, about four hours in length, during which the third party meets separately with each of the two parties. The workshop itself typically lasts about two and a half days, often scheduled over an extended weekend. The participants include three to six Israelis and an equal number of Palestinians, plus a third party of three or more members.

The Israeli and Palestinian participants have included parliamentarians, leaders and activists of political parties or political movements, journalists, editors, directors of think tanks, and politically involved academics, that is, scholars who not only publish academic papers, but who also write for newspapers and appear in the media, who serve as advisors to political leaders, and some of whom move back and forth between government and academia. Some of our participants have been former diplomats, officials, or military officers, and many were later to become negotiators, ambassadors, cabinet ministers, parliamentarians, and leading figures in the media and research organizations. We look for people who are within the mainstream of their societies and close to the center of the political spectrum. At the same time, they have to be people who are at least willing to explore the possibility of a negotiated solution and to sit down as equals with members of the other party.

We are cognizant of the asymmetries between the parties that exist in the real world—asymmetries in power, in moral position, in reputation. These play important roles in the conflict and, clearly, must be taken into account in the workshop discussions. But the two parties are equals in the workshop setting in the sense that each party has the same right to serious consideration of its needs, fears, and concerns. Within the rules of the workshop, the Israeli participants, for example, cannot dismiss the Palestinian concerns on the grounds that the Palestinians are the weaker party and are therefore in a poor bargaining position; nor can the Palestinian participants dismiss the Israeli concerns on the grounds that the Israelis are the oppressors and are, therefore, not entitled to sympathy. Each side has the right to be heard in the workshop and each side's needs and fears must be given attention in the search for a mutually satisfactory solution. One of the tasks of the third party is to try to empower the party that is less powerful in a given context.

The workshop discussions are completely private and confidential. There is no audience, no publicity, and no formal record, and one of the central ground rules specifies that statements made in the course of a workshop cannot be cited with attribution outside of the workshop setting. In the early days of our work, confidentiality was particularly important for the protection of our participants, because the mere fact that they were meeting with the enemy was controversial and exposed them to political and even physical risks. Confidentiality is equally important, however, for the protection of the process that we are trying to promote in workshops. The third party creates an atmosphere, establishes norms, and makes occasional interventions, all conducive to free and open discussion, in which the parties address each other rather than their own constituencies, the record, or third parties, and in which they listen to each other in order to understand their differing perspectives. We encourage participants to think out loud, to experiment with ideas, to explore different options, without having to worry about how others would react if their words in the group were quoted outside. We want them to engage in a type of interaction that is generally not feasible among parties engaged in a bitter conflict—a type of interaction that, indeed, deviates from the conflict norms that usually govern their behavior:

- An interaction that is *analytic* rather than polemical, one in which the parties seek to explore each other's perspective and gain insight into the causes and dynamics of the conflict;
- An interaction that is *problem-solving* rather than adversarial, one in which the parties sidestep the usual attempt to allocate blame and, instead, take the conflict as a shared problem that requires joint effort to find a mutually satisfactory solution.

The agenda of a problem-solving workshop is designed to allow this kind of interaction to unfold. The core agenda of a one-time workshop has four components. First, each side is asked to discuss its central concerns in the conflict—the fundamental needs that would have to be addressed and the existential fears that would have to be allayed if a solution is to be satisfactory. The parties are asked not to debate the issues raised, although they may ask for clarification of what the other says. The purpose is for each side to gain an adequate understanding of the other's needs, fears, and concerns, from the perspective of the other. Once they have demonstrated that they understand the other's needs to a significant degree, we move to the second phase of the agenda: joint thinking about possible solutions. What participants are asked to do in this phase is to develop, through an interactive process, ideas about the overall shape of a solution for the conflict as a whole, or perhaps, a particular issue in the conflict, that would address the needs and fears of both sides. They are given the difficult assignment of thinking of solutions that would meet not only their own side's needs, but the needs of both sides.

Once the participants have developed some common ground in this process of joint thinking, we turn to the third phase of the workshop: discussion of the political and psychological constraints within the two societies that would create barriers to negotiating and carrying out the ideas for solution that have been developed in the group. We deliberately leave the discussion of constraints to the third phase, so that it does not hamper the creative process of jointly generating new ideas. Finally, depending on how much progress has been made and how much time is left, we ask the parties to engage in another round of joint thinking—this time about ways of overcoming the constraints that have been presented. The participants are asked to come up with ideas about what their governments, their societies, and they themselves might do—separately or jointly—that would help to overcome the barriers to negotiating mutually satisfactory solutions to the conflict. A central feature of this phase of the work is the identification of steps of mutual reassurance—in the form of acknowledgments, symbolic gestures, or confidence-building measures—that would reduce the parties' fears of engaging in negotiations with an uncertain or risky outcome.

The third party in our model enacts a strictly facilitative role. It does not propose solutions, nor does it participate in the substantive discussions. Its task is to create the conditions that allow ideas for resolving the conflict to emerge out of the interaction between the parties themselves. A basic assumption of our approach is that solutions generated in the interaction between the conflicting parties are most likely to be responsive to their needs and to engender their commitment. The facilitative role of the third party, however, is an important part of the process. The third party sets the ground rules and monitors adherence to them; it helps to keep the discussion moving in constructive directions, tries to stimulate movement, and intervenes as relevant with questions, observations, and even challenges. It also serves as a repository of trust for parties who, by definition, do not trust each other: They feel safe to come to the workshop because they trust the third party to maintain confidentiality and to protect their interests.

A special issue that arises in our work is the ethnic identity of the third party—an issue that I have had to face from the beginning, as a Jew working on the Israeli-Palestinian conflict. In many respects, my Jewish identity has enhanced my credibility on both sides. It reassures the parties that I am engaged in this work out of genuine personal concern, rather than some ulterior motives; and that I am a third party who is committed and cares about the issues rather than "disinterested" in the sense of standing above the fray. At the same time, my ethnic identity may raise questions about bias on the Palestinian side and loyalty on the Israeli side. I have tried to deal with these issues in part by working with an ethnically balanced team. The third party in my work has always included at least one Arab member. During the 1990s, for example, I worked closely with Nadim Rouhana, a social and political psychologist who is a Palestinian citizen of Israel. We organized and co-chaired an Israeli-Palestinian Continuing Workshop that met between 1990 and 1993, to be described below (see also Rouhana and Kelman, 1994), and a Joint Working Group on Israeli-Palestinian Relations that met between 1994 and 1999 (described briefly in footnote 2; see also Kelman, 1998a). Having a balanced team strengthens our credibility: We claim and try to be, not a "neutral" third party, but an even-handed one—and ethnic balance on our team is an important indicator of that even-handedness. But beyond the image of a balanced team, I have found it extremely valuable in enhancing the third party's sensitivity to the concerns of both sides and ability to grasp readily each party's reactions to new events or to the nuances of what is being said (and felt) around the table.

Workshops have a dual purpose: to produce *changes* in the individual participants and to *transfer* these changes into the political process. Changes in the participants—new learnings—may take the form of more differentiated images of the enemy, a better understanding of the other's perspective and their own priorities, greater insight into the dynamics of the conflict, and new ideas for resolving the conflict and for overcoming the barriers to a negotiated solution. These changes at the level of individual participants are a vehicle for change at the policy level. Thus, the second purpose of workshops is to maximize the likelihood that the new insights, ideas, and proposals generated in the course of the interaction are fed back into the political debate and the decision-making process in each community.

These two purposes may at times create contradictory requirements, leading to what I have called the dialectics of interactive problem solving (Kelman, 1979). The best example of these dialectics is provided by the selection of participants. To maximize *transfer* into the political process, we should seek out participants who are officials, as close as possible to the decision-making apparatus and thus in a position to apply immediately what they have learned. But to maximize *change*, we should seek out participants who are removed from the decision-making process and therefore less constrained in their interactions and freer to play with ideas and explore hypothetical scenarios. To balance these contradictory requirements, we look for participants who are not officials, but politically influential. They are thus relatively free to engage in the process, but, at the same time, because of their positions and their credibility within their societies, any new ideas they develop in the course of a workshop can have an impact on the thinking of decision makers and the society at large.[2]

Another example of the dialectics of workshops is the degree of cohesiveness that we try to foster among the workshop participants. An adequate level of group cohesiveness is important to the effective interaction among the participants. But if the workshop group becomes too cohesive—if the Israeli and Palestinians participants form too close a coalition across the conflict lines—they may lose credibility and political effectiveness in their own communities (Kelman, 1993). To balance these two contradictory requirements, we aim for the development of working trust—of trust in the participants on the other side, based not on interpersonal closeness, but on the conviction that they are sincerely committed, *out of their own interests*, to the search for a peaceful solution.

Problem-solving workshops, as I pointed out at the beginning of this section, are the primary, but not the sole instrument of interactive problem solving. Other activities, over the years, have been particularly oriented toward maximizing the transfer of ideas generated in interactions between the parties to the wider political process. Thus, on the one hand, in the 1970s and 1980s I organized a series of private, one-to-one meetings between highly influential Israeli and Palestinian political and intellectual figures under conditions of strict confidentiality. There was every reason to expect that what participants learned in these very private encounters would be transmitted to top decision makers. On the other hand, I organized a number of public symposia at Harvard University, within the framework of the Middle East Seminar (which I have chaired or co-chaired since 1977),[3] including a major symposium in 1984 that brought together five members of the Israeli Knesset and five leading figures from different Palestinian communities, as well as a symposium in 1989 that brought together senior Israeli political and academic figures with PLO representatives and academics from West Bank, Gaza, and American universities. Also, as president of the International Society of Political Psychology, I organized two open events at the Society's 1986 meeting in Amsterdam (the presidential session and a "fishbowl" workshop) that featured interactions between major Israeli and Palestinian intellectuals and political figures.[4] Finally, starting in 1977, my own lectures, op-ed pieces, and articles (e.g., Kelman, 1978, 1982, 1982-83, 1987, 1988, 1992b, 1997b, 1998c, 1999, 2000) on the Israeli-Palestinian conflict— presenting policy analyses, embedded in a social-psychological perspective on the nature of international conflict, the role of national identity, and the process of change—have drawn heavily on what I have learned from problem-solving workshops and related activities. Such third-party products contribute in their own way to the transfer of ideas developed in the course of workshops (Chataway, 2002).

In 1990, a major step forward in our workshop program took place when, for the first time in our work, Nadim Rouhana and I organized a continuing workshop. A group of highly influential Israelis and Palestinians—six on each side—agreed to participate in a series of three meetings over the course of a year, and in the end continued to meet (with some changes in personnel) until August 1993 for a total of five meetings (Rouhana and Kelman, 1994). The meetings of this group were punctuated by the Gulf War, the beginning of official negotiations in Madrid and then in Washington, and the election of a Labor Party government in Israel. In 1991, with the onset of official negotiations, four of the six initial Palestinian participants in this group became key members of the Palestinian negotiating team. In 1992, several of our Israeli members were appointed to ambassadorial and cabinet positions in the Rabin government. These were very exciting developments from our point of view, in that they enhanced the political relevance of our unofficial efforts, but they also created conflicts of interest for some of our participants (Kelman, 1998a).

As our work moved from the prenegotiation to the negotiation phase of the conflict, all three parties agreed that there was still a great need for maintaining an unofficial process alongside of the official one, although the purpose and focus of the work would need to change. When negotiations are in progress, workshops can contribute ideas for overcoming obstacles to staying at the table and negotiating productively, for creating a momentum in the negotiations, for addressing long-term issues that are not yet on the negotiating table, and for beginning the process of peacebuilding that must accompany and follow the process of peacemaking. The meetings of the group after the start of the official negotiations focused on the obstacles confronting the peace process at the negotiating table and on the ground, and also addressed the question of the function and composition of the continuing workshop in the new political environment. The final session of the continuing workshop took place in August 1993, ending just a day or so before the news of the Israeli-Palestinian breakthrough that was achieved in Oslo began to emerge.

Interestingly, the onset of official negotiations increased the receptivity to our unofficial efforts on both sides. The involvement of members of our continuing workshop in the official process, and the awareness that the issues we were discussing may soon be on the negotiating table, increased the felt relevance of our efforts. At the same time, there was a heightened concern about maintaining the distinction between our activities and the negotiations, in order to make sure that our unofficial efforts in no way undermine the official process. Moreover, there was increased attention to the issue of transfer of ideas developed in the course of workshops to the official negotiations. By 1993, participants felt that the time had come to produce and publish joint papers. Accordingly, in the wake of the Oslo accord, we initiated the Joint Working Group on Israeli-Palestinian Relations, with the express purpose of producing joint concept papers on the final-status issues (see footnote 2).

The Oslo Agreement

When the Oslo agreement was announced, various observers credited our work with having laid the groundwork for it. For example, in the wake of the agreement, the then Middle East correspondent for *The Boston Globe*, Ethan Bronner (1993), wrote a piece about my contribution to the process for the newspaper. In it, he quoted Mordechai Virshubsky, a member of the Israeli Knesset at the time who had participated in our 1984 event at Harvard, as saying: "When one day they write the history of how this conflict was solved, they will have to write about Herb Kelman, how he broke ground, how he was one of the initiators." In a similar vein, Sari Nusseibeh, now the president of Al Quds University and one of the Palestinian participants in the 1984 event, told Bronner: "The time will come when people will look back and see things in context. Herb will certainly be regarded as one of the central figures in this process." On the very day the Oslo agreement was signed in Washington (September 13, 1993), I spoke at an "International Conference on Mental Health and the Challenge of Peace" in Gaza. When the late Ibrahim Abu Lughod, a leading Palestinian intellectual and educator and vice president of Birzeit University, introduced me, he used virtually the same words as Virshubski in predicting my future place in the history of the conflict and its resolution.

I must admit that I found such observations gratifying and confirming, and after a while I persuaded myself that they were indeed true. Of course, I made it clear that my colleagues and I had no *direct* involvement in the prenegotiation and negotiation processes that produced the Oslo agreement. I also stressed that our activities must be seen:

within the context of the variety of Israeli-Palestinian meetings and projects that have been organized in recent years—particularly since the onset of the *Intifada*—under different auspices and with different purposes, types of participants, formats, and agendas. Different projects have made different contributions to the recent developments. Some helped by opening particular channels of communication; others explored the feasibility of certain security or economic arrangements. The cumulative effect of this range of activities has helped to create a political atmosphere conducive to productive negotiations (Kelman, 1995, p. 20).

I am well aware that it is impossible to disentangle the impact of our own efforts from this array of unofficial activities at the elite and the grassroots levels.

At the same time, I was—and continue to be—prepared to take credit for having *contributed* to this larger effort. Moreover, I would point to some of the distinct features of our approach to which its particular contributions can be traced:

- Our program represents a sustained, systematic effort—spanning some two decades by the time of the Oslo agreement—to bring together politically influential Israelis and Palestinians; it is one of the earliest and most consistent enterprises of this type and has reached deeply into the political elites of both communities.
- We have been very clear throughout about the political purpose of the enterprise: communication is not viewed as an end in itself, but as a means of developing new ideas and insights that can be fed into the political process.
- The work is based on close knowledge of the two communities and familiarity with their political landscapes; we visit the region frequently, stay in touch with events and people, and have paid special attention to building and maintaining our networks.
- The selection process is carefully devised to identify participants who can both engage in the kind of communication that our workshops call for and feed what they learn into the political process in their own communities. Thus, we seek out individuals who are politically involved and influential; are actively interested in finding a negotiated solution; and, at the same time, are part of the mainstream of their communities, are close to the center of the political spectrum, and have credibility and access.
- The workshops themselves are carefully designed and conducted so as to facilitate the process of sharing perspectives, joint thinking, and creative problem solving; the setting and the ground rules (with their emphasis on privacy and confidentiality), the agenda, the procedures, and the third party's interventions are all geared to making this kind of communication possible.

In sum, I have felt justified in proposing that our work—the sustained, systematic use of an unofficial third-party microprocess as a vehicle for influencing the political debate and official policy at the macro-level—was well-placed to help lay the groundwork for the Oslo Accord. Certainly, in the glow of this breakthrough, I was motivated to accept some of the credit for it. But today, with the breakdown of the Oslo process, it may seem strange to continue claiming my bit of credit for a process that seems to have been so widely discredited. But I have no hesitation in doing so, because I maintain that the Oslo Accord, despite its flaws, was and remains a major breakthrough and that the peace process will ultimately have to return to the basic ideas that formed the building stones of the Oslo agreement. Since our work contributed to the evolution of these ideas, I shall review them briefly before turning to the nature of these contributions.

The Building Stones of the Oslo Agreement

The ideas that paved the way for the Oslo agreement evolved over the quarter century or so between the 1967 war and the negotiations in Oslo. They reflect a number of developments, to some of which I alluded briefly in my historical review: changes in the political environment in the Middle East; events on the ground, such as the Israeli settlement project in the occupied territories and the first *Intifada*; changes in the long-term interests of the key actors; and domestic-political concerns of the top leaders. These developments persuaded leaders on both sides of the necessity of reaching an agreement—of negotiating a historical compromise that would most likely take the form of a two-state solution. There was thus an increasing readiness for new ideas about resolving the conflict, which were in part shaped and diffused in the face-to-face interactions between the two sides—including our workshops and related activities—that took place over a period of more than two decades.

Before being prepared to sign an agreement, however, the parties had to be convinced not only that such an agreement was *necessary*, in light of their changing realities and evolving interests, but also that it was *possible*. In other words, they had to be persuaded that there was a genuine readiness on the other side to make the requisite concessions and that there was a reasonable probability that negotiations would yield an acceptable agreement without jeopardizing their national existence. The Israeli-Palestinian interactions that took place— largely, though not entirely—at the unofficial level were instrumental in the evolution of this sense of possibility.[5]

Table 2.1 summarizes the ideas that, I propose, served as the building stones of the Oslo Accord. It sketches out four ideas relating to what is necessary and what is possible with respect to the process and to the outcome of Israeli-Palestinian negotiation.

The left-hand column presents the evolving ideas with regard to the negotiation process. The upper box refers to the gradual acceptance of the idea that meaningful negotiations can be carried out only between legitimate representatives of the two national groups. Acceptance of this idea, obvious though it may appear, did not come easy, because seeking out legitimate national representation of the other side as negotiating partners meant to recognize the other as a legitimate national actor—which neither side was prepared to do. Instead, each side searched for interlocutors who were congenial to its point of view. Israelis, over many years, looked for alternatives to the PLO and even tried to create an alternative leadership in the West Bank, the Village Leagues, to represent the Palestinian population. Palestinians, on their part, sought contact with anti-Zionist Israelis or at least (by the time of the 1987 meeting of the Palestine National Council) "with Israeli democratic forces that support the Palestinian people's struggle."

Table 2.1. Evolving Ideas for Resolving the Israeli-Palestinian Conflict (1967-1993): The Building Stones of the Oslo Agreement

Focus of the Ideas	Target of the Ideas	
	Negotiation Process	*Negotiation Outcome*
What is Necessary?	negotiations between legitimate national representatives	mutual recognition of national identity and rights
What is Possible?	availability of a negotiating partner	the two-state solution

An interesting learning experience relating to the issue of legitimate negotiating partners occurred in one of our workshops in the mid-1980s. The Israeli and Palestinian participants found that they were able to talk to each other, and developed a degree of working trust. There came a point in the course of the workshop when the Israelis told their Palestinian counterparts: "If only we could negotiate with reasonable people like you instead of the PLO, we would be able to find common ground." In response, the Palestinians insisted very strongly: "But we *are* the PLO," meaning that they identified with the PLO. In a subsequent session, an almost identical exchange took place in reverse, when the Palestinians said, in effect: "If only we could negotiate with reasonable Israelis like you, instead of the Zionists," and the Israelis replied, "But we *are* committed Zionists."

What the workshop participants learned in this conversation—and what Israelis and Palestinians were increasingly coming to understand in other contexts over the years—was that productive negotiations required partners who represent the mainstream of their respective political communities. But, in addition, they learned that identifying such legitimate negotiating partners was not only *necessary*, but also *possible* (as noted in the lower left-hand box of table 2.1). They discovered that it was possible to find PLO-identified Palestinians and loyal, committed Zionists, respectively, in whom they could develop a degree of trust and with whom they could talk seriously, find common ground, and move toward negotiations.

What participants learned in the microcosm of our workshop was one manifestation of the idea that slowly, gradually took hold on both sides over the years: the idea that legitimate representatives of the other side may well be available as partners in serious negotiations. In the 1980s, some Israeli peace activists summed up this idea with the slogan, "there is someone to talk to and something to talk about" on the other side. The second half of this slogan brings us to the right-hand column of table 2.1: what is necessary and what is possible for the *outcome* of potential Israeli-Palestinian negotiations.

The understanding that resolution of the conflict must be based on mutual recognition of the other's national identity and national rights evolved very slowly and in the face of great resistance on both sides. It ran counter to the pervasive view of the conflict as zero-sum in nature, not only with respect to territory, but also with respect to national existence and national identity. Each side has seen the national identity and indeed the national existence of the other as a threat to its own identity and existence and, accordingly, each has systematically denied the other's identity and rights. Recognition of the other was seen as a dangerous step with irreversible consequences. Not surprisingly, it has taken many years to achieve wide acceptance of the idea that mutual recognition is a necessary outcome of Israeli-Palestinian negotiations if the conflict is to be resolved. This idea finally found expression in the letters of recognition exchanged between Arafat and Rabin, which I have always regarded as the most important feature of the Oslo accord (Kelman, 1997b).

In the early 1980s, the idea of mutual recognition came to be phrased as "mutual and simultaneous recognition of both nations' right of self-determination" (see the two New York Times side-by-side op-ed articles by Sarid and W. Khalidi in 1984). This language, though not quite explicit, clearly hinted at a two-state solution. Significant voices on both sides came to advocate such a solution, including Palestinians with impeccable nationalist credentials, such as Walid Khalidi (1978), and Israelis outside of the traditional peace camp, such as former head of military intelligence Yehoshafat Harkabi (1988). In the brief review of the historical background of the conflict earlier in this chapter, I mentioned that—in the wake of the 1967 war and the Palestinianization of the Arab-Israeli conflict—there was an increasing interest on all sides in settling the conflict and a growing recognition that a two-state solution was the best formula for the necessary historic compromise.

But the question remained whether it would be possible to negotiate a two-state solution that would be acceptable to both sides. The obstacles to acceptance of such a compromise were (and in fact still are) enormous. Significant elements within each society were vehemently opposed to compromise, remaining committed to achieving their maximalist goals. Even those elements that favored compromise were deeply distrustful of the intentions of the other side and were afraid that accepting the other's right to a state would jeopardize their own national existence. Gradually, however, the idea that it is not only *necessary*, but also *possible* to negotiate a two-state solution as the political expression of the national identities of the two peoples and as the fulfillment of their respective rights to national self-determination gained increasing acceptance within the mainstream of both political communities (lower right-hand box of table 2.1). Events on the ground and in the region clearly played an essential role in this process, but direct interactions between the two sides—at the unofficial level and eventually at the official level—contributed significantly to persuading each side that formulas for a two-state solution could be negotiated that would meet the needs of the other without threatening their own vital interests.

The idea of a two-state solution acceptable to both sides as the political outcome of their mutual recognition was left only implicit in the Oslo agreement. Still, both leaders and publics on both sides understood that, at the end of the day, there would be a Palestinian state alongside of Israel, provided the interim arrangements worked out and the final-status negotiations succeeded. This understanding was an essential building stone of the Oslo agreement. The failure to make it explicit has proven to be a major flaw of the agreement—though almost certainly an inevitable one: Rabin was not ready to make a final, explicit commitment to a Palestinian state without an interim period to reassure Israel that such a state would be consistent with Israel's security requirements. Nor was Arafat ready to commit to the finality of an agreement without knowing the precise outcome of the final-status negotiations. Israelis and Palestinians committed to the peace process agree that, now, the resumption of negotiations must be based on explicit commitment from the start to a mutually acceptable formula for a two-state solution.

To sum up, the ideas that paved the way for the Oslo agreement were shaped by political realities in the region and on the ground and their impact on the long-term and short-term interests of the parties. Direct interactions between the two sides—often (particularly in the early stages) at the unofficial level, as in our work—played a significant role in generating, formulating, and diffusing these ideas. At the risk of oversimplification, I propose that the parties' interests in the light of evolving realities were primarily responsible for persuading the leadership and the public of the *necessity* of negotiating a historic compromise; and the interactions between the two sides were primarily responsible for persuading them of the *possibility* of such a compromise.

Contributions to the Peace Process[6]

There are three ways in which our work has contributed to the evolution and acceptance of the ideas that served as the building stones of the Oslo agreement: through 1) the development of *cadres* experienced in communication with the other side and prepared to carry out productive negotiations; 2) the sharing of information and the formulation of new ideas that provided important *substantive inputs* into the negotiations; and 3) the fostering of a *political atmosphere* that made the parties open to a new relationship.

Development of Cadres

Over the years, dozens of Israelis and dozens of Palestinians—all politically involved, some of them "pre-influentials" who later moved into positions of leadership and influence, others already political influentials by virtue of their current and former positions—participated in one or more of the workshops or similar opportunities for direct Israeli-Palestinian communication that we arranged.

Many of these individuals played direct or indirect roles in the discussions and negotiations that led up to the September, 1993 accord. Most of the participants in our continuing workshop played central roles, as negotiators or advisers, in the official peace talks that started in November, 1991. Many "alumni" of our other workshops, meetings, and symposia were also engaged in this process in a variety of roles. Similarly, some of the participants in our projects were involved in the various secret explorations (including the Oslo channel) that took place prior to Oslo—and, I might add, since Oslo. Over the years (including the post-Oslo years), they could be found in the Israeli as well as the Palestinian cabinet, parliament, and foreign ministry, and in leading positions in other official agencies.

In short, we *know* that participants in our activities have been well represented in the various phases of negotiation and implementation of agreements. We can only *surmise* that their earlier participation in our workshops and other activities may have helped to prepare them for these roles—in some sense to train them or even "credential" them for enacting these roles—and may have contributed to the productivity of the process.

Several factors account for the contribution of our program to the development of cadres for negotiation. First, given their sheer numbers, the people involved in the more than thirty workshops and similar activities we conducted in the years prior to Oslo constitute a significant proportion of the political elites of the two communities. Second, our criteria and procedures for selection of participants and composition of workshop groups yielded precisely the kinds of individuals (in terms of their personal characteristics and the political groupings they represented) who were natural candidates for negotiations once there was a political readiness for that step. Third, the workshops increased participants' knowledge about the other side and sensitivity to its concerns, and enhanced their experience and skills in communicating with the other side, as well as their commitment to such communication. As a consequence, workshop participation helped to strengthen their qualifications and effectiveness for the negotiating role.

Substantive Inputs

Workshops produced new knowledge, understanding, and ideas, which gradually found their way into the political thinking and the political debate in the two communities. Thus, Palestinians and Israelis had the opportunity to enter into each other's perspective. Each learned about the other's concerns, priorities, sensitivities, and constraints; about the nature of public opinion and the political divisions on the other side; about changes that have taken place and possibilities for further change; and about the elements on the other side that might be open to accommodation, and the forms that such accommodation could take. Through the process of joint thinking that workshops encourage, participants explored new formulations of issues that would make them amenable to solution, ideas for solutions that would be responsive to the concerns of both parties, shared visions of a desirable future, and steps of mutual reassurance (in the form of acknowledgments, symbolic gestures, and confidence-building measures) that would create an atmosphere conducive to negotiations.

These new understandings and ideas were then fed into the political process in each community by way of workshop participants' political discussions and political work—through their public communications in speeches, articles, and media appearances, and through their private communications to political leaders and political colleagues. Such communications, for example, helped to inject into the Israeli political culture an increasing awareness that the PLO is the indispensable partner for Israeli-Palestinian negotiations, that nothing short of an independent state will satisfy Palestinian aspirations, and that Palestinians are ready to accept a state in the West Bank and Gaza, alongside of Israel, as the *point final* of the conflict. On the Palestinian side, in turn, such communications helped to inject an understanding of the political divisions within Israel, of the elements of Israeli society that can be mobilized in support of an agreement based on a two-state solution, and of the limits of what even the Israeli peace camp can accept. Ideas that emerged from workshop discussions were also fed into the political debate through the work of third-party members, such as my own publications and lectures on ways of overcoming the barriers to a negotiated solution.

In sum, the information exchanged and the ideas developed in the course of workshop interactions injected into the two political cultures some of the substantive elements on which productive negotiations could be built: shared assumptions, mutual sensitivities, and new conceptions of the process and outcome of negotiations. In the terms of the building stones of the Oslo agreement that I identified, workshop participants learned and helped their societies to learn what was necessary and what was possible for successful negotiations.

Political Atmosphere

Our workshops, along with various other Israeli-Palestinian meetings and projects, helped create a political atmosphere that became increasingly favorable to negotiations. A new relationship between significant segments of the two communities evolved over the years. This relationship accelerated after the onset of the *Intifada* and it maintained itself despite many setbacks—particularly during the Gulf crisis and war of 1990-1991. The workshops and related activities contributed to a political atmosphere conducive to negotiations and to the gradual evolution of a new relationship between the parties by encouraging—through the interactive problem-solving process—the development of more differentiated images of the enemy; a de-escalatory language that minimizes threat and humiliation; a new political discourse attentive to the concerns and constraints of the other party; a working trust based on the conviction that both parties are genuinely committed, largely out of their own interests, to finding a peaceful solution; and a sense of possibility, based on the belief that a mutually satisfactory resolution of the conflict can ultimately be achieved. The two most important elements of a supportive political environment, to which workshops contributed, are the sense of *mutual reassurance*, which reduces the parties' fear of negotiations as a threat to their existence, and the sense of *possibility*—the perception that there is "a way out" of the conflict (Zartman, 1997), which enhances their belief that negotiations, though difficult and risky, can produce an acceptable agreement.

Renewing the Peace Process

By contributing to the development of cadres experienced in communication with each other, of substantive ideas for resolving the conflict, and of a political atmosphere conducive to negotiation, Israeli-Palestinian interactions over the years—including our problem-solving workshops and related activities—have laid the groundwork for the Oslo accord. When the convergence of long-term and short-term interests on the two sides created the necessity and the political readiness for negotiations—in other words, the ripe moment—the people, the ideas, and the habits to take advantage of this opportunity were at hand.

The Oslo accord materialized because certain key lessons had been learned in the two communities—a learning process to which our activities, among others, made substantial contributions. Sadly, these lessons have been unlearned, particularly since the failure of the Camp David conference in the summer of

2000 and the onset of the second *Intifada*. In my view, these lessons must now be relearned, particularly the underlying assumptions of the Oslo agreement that there is a credible negotiating partner and that the best formula for ending the conflict remains a two-state solution. I believe that this relearning process will take less time than the original learning process, but it calls for a new framework for pursuing peace. Revival of the peace process at this stage will require moving beyond a series of concessions dictated by pragmatic considerations and outside pressures (although pragmatism and active involvement of outside powers remain essential features of the process). What is needed now is a commitment by the parties to a *principled peace*, one that they can embrace with enthusiasm and commend to their publics as a peace that addresses the basic needs of both societies and conforms to their sense of attainable justice. The challenge to our work is to contribute creatively to the parties' relearning of the lessons that made the Oslo agreement possible and shaping them into a new framework for a principled peace.

The relearning process made significant headway in 2003, with the appearance of two initiatives—quite different from each other, but each the product of unofficial, joint Israeli-Palestinian efforts—that have effectively challenged the claims of both sides' dominant narratives of recent years that there is no negotiating partner on the other side willing to agree to a mutually acceptable two-state solution. The first is the "People's Voice" initiative, launched in June by Ami Ayalon, former commander of the Israeli navy and former head of the Shin Bet security services, and Sari Nusseibeh, president of Al Quds University and former representative of the Palestinian Authority in Jerusalem.[7] They formulated a statement of principles for a two-state solution (see Ayalon-Nusseibeh Statement of Principles, 2003) for which they have so far gathered tens of thousands of Israeli and Palestinian signatures. The purpose of their campaign is to mobilize enough public support for an agreement embodying the principles they have outlined to create both the legitimacy and the pressure for decision makers to negotiate such an agreement. The campaign is also designed to gain international support for these principles, encouraging the relevant outside powers to put their weight behind them.

The second initiative, the "Geneva Accord" (for the full text, see Geneva Accord, 2004) was first made public in October of 2003 and formally launched in Geneva at the beginning of December. It was spearheaded by Yasser Abed Rabbo, former minister of information and culture in the Palestinian Authority, and Yossi Beilin, minister of justice in the Barak administration—both leading figures in the negotiations that ended in Taba, Egypt, in January 2001. The Geneva Accord takes the form of a draft of a permanent status agreement, embodying principles very similar to those outlined in the Ayalon-Nusseibeh initiative. The Geneva Accord, however, actually spells out the terms of the agreement on most of the key issues—including borders, Jerusalem, refugees, security, and monitoring arrangements—in great detail, as they might be found in an official treaty. The text was "negotiated" over a period of nearly three years, with facilitation by Swiss governmental and nongovernmental agencies (in a process similar in many respects to the Norwegian facilitation of the Oslo agreement). A diverse group of Israelis and Palestinians—including Israeli military, political, academic, and literary figures, and Palestinian political figures, community activists, and civil society leaders—participated in negotiating and promoting this document and thus added to its credibility. The agreement has no official status, nor do its authors make such a claim. However, the detailed provisions and the list of sponsors provide an impressive, concrete demonstration that a mutually acceptable formula for a two-state solution can be devised by mainstream Israelis and Palestinians, including individuals who were in the past and may again be in the future negotiating on behalf of their governments.

Opinion polls suggest that majorities of the two populations still favor a two-state solution and are willing to make the compromises it would require—although they do not trust the other side's readiness or ability to come to an agreement. Even among the pro-negotiation segments of the populations, there is concern about some of the provisions of the Geneva Accord, such as those regarding the resolution of the Palestinian refugee problem or the allocation of sovereignty in Jerusalem. These concerns may be exacerbated by the way in which proponents of the accord present it to their respective populations. For understandable reasons, each side may emphasize to its own constituencies how favorable the accord is to their own interests and how much the other side has conceded. These are important messages to convey to their own population but, when they are heard on the other side, they may well reinforce the prevailing distrust. For example, when Palestinians hear Israelis stress that Palestinians have in effect given up the right of return of refugees, and Israelis hear Palestinians deny that they have given up the right of return, both may come to feel that this is a bad deal or that there is enough ambiguity to allow the other side to exploit the agreement to their own side's disadvantage.

To build on the enormous achievement represented by the Geneva Accord and the People's Voice initiative, it is now essential to garner widespread support for these proposals in the two communities by capturing the public's imagination and generating trust and hope. To this end, as I have proposed above, the initiatives need to be framed in terms of a *principled peace* that represents not just the best available deal, but a historic compromise that meets the basic needs of both societies, validates the national identity of each people, and conforms to the requirements of attainable justice. Common messages along these lines need to be jointly constructed and brought to both populations to ensure that proponents of peace initiatives avoid working at cross-purposes as they seek to mobilize their own constituencies.

I envisage three central elements in a jointly constructed framework for a principled peace:

- *Acknowledgment* of the other's nationhood and humanity. Acknowledging the other's nationhood requires explicit recognition of each people's right to national self-determination in a state of it own, acceptance of each other's authentic links to the land, and rejection of language that denies the other people's political legitimacy and historic authenticity. Acknowledging the other's humanity requires words and actions demonstrating that the other side's lives, welfare, and dignity are considered to be as valuable as one's own. In this spirit, it is necessary to reject acts of violence, especially against civilian populations; all forms of humiliation, harassment, destruction of property, confiscation of land, violation of rights, and dehumanizing treatment; and language of hate, denigration, and dehumanization. A corollary of such acknowledgments is willingness to take responsibility and express regret for harm done to the other over the course of the conflict.
- *Affirmation* of the meaning and logic of a historic compromise. The agreement needs to be clearly framed as a commitment to ending the conflict by sharing the land that both sides claim, through the establishment and peaceful coexistence of two states, in which the two peoples can fulfill their respective rights to national self-determination, give political expression to their national identities, and pursue independent, secure, and prosperous national lives. The implications of such a commitment must be clearly spelled out in terms of the costs and benefits that it entails. On the one hand, the logic of the historic compromise imposes significant costs on each side—such as the removal of Israeli settlements from the Palestinian state and limitations on the return of Palestinian refugees to Israel—in order to safeguard the identity, independence, and viability of both states. On the other hand, the historic compromise establishes a principled peace that allows each people—through its independent state—to fulfill its national identity, to satisfy its fundamental needs, and to achieve a measure of justice.
- *A positive vision* of a common future. A peace agreement needs to be framed in positive, visionary terms, as an opportunity for the two peoples to create a common future in the land they share, enhancing peace, justice and the welfare of both populations, rather than an arrangement that is being forced on them by outside pressure and the unending cycle of violence. Such framing is consistent with the high degree of interdependence that characterizes the two societies and the emotional attachment that both peoples have to the entire land even though each can establish its national state in only part of the land. Thus, the agreement should be presented to the two populations as the foundation of "a future relationship based on mutually beneficial cooperation in many spheres, conducive to stable peace, sustainable development, and ultimate reconciliation," with the understanding that "the scope and speed of expanding and institutionalizing cooperative activities must be determined by experience—by the extent to which such activities meet the needs of both parties, enhance mutual trust, and reduce inequalities between the parties" (Joint Working Group, 1999, abstract).

I have proposed that peace initiatives, such as the very impressive Geneva Accord, need to be brought to the Israeli and Palestinian publics within a framework of a principled peace, featuring the three elements that I have outlined. To be maximally effective, this framework should be captured in common messages, jointly constructed by thoughtful, credible representatives of the two sides. Joint construction is essential in order to make sure that these formulations are responsive to the concerns and sensitivities of each side without unduly threatening the other side. I believe that the methods of interactive problem solving are especially suited to facilitating such a joint effort of creating a new framework for the peace process and developing common formulations of a principled peace.[8]

In particular, problem-solving workshops can provide an arena for the "negotiation of identity" (Kelman, 1992b, 2001), which is precisely what the current stage of the peace process calls for. Negotiating identity means finding ways, through an interactive process, whereby conflicting parties can accommodate their collective identities, and the associated national narratives, to one another—at least to the extent of eliminating from their own identities the negation of the other and the claim of exclusivity. Such identity changes are possible only if "they leave the core of each group's identity and national narrative—its sense of peoplehood, its attachment to the land, its commitment to the national language, welfare, and way of life—intact" (Kelman, 2001, p. 210). Thus, the key to effective negotiation of identity is to find ways of accommodating the two groups' conflicting identities without jeopardizing the *core* of their separate identities. This can best be accomplished in a context of reciprocity, in which acceptance *of* the other occurs simultaneously with acceptance *by* the other. Change in a more peripheral element of identity thus becomes a vehicle for affirmation of the core of the identity.

In sum, the challenge to our work at the current stage of the peace process is to contribute to the development of a new framework for a two-state solution whose parameters are by now widely known and accepted—a framework that would persuade the two publics that such a solution is not only necessary, but that it is possible, that it is safe, that it is fair, and that it promises a better future. The methods of interactive problem solving have been used effectively at the prenegotiation and paranegotiation stages of the Israeli-Palestinian conflict. I propose that they can now contribute, with emphasis on the negotiation of identity, to the revival of a peace process that has broken down.

Notes

1. This and the next section draw extensively on pp. 188-190 and pp. 198-200 of my chapter in *Social Identity, Intergroup Conflict, and Conflict Resolution*, edited by Richard

D. Ashmore, Lee Jussim, and David Wilder, and published by Oxford University Press (Kelman, 2001).

2. In our work up to 1993, transfer was left to the individual participants. Depending on their positions in the society, it may have been effected through their writings, their political leadership, or their advice to decision makers. There was no effort in these workshops to create joint products, although on some occasions the participants themselves decided to do so (cf. Sarid and Khalidi, 1984; Ma'oz, 2000). In 1994, for the first time in our work, Nadim Rouhana and I organized a Joint Working Group on Israeli-Palestinian Relations with the express purpose of producing joint concept papers on the final-status issues in the Israeli-Palestinian negotiations (Kelman, 1998a, pp. 21-24). This group (and working sub-groups) met on a regular basis until 1999 and produced four papers, three of which have been published (Alpher, Shikaki, et al., 1998; Joint Working Group, 1998, 1999).

3. The Middle East Seminar, now cosponsored by the Weatherhead Center for International Affairs and the Center for Middle Eastern Studies at Harvard University, covers a wide range of topics relating to Middle East politics and society, but it has devoted many sessions to the Arab-Israeli conflict. Speakers have included Israeli, Palestinian, and other Arab diplomats, political leaders, academics, and writers. Perhaps the most dramatic event in the history of the seminar was a presentation in 1979 by Shafiq Al-Hout, head of the PLO office in Beirut—probably the first time that a senior PLO official spoke at a semi-public event (the seminar is open, but off-the-record) in the United States.

4. For example, the speakers at the presidential session (in addition to myself) were the late Edward Said—the renowned Palestinian intellectual and Columbia University professor—and Mordechai Bar-On, an Israeli historian, peace movement leader, and, at the time, member of the Knesset.

5. In a similar vein, Pruitt (1997) speaks of the motivation to de-escalate the conflict (motivational ripeness) and optimism about reaching an acceptable agreement as the two broad determinants of readiness for conflict resolution. He proposes that optimism grew incrementally over the course of the parties' interactions at Oslo.

6. This section draws extensively on pp. 21-23 of an article published in the *Negotiation Journal* (Kelman, 1995).

7. Sari Nusseibeh, as noted earlier, participated in a major Israeli-Palestinian event at Harvard University that I organized in 1984. Ami Ayalon, as a mid-career student at Harvard's Kennedy School of Government in 1991-92, took my seminar on International Conflict, which included a full-scale Israeli-Palestinian problem-solving workshop, in which the seminar students participated as apprentice members of the third party. They illustrate the extent to which our work reached into the political elites in both communities. Unfortunately, in adherence with our promise of confidentiality, the names of many other participants in our workshops and related meetings cannot be mentioned at this time.

8. I am very grateful to Harvard University and to the U.S. Institute of Peace for their financial support of my current work, and to the Weatherhead Center for International Affairs, Harvard University, for continuing to provide logistical support and a most hospitable environment for this work.

3

The Maryland Problem-Solving Forums

Edward Azar's Lebanon

George Emile Irani

As a Lebanese-American scholar in conflict management and one the founding fathers of interactive conflict resolution, together with his colleague John Burton, Edward Azar dedicated some of his energies, when he was at the University of Maryland, to finding possible solutions to the Lebanese War. His efforts on behalf of Lebanon culminated in two problem-solving workshops or forums held in May and October 1984.

This chapter is an attempt to describe and frame how Azar's unofficial Track Two efforts influenced efforts towards resolving the civil war in Lebanon. I will first briefly describe the nature of the conflict in Lebanon looking at the principal parties' issues, positions, goals, and underlying needs. Second, I will sketch the various attempts at major settlement plans. I will then look at Azar's role as a third party at the Lebanon problem-solving forums and focus on his goals and the nature of the intervention. Finally, I will draw an initial and tentative assessment on the nature of the transfer that took place, comparing what was achieved in Maryland to the 1989 Taif Accord that ended the strife in Lebanon.[1]

The Lebanese War: Nature of the Conflict

Because of its formation as a federation of ethno-religious communities (eighteen communities, Christian, and Muslim), Lebanon cannot be considered a nation-state. The major communities that constitute Lebanon's basic population are, on the Christian side, the Maronites, the Greek Orthodox, and the Greek Catholics; and on the Muslim side, Shi'a Muslims, Sunni Muslims, and the Druzes (Rabbath, 1973; de Bar, 1983). Lebanese communities, each jealous of its socio-religious traditions and prerogatives, have never evolved from a confessional, sectarian mosaic to form an integrated political system (Suleiman, 1967; Rabbath, 1973).

Coexistence between Christian and Islamic communities was first sanctioned by the Lebanese Constitution of 1926 and by the unwritten National Pact of 1943 (mithaak al-watani). The National Pact was more of a political act aimed at the lebanonization of Muslims and the arabization of Christians. It was based on the premise that the Maronites would renounce their allegiance to French protection and the Muslims would forego their dreams of unity with Syria. The National Pact reflected also the population balance that existed at that time which exhibited a slight advantage for the Christian communities. This situation was reflected in a verbal agreement between Lebanon's elites, whereby the president of the Republic of Lebanon would always be a Christian Maronite, the prime minister a Sunni Muslim, and the speaker of the parliament a Shi'a Muslim.

The National Pact was one of the fundamental casualties of the civil war in Lebanon. By the mid-1970s, the Muslim population of Lebanon had achieved a relative majority, even if this fact has not been sanctioned by an official population census—since 1932, no formal census had been carried out to analyze the demographic weight of the various communities in Lebanon. As an alternative to the failure of the National Pact, several Maronite personalities advanced solutions ranging from the creation of a federal or a confederal state in Lebanon to the outright partition of the country.

Since the beginning of the civil war in 1975, the most important group that embodied and defended Maronite and Christian aspirations in Lebanon is the Phalangist Party (hizb al-kata'ib al-lubnaniyya). Pierre Gemayel, a leading figure in Maronite and Lebanese politics, established this political formation in 1936. During the Lebanese war (1975-1989), the Phalangists staunchly opposed the military involvement and political meddling of Palestinian (PLO) guerrillas in Lebanese politics. In 1976 the Phalangists joined a larger coalition of major conservative parties known as the *Lebanese Front*. The Lebanese Front's charter stressed "the need to maintain the unity of Lebanon, to reestablish the authority of the law, and to respect private enterprise in the economic sector" (MECC, 1979; Picard, 1980). The militias controlled by the member parties of the Lebanese Front were unified in 1980 in the *Lebanese Forces* (LF) (Snider, 1984).

In order to preserve their presence and survival during the civil war, the Phalangists and their allies called first on regional powers, then on global intervention, to defend the integrity of the state of Lebanon. In the summer of 1976, the Syrian regime of Hafez al-Assad was invited to intervene on behalf of the Christian militias in Lebanon to forestall an imminent victory by the Islamic-Leftist-Palestinian coalition.

The outbreak of the civil war in Lebanon was perceived as a threat to Syria's military and political position against Israel. During the conflict in Lebanon, the Syrian leadership's goals in Lebanon were threefold: (1) to prevent a leftist-Palestinian takeover in Lebanon, which would have inevitably led to a war between Syria and Israel, (2) to thwart any attempt toward the partition of Lebanon that could threaten the integrity of Syria itself, and (3) to maintain a state of controlled tensions between the Lebanese warring factions (Dawisha, 1980; Haley and Snider, 1979; W. Khalidi, 1979).

The Syrian-Lebanese conservative Christian harmony did not last very long—less than two years. In order to counter the Palestinian and Syrian presence in Lebanon, the Christian-dominated militias or some among them decided to establish close ties with the Israelis. The Israelis came to the Lebanese Christians' rescue because of the latter's status as a threatened minority in the Near East. The Israeli-Maronite connection goes as far back as the 1930s when some prominent Maronite Christian leaders, mostly the patriarch, then Monsignor Arida, advocated the creation of a Christian homeland similar to the Jewish homeland promised to the Jews in the Balfour Declaration (Irani, 1989). Israel's objectives in Lebanon were not too different from those of Syria in that both countries' leaderships loathed any radical change in the Lebanese formula of 1943 (the National Pact). For the Israelis, the PLO should not be allowed free hand in southern Lebanon to disrupt the northern Israeli settlements. By the spring of 1976, the Israelis were praising the Syrian intervention in Lebanon, given Damascus's heavy hand against the PLO and its Lebanese allies.

In 1982, Israeli objectives in Lebanon were given a new impetus with the advent of a Likud-dominated coalition government in power. At that time, the then defense minister, Ariel Sharon, formulated a three-pronged policy towards the invasion of Lebanon in June 1982. The objectives of this second major Israeli invasion of Lebanon (the first was in 1978) were to (1) destroy PLO bases in Lebanon, (2) undermine and defeat Syrian troops in Lebanon, and (3) install a friendly Phalangist-dominated regime in Beirut. By the fall of 1982, Sharon's grandiose schemes ended following the tragic massacres of Palestinian and Lebanese civilians in the refugee camps of Sabra and Shatila (Schiff and Ya'ari, 1984; Kapeliouk, 1982).

Together with the Christian communities in Lebanon, Muslim communities have played an ever-increasing role in Lebanese politics. During the Lebanese war, the Muslim communities in Lebanon did not present a unified front. Nevertheless, both conservative and radical elements were in agreement on fundamental issues. Given the demographic changes that occurred in their favor since the formation of the Republic of Lebanon in 1920, Lebanese Muslims claimed that the distribution of power in Lebanon was to their disadvantage. The other issue that united the Muslim communities was their total opposition to the partition of Lebanon and their stress on the Arab identity of the country.

Additional objectives that united Lebanese Muslims included (1) the consolidation of relations between Lebanon, the Arab countries, and the Third World; (2) solidarity with the Palestinian people, through rejecting its permanent settlement (tawteen) in Lebanon; (3) the end of all cooperation with Israel; and (4) the dismantlement of the militias (Khuwayri, 1975-1981; W. Khalidi, 1979). Furthermore, the Muslims in Lebanon advanced two requests: (1) a major role for the prime minister, who, until the war ended in 1989, was considered a rubber stamp to the president's decisions; and (2) a better distribution of economic wealth.

From the military standpoint, the Maronite-dominated Lebanese Front was confronted during the war by the Muslim-Leftist coalition known also as the Lebanese National Movement (LNM; al haraka al wataniyya al lubnaniyya). One of the main objectives of the LNM was to be an active and militant advocate for dispossessed Lebanese living in the misery belt around Beirut (Zhibian, 1977). The radical Islamic-Leftist coalition found in the PLO presence in Lebanon a golden opportunity to upset the sectarian equilibrium in the country. Nevertheless, the LNM aims were thwarted by the pervasive confessional nature of the Lebanese body politic, the policies followed by the Assad regime in Syria, and in the internal bickering that marred relationships between the various Muslim groups and between them and the Palestinians.

In the course of the Lebanese civil war, several atrocities were committed against innocent civilians. This led to the internal displacement of communities and wanton acts of violence between and within each of the communities in Lebanon. The conflict in Lebanon was further compounded by regional and global interventions that led to the escalation of the conflict.

Settling the Lebanese War: Brief Sketch

To place Edward Azar's Maryland forums in perspective it is important to sketch the various mediation attempts at settling the Lebanese conflict, which were almost as frequent as the cease-fire violations. Throughout the civil war the countries and parties that were very involved in settling the civil strife in Lebanon included the League of Arab States, Syria, Saudi Arabia, France, the Holy See, and the United States.

Until October 1989 when the Lebanese Parliament approved the Taif Accord that put an end to the war, numerous attempts at settling the conflict failed. Overall, the conflict in Lebanon was predicated on two important components. The first component evolved around the issue of power-sharing that involved political and socio-economic reforms. The second component was mostly related to Lebanon's relations with its regional and global environment, especially its relationship with Syria and the question of Palestine.

The most important attempts at mediation and agreement plans included the National Dialogue Committee (September-November 1975); the Constitutional Document of President Sulayman Faranjiyyah (February 1976); the Riyadh and Cairo Arab summits (November 1976); the Lebanese Parliamentary Document (April 24, 1978); the Fourteen Points of Consensus for a National Accord (March 1980); the May 17, 1983 agreement between Lebanon and Israel; the Geneva and Lausanne National Reconciliation Conferences (1983); Ministerial Declaration of the National Unity Government (May 23, 1984); the Damascus Tripartite Agreement (December 28, 1985); and the Murphy-Glaspie missions (Fall 1987 to Summer 1988).

Efforts at settling the conflict in Lebanon failed for several reasons: an exclusive focus on internal reform and power-sharing issues, a lack of balance between presidential prerogatives, Lebanon's relations with Syria and Israel, and the issue of confessionalism. The Taif Accord succeeded because it reflected the convergence of regional (Syria, Saudi Arabia, and Egypt) with international support and efforts (mostly U.S. but with French and Vatican backing) to consolidate the power of the central government in Lebanon. Last but not least, Taif was a somewhat successful attempt at settling the conflict in Lebanon because it balanced domestic Lebanese issues with regional realities (ATFL, 1991).

The Nature of the Intervention

Before delving into the nature of Edward Azar's intervention in the 1984 University of Maryland's workshops, a background on Azar's perceptions of a solution to the conflict in Lebanon and his relationships with Lebanese factions is in order. To understand Edward Azar's views of Lebanon one has to place his presence at the University of Maryland in the context of Lebanese politics. In the late 1970s, the Lebanese Forces (LF) headed by the late Bashir Jumayyil, dispatched to Washington an engineer and a member of the Phalanges Party to establish a Lebanese Information and Research Center (LIRC). The purpose of this presence was to organize the Lebanese community in the United States and create a lobby in favor of the conservative Christians' vision and solutions for the war in Lebanon. An important caveat needs to be added here: Edward Azar had broader interests than those of the LF and was always keen to maintain, at least in public, his distances between the Center for International Development and Conflict Management (CIDCM) and the LF. Azar had reached an agreement with the LF that they would not use his academic position to lobby on behalf of their agenda.[2]

At that time, President Ronald Reagan was in the White House and some officials in his administration sympathized with the Lebanese Forces (LF) vision for Lebanon, that is, that a resolution to the civil war in Lebanon will go a long way to bring stability to the Middle East. The conservative Christian militia's perspective was that together with Israel and the United States, Lebanon could become an important linchpin to fight all those forces opposed to U.S. peace-making efforts in the Middle East and to oppose Soviet inroads in the region.

Thus, the fundamental message of the LF in Washington was that peace within Lebanon would bring peace to the region. This philosophy was later reflected in the Reagan administration's statement that Lebanon was a "vital" component in U.S. foreign policy in the Middle East (Boykin, 2002). In sum, the LF objectives in Washington were threefold: (1) influence U.S. foreign policy through the efforts and contacts that Professor Azar had in U.S. academic and government circles; (2) promote the LF policies on how to find a solution to the war in Lebanon that would be to the conservative Christians' advantage; and (3) showcase the LF political program in the U.S. and lobby for the election of Bashir Jumayyil as the president of Lebanon in 1982.

Edward Azar had been at the University of Maryland since 1981 and had established the CIDCM where together with his collaborators he studied identity-driven protracted conflicts, such as Cyprus, Northern Ireland, Spain, India, and Sri Lanka. For the Lebanese Forces (LF) and their Washington representative, Edward Azar's presence and prominent role in a major U.S. academic institution was a godsend for their political lobbying aims. In a personal interview, the director of the LIRC office at that time told me that the LF helped identify funds to support Azar in his efforts to publicize his writings and efforts on behalf of Lebanon.[3]

In a speech he delivered in 1984 at the University of Maryland, Edward Azar outlined his solutions to the conflict in Lebanon. Fundamentally, Azar stated that "the Lebanese have only each other" and that they ought to count on themselves to save their country. Azar went on to tackle Syria and Israel's roles in Lebanon. As for Syria, Azar wondered: "Are there Lebanese who believe that the Syrians have *Lebanese* [underlined in original document] interests at heart after so many years? How can a Lebanese show one iota of trust or respect to the Syrian regime?"

Azar was as scathing in his assessment of the Israeli government's intention towards Lebanon. In his 1984 speech Azar said about Israel's intention, "let no Lebanese kid himself, Israelis do not think that all Lebanese Christians wish it well either. Israelis did not really, in the full psychological sense of the word, distinguish between different Lebanese groups except as factions to be encouraged or pitted against one another to serve Israeli interests." Azar went on to chide the LF and their illusion of befriending the Israelis as potential liberators of Lebanon from the PLO, the Syrians, and their allies. His words were really dramatized when he stated that he was disappointed that "the Lebanese nationalists [this is how Azar defined the members of the LF] did not do enough to convince the Israelis of the shortsightedness of these perspectives in the case of Lebanon" (Azar, 1984). At this point in time, the conflict had experienced an escalation from political differences over the degree and nature of change required to a vicious war among sectarian militias with the involvement of outside parties and shifting alliances among the players. Intractability was therefore at a high level.

The Lebanon problem-solving forums took place in May and October 1984 at the University of Maryland, College Park. This venue provided an informal and neutral setting in an academic atmosphere, although the proximity to Washington, D.C. compromised its seclusion somewhat. These workshops were informal meetings between influential individuals who were involved with the various factions embroiled in the Lebanese war.

The participants, who were mainly academics, were nominated by their respective leaders, and represented the major confessional groups—the Maronite Christians, the Druzes, and the Muslim communities. Seven informal representatives attended the first meeting and eight came to the second, and most of the latter were at a higher level of influence. Only two participants attended both meetings. Azar notes that during the May 1984 meeting, the focus was on "*whether a united Lebanon* [italics in original] was desired as the homeland for the conflicting Lebanese communities." As for the second meeting in October 1984, the focus according to Azar was on "*what kind of Lebanon* [italics in original] was desired" (Azar, 1986, p. 126).

Before delving further in to the activities and results of the two Lebanon workshops, it would be useful to briefly present the approach and thinking lying behind the Azar-Burton problem-solving forums at the University of Maryland. In one of his books, Azar states that these forums are an alternative to the power-based (win-lose) approach, which underlies most traditional diplomatic negotiations (Azar, 1990). For Burton there are four fundamental conditions underlying the process of these problem-solving forums. First, "the process must be independent of traditional diplomacy. . . . Second, the parties must not feel obliged to come up with agreements. . . . Third, it must be established that the representatives of the opposing sides are independent decision-makers." The fourth condition according to Burton is that "the outcome of the interaction be satisfactory to the representatives as well as to their constituents" (Azar, 1990, p. 31).

The Azar-Burton version of track-two diplomacy was "led by a panel of facilitators schooled in conflict analysis, management techniques, or human behavior" (Azar, 1990, pp. 35-36). Panel members were chosen based on their knowledge of protracted social conflicts, their cross-cultural sensitivity, and their ability to work in an interdisciplinary team. In contrast to Burton, Azar (1990) maintained that facilitators should have close or even intimate experience with the conflict in question, so that they could appreciate the communal needs of the parties. The role of the third party is to facilitate a mutual understanding of perception, grievances, and needs. To accomplish this, panel members need to ask questions that reveal the true nature of the relationship and to introduce information from comparable cases, including potential solutions. In the first workshop, four members from CIDCM acted as a panel of experts, while in the second workshop there were five members from CIDCM. Two of the panel members—Azar and Burton—were more experienced in workshop facilitation, while the others brought regional knowledge and understanding of international relations. As a Maronite Christian of Lebanese heritage, Azar was identified with one of the main parties, but he apparently was able to transcend this and enact the role of an impartial facilitator.

Azar (1990) indicates that the sessions were informal and exploratory, with frank and serious encounters focusing on the analysis of the conflict and its potential resolution. In the first meeting, most Lebanese participants unanimously "identified with the State of Lebanon . . . Lebanon should be independent, and removed from regional conflicts, while maintaining and developing its commercial, cultural, and other links with the outside world" (Azar, 1986, p. 132). Moreover, the participants reached a consensus on their shared needs, values and conflicting interests. In his report on the two seminars Azar wrote that in the shared needs and values participants included the need for security, such as the "preservation of communities as identities," and security from external or internal threats. Other needs and values included the issue of Lebanon's identity, economic equality and distributive justice, and the issues of political participation and power sharing and a guarantee of basic freedoms. Conflicting interests focused on the issues of "economic privilege, leadership roles, property rights, displaced persons (internal refugee) rights, war-time interests and roles" (Azar, 1990, p. 53).

In the second seminar (October 1984), the focus was on what kind of Lebanon do the Lebanese desire to live in. What is very interesting to underline is that in the second seminar, the focus was mostly on domestic factors while regional and international factors were virtually ignored. External actors (Syria, Israel, United States, etc.) were perceived to be "the source of strife and violence more than the agents of reconciliation and coexistence" (Azar, 1986, p. 137). At the end of the second forum in October 1984 the participants agreed on a declaration containing twenty-two principles. Some of these principles were:

- In the hierarchy of political values, the highest is the preservation and development of the State of Lebanon.
- By a Lebanon State is meant a united, Arab, independent State which is a meeting ground for Christianity and Islam.
- The State of Lebanon should develop into a non-communal political system.
- It is acknowledged that the need for security may lead to tactics that tend to destroy the independence of Lebanon. The above definition of the united and independent Lebanon implies an obligation on all who support

it to refrain from seeking external alliances in their quest for security through power.

- Justice requires (a) that all kidnapped persons be unconditionally freed; and (b) that all Lebanese displaced citizens have the opportunity to return to their previous abodes as soon as security permits.
- The armed forces of the government of Lebanon should be under the command of government authorities, and should be reformed, retrained, and re-equipped for their policing role; and should cooperate with local forces and police until such a time as local forces become redundant.
- Transition steps are not complete in the absence of a clear vision of future political, social and economic reforms, which are to be ratified by a freely elected representative body.
- Stability and peace in Lebanon will contribute to a just and lasting peace in the Middle East. (Azar, 1990, pp. 55-56)

Some of these principles were already present in previous failed agreements to end the civil war in Lebanon. They covered the issue of Lebanon's identity, independence, inter-communal relations, role of the government and Lebanese armed forces, the fate of the internally-displaced and kidnapped Lebanese, transitional steps required to consolidate peace in Lebanon, social and economic issues, and finally the relationship between peace in Lebanon and the Arab-Israeli-Palestinian conflict (Azar, 1990).

The Nature of Transfer

A mixed picture emerges when one considers the impact or the transfer effect of Edward Azar's two Lebanon workshops in 1984 and the Taif Accord that ended the Lebanese war in 1989. The first issue is the question of time. More than five years separate the two Maryland workshops and the Taif Accord. Certainly, the steps and recommendations included in the declaration issued at the end of the second workshop (October 1984) have some similarities with the essential elements of the Taif Accord. Between the time of the workshops and the signing of the Taif Accord, Azar (1990) indicates that an informal network of communication was established among the parties that came to include a much larger number of individuals than the participants. In the spring of 1988, the network produced a National Covenant Document, which proposed "ideas for beginning the reunification of all Lebanese and initiating a much needed healing process" (Azar, 1990, p. 110). Azar viewed this document as a means of continuing the dialogue and gaining more attention from U.S. decision makers, but apparently these objectives were curtailed by Azar's illness and untimely death. The degree to which the National Covenant Document influenced either the process or the substance of the Taif Accord unfortunately remains unknown.

The Taif Accord, signed and ratified by the Lebanese parliament in 1989, introduced sweeping constitutional changes and instituted structural political amendments on August 21, 1990. It established the foundations for the Second Republic and altered the content, form, and substance of political discourse in Lebanon. Specifically, the Taif Accord promised 1) restoration of Lebanese national political and administrative institutions; 2) structural and institutional reform of the Lebanese political system; 3) restitution of Lebanese independence, sovereignty and territorial integrity by devising a framework for the withdrawal of all foreign troops from Lebanon; and 4) forging a special relationship between Lebanon and Syria that "derives its strength from the roots of blood relationships, history, and joint fraternal interest" (ATFL, 1991, pp. 154-155). The main themes of Lebanon's new constitution included the elements of sovereignty, independence and unity of land, people and institutions; identity which has always been a nagging issue in the country's history since its independence; social justice and economic development; abolition of political confessionalism; institutional reforms that would include the executive, legislative, and judiciary; and lastly administrative reforms.

The interesting similarities that exist between the Maryland workshops and the Taif Accord can lead the observer to talk about a possible transfer of topics between the two meetings. For instance, the participants in Azar workshops in 1984 tackled fundamental issues that ended up being addressed later in Taif. Some of these issues included the question of Lebanon's identity, political system, the role of the government and the army, the issue of economic, political, and social reforms, the fate of the kidnapped and the internally-displaced people, and last but not least Lebanon's stability and its impact on regional politics. The basic difference though is that the Maryland workshops were mostly an academic exercise while the Taif Accord, despite its flaws, gave Lebanon its new constitution.

A second and very important distinction where direct transfer did not take place is the nature of the participants (mostly intellectuals and representatives of various Lebanese warlords) in the Maryland workshops and those who attended the meeting in Taif (Saudi Arabia) who were elected members of the Lebanese parliament.[4]

In an interview with Husayn al-Husayni, speaker of the Lebanese parliament (1984-1992) and one of the architects of the Taif Accord, Husayni dismissed the Maryland declaration as a set of "dissertating words" with no relevance to what happened in Taif.[5] He underlined the fundamental differences between the principles adopted in Maryland and Lebanon's new constitution. First, Husayni stated that the Maryland principles reflected the power of the militias in Lebanon at that time. He mentioned that the Maryland principles were very similar to the Damascus Tripartite Agreement that was signed in December 1985 by the representatives of three major militias—the Lebanese Forces, the Shia-dominated Amal, and the Progressive Socialist Party (PSP). The Damascus agreement gave Syria a number of prerogatives and defined bilateral relations between the two countries. Some Christian leaders perceived it as a sellout of Lebanon's sovereignty to Syria. In addition to the warlords, Husayni mentioned what he called "milishya al-maal," the moneyed militias, specifically Mr. Rafiq al-Hariri (Lebanon's current prime minister) and influential Lebanese pro-Syrian politician, Michel Murr.[6]

The second fundamental difference Husayni raised is the fact that government authority and state institutions were totally absent from the Maryland principles. Husayni brought to my attention point 17 in the 1984 Maryland declaration. It states that "the transition from war to stability and peace requires the recognition of *the authority of the existing political coalition of leaders and their mutual cooperation*" (my italics, Azar, 1990). According to Husayni this totally flies in the face of the spirit of the Taif Accord, that is, the consolidation and strengthening of the state's central authority and institutions, including the executive, legislative, and judiciary.

The last point raised by Husayni is the fact that the militias in Lebanon did not believe in a free market economy as stated in the Taif Accord. Warlords in Lebanon used the war to enrich and enhance their own personal coffers and that of their communal clientele.

In his commentary on the Maryland forums, Azar wrote that the definition of "Lebanon's identity and the discussion of what type of society the country should develop were highlights in these meetings" (Azar, 1990, p. 58). One issue on which all the participants were in agreement was the rise of radical Islamist movements in the Middle East and their impact on Lebanon's future. Azar wrote that both Lebanese Christian and Muslim participants seemed to argue that fundamentalism—and the terrorism that is sometimes associated with it—are a function of denial of needs and rights, and of fears of the future. Both sides argued that the lack of national integration and the weakness of the army permit terrorism" (Azar, 1990, p. 58). In his synthesis of the Maryland workshops, Azar highlighted fundamental issues that were to be later dealt with in Lebanon's new constitution. In their quest for peace the Lebanese needed to address the following issues:

1. Definition of national identity and its reflection in the constitutional structure;
2. Security and the means for harmonizing communal militias and the national army;
3. Power structure and the demarcation between central and local authorities;
4. Healing the scars of war and promoting positive participation by the young population; and,
5. Promoting economic reconstruction and development. (Azar, 1990, p. 59)

Azar was very much aware of the Lebanese dependent need to always rely on outsiders either to help them get out from the quagmire their country has fallen into or seek external alliances to defeat rival factions. In a prophetic realization that demonstrates Azar's sophisticated understanding of ethnopolitical and inter-communal conflicts he wrote that the "Lebanese will have to rely upon themselves. They can only resolve their problems through mutual accommodation and not through force. Of course, this is easier said than done." Underlining Lebanon's ongoing plight as an occupied country, Azar observed that "Lebanon will not be able to work out a lasting solution to its problems either under occupation or while it is manipulated by its neighbors and other external powers and groups" (Azar, 1990, p. 61). In his final comments, Azar wrote that in addition to institutional reforms there was also an urgent need for reform in attitudes and behavior: "The first steps in effective conflict management must therefore involve redressing the negative psychological effects of protracted social conflict in order to provide a basis for long-term peace-building" (Azar, 1990, p. 62).

It is a tragedy that Azar passed away prematurely but this does not mean that his efforts went for naught. One possible alternative for the continuation of the workshop process would have been to involve a mixed group of participants that would have included in addition to representatives of the various warlords, intellectuals, prominent scholars, and elected members of the Lebanese parliament. Another set of workshops to complement Azar's efforts would have included victims of the war—from the displaced, to women, to members of civil society at large—in order to explore and implement a process of policing the past that would lead to national reconciliation in postwar Lebanon. As of this writing, there has not yet been an effective process of national reconciliation in Lebanon. Thus, Azar's recommendations are still as relevant today as they were relevant twenty years ago following the end of the Maryland Lebanon forums.[7]

The effectiveness of transfer in the case of the Lebanese war was made more complicated by larger regional and global interests. The final chapter that ended the civil war in Lebanon was written in Damascus, Washington, and Ryad and not in Beirut. Maryland could have been an important location had Azar lived, widened his circle of participants, and held a continuing series of workshops.

Notes

1. I would like to thank Professor Ronald Fisher for his encouragement to write this chapter. I am also grateful to Mr. Alfred Madi, Mohammad Mattar, Nawaf Salam, Robert Pranger, Robert Murphy, Amb. Richard W. Murphy, Amb. John McDonald, and President Husayn al Husayni for all their help in piecing together this study. Appreciation is also expressed to the Center for International Development and Conflict Management at the University of Maryland for kindly providing what information was available on the 1984 problem-solving forums. I take the opportunity to call on the community of scholars involved in conflict analysis and management to revive the work of Edward Azar, and to help in setting up an archive of his papers, which as of today is still unavailable.

2. Personal interview with Mr. Alfred Madi, 12 June 2003.

3. Personal interview with Mr. Alfred Madi, 12 June 2003.

4. Thirty-one Christian and thirty-one Muslim deputies out of the seventy-three surviving members of the 1972 parliament attended the meeting in Taif. Its purpose was to explore and discuss plans for constitutional reforms in Lebanon.

5. Personal interview, 2 February 2004.

6. Hariri made his fortune in Saudi Arabia (he is also holder of Saudi citizenship) and played a role in financing several Lebanese militias during the war. He was instrumental in setting up the Taif meeting. Murr, who was member of the Lebanese parliament, held several government positions, and was very active in supporting financially the election of Maronite warlord Bashir Gemayel to the presidency of Lebanon.

7. In April 1994, and with funding from the United States Institute of Peace (USIP), I organized with my wife, Dr. Laurie King-Irani, a conference on "Acknowledgment, Forgiveness, and Reconciliation: Alternative Approaches to Conflict Resolution in Lebanon." As a result of this conference we edited a book-length manuscript entitled *Lessons from Lebanon: The Relevance of Acknowledgment, Forgiveness and Reconciliation to the Resolution of Protracted Inter-Communal Conflicts*. In 1996, the Lebanese American University published an Arabic translation of this manuscript as a book.

4

Learning from the Mozambique Peace Process

The Role of the Community of Sant'Egidio [1]

Andrea Bartoli

The Successful Peace Process in Mozambique

Mozambique is now at peace. It is an independent, unified and democratic country. It is playing a significant role regionally to insure peace and security. This is a remarkable achievement for a country that was ravaged by an intense civil war that lasted more than sixteen years and caused extraordinary damage (Stedman, Rothchild and Cousens, 2002). After more than a million deaths, and the terrifying experience of more than four million refugees and internally displaced people, Mozambique is still recovering while struggling to respond to the present challenges, especially natural disasters such as floods and AIDS, made worse by the lack of adequate infrastructures. Yet, the conflict is over and the prospect for the successful continuation of the state formation process, which started with the peace agreement, is very high (Hume, 1994). A presidential democracy with a strong role for parliament, Mozambique has undergone significant changes in its political structure that account for much of its success in other sectors. Political stability has created the conditions for foreign investment, thus encouraging significant economic growth. Food production, helped tremendously by the end of the hostilities, has increased and the macro-economic indicators are very positive. For several years, Mozambique has seen a double-digit increase of its GDP,

79

and if it were not for the AIDS epidemic, conditions would be even brighter (IMF, 2004).

There is little doubt that in Mozambique, peace has created the conditions for development. This chapter will argue that this is particularly true because of the ways peace was achieved. The country found its way out of violence not through a military victory or an "only-power-counts" solution. Rather, a prolonged investment in communication, problem solving and institution building made possible a cooperative peace, which is lasting and so far is highly successful (Morozzo, 2003). The enemies, who were fighting for years on the battleground, found a way to communicate constructively and channel their differences into a healthy and sustainable political system. The possibility of peace was transferred from Rome—where representatives of the parties met for more than two years—to Mozambique (Synge, 1997).

Wars do not end by chance. The successful conclusion of violent deadly conflicts occurs when parties find it in their interests to explore a political way to address their grievances and work cooperatively. In Mozambique, the challenges to this political constructive integration were many. The country was never independent, unified and at peace (Alden, 2001). Located in the southern region of Africa, Mozambique was (and still is) ethnically very diverse. Colonized by the Portuguese at the end of the fifteenth century, Mozambique did not experience the decolonization process that peaked in the 1960s (Newitt, 1995). Portugal relinquished control over the colonies only after a military coup in Lisbon that prompted a very hasty transition of power to Frelimo (Frente de Liberacao de Mocambique), the independence movement that took the name in 1963 when three major nationalist groups united under the leadership of Eduardo Mondlane (Alden, 2001). After the assassination of Mondlane, Frelimo was led by Samora Machel, a representative of the tribe in the south of the country who favored a radical policy aimed at not only challenging the Portuguese, but also liberating people from traditional authorities. Machel became the first president of the newly independent Mozambique (Bartoli, 1999), a country of great diversity in terms of tribal, regional, racial, and religious elements that was for the first time called to a national project. The ideological preference was clearly at the same time nationalist and socialist. Both these approaches clashed with traditional identities and local structures of power. The tension became significant after the government's nationalization of the economy, the establishment of new property regulations, and the establishment of nationwide offices of the state.

Under Machel's leadership, Mozambican tribal, regional, racial, or religious identities were downplayed and a new nationalist, socialist identity was promoted. The government was particularly harsh on traditional local authorities. The government nationalized much of the economy, and directly controlled property and many of the country's functions. "While the Frelimo government was able to set the tone for a liberated Mozambique, it was also forced, by a lack of resources and some ideological rigidity, into an impasse" (Bartoli, 1999). The dissatisfaction created by the clash of traditional structures and ideological inno-

the cause of the conflict.

vation led to the development of an armed movement. Renamo (Resistencia Nacional Mocambicana), previously called Mozambique Military Resistance, was the result of both internal and external factors. The most significant among them was probably the involvement of Mozambique in the Rhodesian conflict on the side of the liberation forces led by Mugabe against the regime. This resulted in support for Renamo from Rhodesia and later South Africa. In a moment in which the whole region was struggling for freedom and independence, the ideological clarity of the Frelimo regime served them well in the long-term investment that secured independence. However, it provoked reactions that were highly destructive and that would force the government on the defensive (Abrahamsson and Nilsson, 1995; Flower, 1987; Birmingham, 1993; Henrikson, 1983). As noted by Bartoli (1999), under the leadership of Afonso Dhlakama,

> Renamo exploited the discontent of the traditional authority structures. Dhlakama was himself a member of the Ndau tribe in the center of the country, and was connected with the Shona tribe, which constitutes the largest ethnic group in Zimbabwe. Renamo's aim during the entire war was to make it impossible for the Frelimo government to function properly. Almost no military confrontation between armies on the battleground was ever recorded during the war in Mozambique; Renamo preferred to attack villages and infrastructure by demolishing houses, schools, bridges, hospitals, and roads. The war was bloody and very destructive. Many civilians were killed, and many more were forced to flee from their homes. (p. 254)

Many of these people found refuge in neighboring countries, especially Malawi and Zimbabwe (Gersony, 1988; Human Rights Watch, 1992; Nordstrom, 1997). At the time, Renamo had neither an articulated ideology nor an organizational structure with which to promote any political platform (Magaia, 1988; Minter, 1989, 1994). As essentially a military insurgent movement, Renamo was unable to develop any significant political strategy (Bartoli, 1999; Geffray, 1990; Msabaha 1995).

If it is plausible that the conflict between Frelimo and Renamo had one of its causes in the ideological rigidity of Frelimo, it is also true that the regime experimented quickly with pragmatic responses, especially in the area of foreign policy. It must be noted that Samora Machel himself won the support of President Ronald Reagan and Pope John Paul II, both of whom he visited in 1985. Pragmatism was indeed a significant component of Frelimo strategy that at times was at odds with its ideological purity while at other times was at the service of it.

This more pragmatic approach within the Frelimo leadership was probably best represented by the foreign minister in Samora Machel's government, Joaquim Chissano. He had studied in Paris, spoke many languages, and was very well-versed in the art of international diplomacy. A representative of the Shangana tribe of the south, he was chosen as a successor to Samora Machel when he died in a plane crash. Since being selected to lead the country in October 1986, Chissano guided the country through the difficult challenges of the moment, finally leading it to a peaceful transition (Hoile, 1994).

The credit for this peace falls mostly to the Mozambicans themselves, their parties, their leadership and most importantly, the population at large. There is no doubt that the people of Mozambique were ready for peace for a long time. The human suffering caused by the war, the impossibility of any investment for the future (Egero, 1987), and the constant condition of fear and despair, had motivated millions for a long time to seek and demand peace (Cahen, 1987). However, the political system—partially hardened by centuries of colonialism, a prolonged independence war and the consequences of the ideological divide of the Cold War—was unable to represent those demands fully. Once international and regional conditions developed favorably—the end of communism and the change in South Africa—the opportunity was provided for the Mozambique leadership to conceive a plan to reach out to the sectors that had been fighting for a long time. This investment was matched by the willingness of the Renamo leadership to consider ways in which they could transform themselves from a military force to a political party participating in the construction of a democratic and inclusive Mozambique (Cahen, 1997; Hume, 1994).

The peace process in Mozambique has been a success, because of the Mozambicans themselves (Chan and Venancio, 1998; Finnegan, 1992). However, this participation in the peace process should not be identified with unanimity or consensus. Rough spots, disagreements, tensions, and breakdowns were part of it, and still continue to mark the difficult transition from war to peace, and from violence to coexistence. Some could argue, paradoxically, that the very existence of these difficulties is the demonstration that the process is effective, and "the spirit of Rome" is still alive. A successful peace process in fact aims at addressing those very tensions, incompatibilities, and apparent antinomies, creating the space to consider alternatives to them. Problem-solving interventions would be meaningless if there were no problems to solve! A peace process makes sense only in the presence of war. A conflict resolution exercise is effective only as far as it addresses the conflict in its multifaceted expression (Edis, 1995; Morozzo, 2003).

Too often, external observers seem to identify the presence of tensions as a symptom of a "non-working" or "non-successful" peace process. This could be incorrect. Success is determined by the final results: An effective process produces tangible and verifiable results, which intentionally address the tensions that caused the conflict. Mozambique is certainly, so far, a case of success, because the parties were able to identify a process and to produce results that made peace attainable, and sustainable.

The Peace Process and Interactive Conflict Resolution

Together with the Mozambicans themselves, there were actors who facilitated, accompanied, and nourished the peace process. Significantly, the array is larger than usual. Along with state actors, representatives of international and regional organizations, and private sector representatives, there is one agent of change that played a central role: the Community of Sant'Egidio (Appleby, 2000). Two members of the Community (its founder, Andrea Riccardi, and the first priest emerging out of its ranks, Matteo Maria Zuppi) were part of the informal third-party team that for more than two years led the process in Rome towards its successful conclusion. However, early stages of the Community's involvement and its service prior to the negotiation itself are less studied. This chapter addresses the prenegotiation process, analyzing key episodes that many have identified as cornerstones to the whole peace process. The chapter identifies key elements that could lead to further research in the areas of prenegotiation, transfer and sustainability, especially in relation to the characteristics of Interactive Conflict Resolution (ICR).

It is my conviction, as a member of the Community and a limited contributor to the process, that the role of the Community of Sant'Egidio in the peace process in Mozambique can be analyzed along the lines of the broader definition of ICR as facilitated face-to-face activities in communication and consultation (see Introduction, this volume). However, it is important to note that this intervention was long and complex. The preparation time, allowing for an extraordinarily intense relational investment, was crucial to the success of the enterprise. These relationships continued during the negotiation and in its aftermath. Significantly, the Community of Sant'Egidio, which has been involved in Mozambique since the mid-1970s, is still very active in the country through both a growing grassroots movement and an innovative project to address the HIV-AIDS epidemic.

Transfer does not occur in a void; it is made possible by relations which are challenged and strengthened over time and thrive in achieving a common purpose. When the purpose is peace and the well-being of millions, it becomes apparent that the responsibility and caring underlying those relationships is the key element that allows the necessary change to occur. This is why it is productive to analyze the case of Mozambique more as a "morphing" process, from the unofficial to official interactions, rather than a "transferring" one. The chapter begins by analyzing one particular moment of the prenegotiation phase, which is a paradigmatic example of a series of similar strategic, creative choices that constitute the successful process as a whole.

The Role and Nature of the Community of Sant'Egidio

Mozambique was controlled by the Portuguese during the colonial period that lasted more than 400 years, and achieved independence in 1974. At that time, the Holy See was able to implement the change in its policy of appointing bishops made by the II Vatican Council a few years before. Rather than continuing to have white, Portuguese bishops in the colonies, new, native, local bishops were to be selected. In the case of Mozambique, the number of priests who could be considered for the position was very small. One of the candidates was a friend of the Community of Sant'Egidio. Jaime Gonçalves, as a young student originally from Beira, happened to be a friend of a member of the Community, don Ambrogio Spreafico. However, at the point of Msgr. Gonçalves' ordination, the Community was an almost unknown small youth group in Rome. Created in 1968 in a public high school, it was founded as an attempt to live the Gospel fully in prayer, service and friendship. It took its name form the church of Sant'Egidio (St. Giles in English), which was given to the Community in 1973 (Riccardi, 1999).

Msgr. Gonçalves came to the Community after a few years in Mozambique, and shared some of the difficulties he and the Catholic Church were encountering in the country. The Frelimo government was ideologically unsympathetic with religious contributions to public life. Being a Marxist-Leninist entity, it viewed religion as a relic of the past to be overcome. In particular, it viewed the Catholic Church as allied with the former colonial Portuguese power, and therefore as unreliable and potentially hostile. These assumptions became even more dramatically relevant after the emergence of Renamo, a resistance movement that was supported by the racist neighboring Rhodesia and South Africa. Frelimo stressed the necessity of national unity against the external and internal threats. This policy augmented the animosity against the Catholic Church and its institutions, thus fostering a period of significant tensions between the government and the church, both nationally (with the newly constituted bishop conference) and with the Holy See in Rome. Diplomatic relations were severed and bishops, including Msgr. Gonçalves, were not free to exercise their ministry.

In the early 1970s, the Community of Sant'Egidio was a very young entity with no power or influence. However, the web of relationships in which it was born was extraordinarily rich. The Community was part of the Catholic Church, which has its center in Rome, and always stressed this belonging, as a part of the whole rather than a separate piece. The riches of this approach cannot be underestimated. While officially not recognized by the Holy See until the mid-1980s, the Community ceaselessly struggled with questions of self-identity such as "Why here? Why now?" Both location and historical moment were in fact highly significant.

On one hand, Rome as the center of the Catholic Church was rediscovering its universality. No longer the center of an empire, marginal in reference to major world powers, Rome was still the locus of an extraordinary rich web of relationships that linked the young Community to the world, thus allowing for a learning process, made up of study and friendly encounters. Bishops, religious people, and occasional visitors, as well as members, were the participants in the Community's interactions. The Community gathered for prayer every night in its church and many visitors, especially Roman Catholic, were evidently very pleased by the welcoming atmosphere. A meal frequently followed the encounter, adding a conversational setting that allowed for an exploration of many concerns. The setting allowed for the Community "growing" a conversational web, as a relational center where concerns were shared and responses imagined. The Community, and especially its founder, Andrea Riccardi, were very gifted in reading the potential of the setting properly and creatively identifying strategies of response that were very positive and constructive. This reflection on the very constructive interaction between the Community and its environment is of importance in appreciating the kind of change that occurred later in the Mozambique peace process—a change which was a function not only of intellectual and political calculation, but of an environment conducive to the appreciation of peacefulness and nonviolent alternatives to violent conflict (Johnston and Sampson, 1994).

The second element of Sant'Egidio's self-inquiry was "why now," and it refers especially to the birth of the Community after the II Vatican Council, which cannot be underestimated as a moment of significant change in the life of the Catholic Church, especially in its relation with the world. Following the leadership of Angelo Giuseppe Roncalli, Pope John XXIII, the church undertook a profound period of renewal that emerged not out of a controlled, centralized structure, as some more conservative quarters in the Vatican would have liked, but out of an open and creative exchange, which took the Council and then the Church, toward innovative reforms. Notions of religious freedom were embraced at the same time as the Church abandoned a hostile approach against non-Catholics. Human dignity was reaffirmed and the reading of the Bible—not common practice among lay Catholics—was encouraged (Riccardi, 1990).

The Community of Sant'Egidio would not have been possible before the II Vatican Council. It is a synthesis of sustained ecumenical commitment, of actual work with the poor, of open inter-religious dialogue, of non-proselytizing testimony, which would have been very difficult prior to the transformation. Change was therefore seen and experienced by the Community members as normal, non-threatening, and non-conflictual. These sensitivities contributed to the creation of a setting that was operative during the prenegotiation, negotiation, and post-negotiation phases of dealing with the conflict in Mozambique.

Another element that should not be underestimated is the religious character of the Community. Motivationally, it would be very hard to grasp the intensity and commitment of the Community without any reference to its religious roots. As a Christian experience, the Community holds the belief that individuals can change through caring, committed, communicative human exchanges. Words are essential components of this possible transformation. Aware of the Gospel commandment of "do not judge," the Community has been extraordinarily free from the self-imposed constraints of many who, using necessary reference to positive law, argue in favor of punishment, exclusion, and marginalization for anyone involved in criminal activities. The implications of the Community's attitude, which is open to listening and talking to anyone, are significant. Listening in Sant'Egidio's experience is both a daily practice and an art. People from very different paths of life, rich and poor, powerful and powerless, are invited into conversations that are not instrumental, yet not merely social. A more profound human contact, which the Community calls *friendship*, is sought after and nourished in relationships, which are not intended to cease, but rather to last until the end. This openness to the other through listening, this eagerness not to close the relationship in the box of social convention, this investment in possible expressions of the future, all contributed significantly to the successful relational investment which occurred in Mozambique.

Another important element of Sant'Egidio is the intensity of the exchange within the Community. Each day in relevant cases, such as the Mozambique peace process, each action may be reviewed, searching for reasons to celebrate and be thankful as well as sentiments of sorrow and failure. The daily prayer, usually at night, allows for a fundamental moment of self-reflection, in which each member of the Community is invited to honestly and personally respond. The prayer and reflection offers a moment for an intense social interaction in which all meaningful elements of the day are quickly and informally exchanged. This form of communication has several advantages vis-à-vis the more structured, written modality used in official circles. Each relevant piece of business is treated in this setting as the centerpiece of common concern. These exchanges encourage a Community of several hundred members to share information rapidly, to find a common focus, to celebrate successes when they occur, and to respond to unexpected challenges collectively and promptly.

Both the prayer and the informal conversations are at the same time open and intimate. While the prayer is open to the general public and anyone can participate, no one is necessarily invited, much less forced, to come. Prayer is seen more as an intimate, precious moment that should not be imposed on anyone, but rather offered as a welcoming space in case it is needed. The informal conversations are for members only at first, because they are based on shared assumptions, previous experiences and common patterns of communication and work. However, very frequently non-members are "brought into" the informal modality with amazing results. Some made the observation—watching senior American diplomats talking informally but very substantially with members of the Community of Sant'Egidio—that "those conversations were the foundations of the agreement" in Mozambique. Such moments are crucial in the informal brainstorming modality, wherein information is shared, authenticated and assessed in terms of relevance and the need for response. If someone speaks about his situation in a newly independent country where the Church is not allowed to function fully, it is a shared belief among the members of the Community—as it was in the mid-1970s—that time should be allowed for the speech to proceed, and for an understanding to develop.

The elicitive approach identified by John Paul Lederach occurs informally in the setting of the Community of Sant'Egidio. Elicitation happens in the moment and continues over time, and its first function is to identify a set of shared facts. Through this process assumptions are made, challenged and verified. Next, the conversational elicitation calls for and encourages the exploration of responsible, but hypothetical non-binding responses. These may contain a significant degree of creativity and may help facilitate a shift from negative to positive attitudes—the first building block of a successful peace process. Successful peace processes can be described as a sequence of creative responses to unique conflictual situations. Responses to a single problem, however, can be infinite and many of them might be positive. How could we determine the "right" course of action? Are there rules that can be applied? The experience of the Community of Sant'Egidio seems to go in the direction of an artistic response that makes sense of the whole through a meaningful association of elements that may appear disparate at the beginning. It could be argued that the *proper* course of action is the one that optimizes the possibility of a new gestalt, a new understanding, a new perception of the situation, and therefore a change in attitude.

If we examine the first of many responses to conflictual situations that the Community developed over time, we can see some of these elements at work. When the old friend Jaime, at that point, His Excellency Msgr. Gonçalves, visited the Community, he certainly did not have in his mind a clear plan that would lead the country out of war sixteen years later. Nor was he asking for much. He was sharing a burden of life. He was making his friends aware that in a certain corner of the world people were suffering. The Community perceived his sharing with an acute awareness of the linkage that through their friendship, through their common humanity, and through the ties of the Catholic Church, they were linked to that suffering. The response was: "Let us help you to meet the Secretary General of the Italian Communist Party, Mr. Enrico Berlinguer, to explore the possibility of an intervention from Italy towards the establishment of religious freedom in Mozambique." This response was creative in that there was no link between the Community and the Italian Communist Party, and there were no personal connections with Mr. Berlinguer.

If the reaction of Gonçalves had been skepticism, no process would have started. So, positive feedback is essential when a party in the conflict is offered a new possibility, something that s/he was not aware of or not in the position of conceiving. Yet, the responsibility of moving ahead does not reside in the proponent, but rather in the party itself. The role of the third party is not to impose solutions that seem reasonable, rational and perfectly doable, but rather to encourage the party in the conflict to see itself in a new situation in which the conflict may be managed. The third party acknowledges and empowers a party in conflict every time it seeks feedback. So while the "production" of alternatives is imperative of any third-party intervention, the respectful engagement that allows for the parties to own the process by giving feedback to any of those "responses" is crucial. Another reason for the importance of feedback is that the implementation of an idea of the magnitude of "Let's meet Mr. Berlinguer" requires the active participation of the actors. Having created a challenge, the participants, both the parties and the third party (Ury, 2000), have to demonstrate that the action is doable, the risks associated with it are reasonable and that the expected results will likely exceed the investment.

So after the initial sharing, the elicitation, and the tentative response, an ongoing process of trial and error took place, opening the way to a series of unexpected consequences of the previous actions. The meeting between Mr. Berlinguer and Msgr. Gonçalves was very constructive. The communist leader listened carefully to the situation described by the bishop and responded very thoughtfully quoting Gramsci and his theory of hegemony, explaining how, in a moment of construction of the national project, an alliance of all positive forces was necessary. The indirect reference—somehow more meaningful for Italy than for Mozambique—was to the *"compromesso storico,"* a policy proposed by Mr. Berlinguer for an alliance of Catholics and communists to govern Italy together. Mr. Berlinguer promised to intervene with Frelimo through a delegation of Italian communists who were to visit Mozambique in the near future. The bishop was very thankful for the opportunity to learn about distinctions within the communist block. The Community was very pleased that the meeting opened the way for further action (the Communist Party delegation to Mozambique) and a new understanding by Msgr. Gonçalves towards the Mozambique government (Morozzo, 2003).

Following the meeting, Msgr. Gonçalves had a conversation with some members of the Community to assess the event. A sense of future direction, different from the moment in which Msgr. Gonçalves entered Sant'Egidio after his first period in Mozambique, was achieved. The question is: how did it evolve into something more significant? The Community's sensitivity to suffering and its endurance are both qualities that explain how the meeting of Msgr. Gonçalves with Mr. Berlinguer became such a significant turning point. On one hand, the meeting demonstrated that the "possible" was much more than previously imagined. On the other hand, it strengthened the discovery by the Community of a role that it could play. To convene, to listen, to respond positively, became a real possibility—an interactive modality that could be fostered by a creative response and sustained through long-term dedication.

Continuity is also a very significant characteristic of the Community of Sant'Egidio's work. Responsibilities are shared among members who continue to follow a situation for years through an ever increasing web of relationships. While academic institutions and nongovernmental organizations must find resources to operate before action is planned, the Community can sustain years of work without much of an investment due to its voluntary nature. The Community's direct service work on social justice (schools, hospitals, food programs, etc.) provides a context of more traditionally development activities—to which conflict resolution can easily be added.

The encounter between Bishop Gonçalves and Mr. Berlinguer provides a paradigmatic example of a series of episodes with the same creative and transformative qualities. The same pattern appeared in the case of the subsequent visit of Mr. Dhlakama to Italy. In the second half of the 1980s, after the death of President Samora Machel, it became clear that the government of Mozambique was ready to engage Renamo in a serious effort to end the war. However, a significant obstacle was in its way—the lack of communication channels with the Renamo leadership. Encapsulated in a military struggle played out in the jungle, the Renamo leadership was almost unknown and completely out of touch with the international community. In contrast, the Frelimo government was very successful in cultivating proper official relationships with all western powers, while the support for Renamo was confined to marginal groups. While important for the government, this political isolation of Renamo started to backfire at the moment when stronger ties were needed to establish a peace process. The Mozambique government—at that point led by President Joachim Chissano—decided to involve religious leaders in their search for contact with Renamo (Sengulane, 1994). Initial moves were encouraging, but a more direct assessment of the actual availability of Mr. Dhlakama was needed. The opportunity was offered by his visit to Europe in 1990. Due to its political isolation based partly on a legacy of violence, Renamo was not officially welcome in Lisbon or Rome. The Community was made aware of the negative impact that a failed visit would have on the fragile orientation for peace on the part of the Renamo leadership. We decided to respond to these concerns by proposing high-level meetings at the Italian Foreign Affairs Ministry and a luncheon at the Sant'Egidio headquarters. Both proposals were accepted, and the visit to Rome became a significant turning point. Mr. Dhlakama felt respected and able to present his political demands without being overwhelmed by objections. The transformation of a military commander into a political leader had begun.

The Nature of the Intervention

What was the nature of the intervention by the Community of Sant'Egidio? It was relational. It was an attempt to respond to positive openings by including them into a larger, more creative interpretative framework. This constant presence brought the two parties to speak with the members of the Community, and only later between themselves directly. This was done through an incremental process of exploration of possibilities that gradually bridged the gap between the two. It must be noted that the level of enmity between the two sides was very high due to differences in ideologies (the Frelimo with a Marxist-Leninist out-

look versus Renamo with a pro-democracy outlook); differences in military
strategies (the killings were brutal and the level of violence very significant);
lack of direct contact; and distinct tribal affinities.

Through different paths the two parties established independent trust relations with the Community of Sant'Egidio. These relationships were long-term,
open, transparent, respectful and allowed for the exploration of political options
not otherwise available. While the quality of some personal contacts, especially
with Bishop Jaime Gonçalves, was an essential component of the lasting effect
of Sant'Egidio's involvement, it is without a doubt that the availability of these
relationships to explore alternatives to specific constraints of the Mozambique
political scene contributed greatly to the success of the peace process. This was
particularly true when other such options were neither easily available nor even
conceivable. Sant'Egidio helped both parties relationally by encouraging creative responses to a very challenging crisis. The two paths followed very different
lines (the relationship with Frelimo was much longer and complex, while the
one with Renamo was more intense, especially in the period leading to the negotiations).

In the case of Frelimo, the most relevant steps in this growing relationship
with the Community of Sant'Egidio, as mainly represented by its founder, Prof.
Andrea Riccardi and don Matteo Maria Zuppi, included a number of significant
meeting and events. The meetings of Msgr. Jaime Gonçalves with Mr. Berlinguer in 1982 and 1984 explored new interpretative frameworks of the internal
political dynamics of Mozambique and of the region. These meetings, which
occurred in the presence of other high-level officials of the Italian Communist
Party, had a transformative impact on how the young bishop was conceptualizing the possibilities of political intervention. Away from a confrontational stand,
a firm but pragmatic approach emerged, where values and principles were expressed less by hard rhetoric and more by possible, incremental and positive
moves that could benefit all actors. In both cases, the conversations were equally
very practical and very rhetorical, offering a good array of possibilities that
would have been otherwise beyond the reach of individual participants. These
meetings also allowed for a growth of stature and self-recognition among the
participants involved, especially Bishop Gonçalves and the members of the
Community. Significantly, these meetings marked the beginning of the ongoing
secretariat led by don Matteo Maria Zuppi, which followed the developments in
Mozambique on a daily basis.

In August 1984, the founder of the Community of Sant'Egidio, Andrea Riccardi and don Matteo Maria Zuppi went to Mozambique for an *official* visit,
bringing two planeloads of humanitarian aid. They were received by three ministers (Aranda da Silva, minister of commerce; Chissano, minister of foreign affairs; and Monteiro, minister of interior). The visit was a fundamental turning
point in the relationship between the Frelimo government, which at that point
was interested in broadening their international outreach, and the Community of
Sant'Egidio, ready to engage the government and the church in Mozambique

more fully. The strategy that emerged was of respectful engagement. The Community would work in Europe to enhance the understanding of Mozambique and its policies, and the Frelimo government would entertain conversations regarding the role of religious freedom in the newly independent country. Following these discussions, the Community started several projects in development and cooperation between 1984 and 1988—among them agricultural assistance, textile production and cultural exchange. This last effort was especially well received and supported by the Frelimo leadership, who was eager to present a new image of Mozambique, not as a dependent country, but as a vibrant, productive country of rich cultural heritage and talents.

During this period, the contacts, both at the medium and high level, between the government of Mozambique and the Community grew significantly, culminating in the facilitation of the meeting of President Samora Machel with Pope John Paul II in Rome on September 28, 1985. It is important to note that the Holy See had a very prudent assessment of the work of the Community of Sant'Egidio, which was considered at times too daring. While all efforts to facilitate peace in Mozambique were supported, especially by Msgr. Achille Silvestrini, at that time the secretary of the Council for the Public Affairs of the Church, a direct involvement was frequently seen as potentially too dangerous. The Holy See consistently advised in favor of involving state actors in the peace process and the Community was able to welcome those suggestions, including the more formal channels as appropriate during the evolution of the process.

President Samora Machel died (in circumstances still unclear) a little more than a year after the visit to Pope John Paul II; Joachim Chissano was elected president and initiated and continues a policy of opening up to the West to bring Mozambique closer to Europe and the United States. These factors proved very significant in sustaining the course towards the possible direct contact between Frelimo and Renamo. While the credit for the peace process rests with the Mozambicans and their leadership, there is no doubt that the participation and pressures of external actors had a great impact in reducing the chances of a continuation of the hostilities, while also offering alternatives to serious problems in terms of physical security, military strategy, political interactions and international recognition. Pope John Paul II had two meetings with President Chissano, and on both occasions reiterated the necessity of a peaceful solution. Thus, internal and external forces converged in forcing the leadership to recognize that peace was no longer an impossibility. For a long time Frelimo had stated that Renamo was simply a group of *bandidos armados* (armed bandits) with no legitimacy, no popular support, and no policy. It was impossible (and a crime) for any Mozambican to even suggest the possibility of an agreement that would give Renamo recognition as a political force. The refusal to consider the possibility of negotiations in any form was strongly supported by large sectors of the party.

The peace process moved a step further with the 1987 visit of Cardinal Etchegaray to Mozambique, along with Matteo Zuppi, in preparation of the pontiff's visit the following year. Although it is a relatively small group in Mozambique, the Church (always in close relation with other Christian and religious leaders) was able to challenge the strongly stated assertions supporting no negotiations. The Church advocated for a long time the necessity of a negotiated solution, both privately and publicly. The Community reinforced this strategy, both directly and indirectly, by supporting Bishop Gonçalves' and Cardinal dos Santos' work, as well as offering unprecedented access to European decision makers. This synergy enhanced the stature of the Church in Mozambique, and allowed for a proactive role in advocating for a peaceful solution of the conflict.

In January 1988, President Chissano, in a meeting with a group of Catholic bishops, asked informally to seek contacts with Renamo (Venancio, 1993); it was the formal beginning of a process that had been in preparation for a long time. The willingness of the Frelimo leadership to use religious channels was a decisive departure from previous positions and was accompanied by official denials and qualifications. However, the relationship between church and state was steadily improving, with the elevation of the first native bishop of Maputo to the position of Cardinal. When dos Santos went to Rome for the ceremony, the first Mozambican to be so invited, the government sent Minister Cabaco as its representative. This visit offered further opportunities to negotiate the restitution of properties and opened the possibility of diplomatic relations. Some politicians in Mozambique started speaking about the "collaboration of men of religion in the name of unity." In July 1988 Riccardi spoke at the fifth Frelimo congress; his speech was brief, but significant and very well received. He strongly encouraged a bold move in favor of negotiations and sensed a "pervasive desire for peace" not only among the people but also among the leaders participating in the congress. The message became a key element of the September 16-18, 1988 visit of the Pope to Mozambique. During his discussions with President Chissano, the Pope spoke about peace and strongly pushed for a "path of reconciliation and dialogue."

It was after all these events, in April 1990, that the Community received a confidential request through a young and very talented minister of Frelimo, Aguiar Mazula. The proposal called for secret talks with Renamo without preconditions. It was a breakthrough, prior to which Frelimo had always contended that Renamo had to stop the violence and accept to meet in Mozambique. Renamo always refused, fearing for their safety, and because of their request to be recognized as a political interlocutor. The Community's response was—as always—welcoming but prudent. Minister Mazula was invited to meet Vatican officials as well as selected Italian politicians. At the same time, more confidential discussions around format and content of the talks started with don Zuppi. These conversations were productive, and the blueprint suggested to President Chissano was accepted (most probably with the intention of moving the talks later to Africa). The Frelimo delegation of four came to Rome at the beginning of July. Mazula was a member, but not the leader of it. The first meetings were so successful that both parties agreed to give formal notice through a joint Com-

Communiqué. It was the beginning of the dialogue and negotiation process that would lead to the successful end of the war with the signatures on the general agreement in Rome, October 4, 1992.

Before describing the evolution of the relationship between Sant'Egidio and Renamo, it is essential to note that the Community played a very significant role in supporting the involvement of the Mozambican church with the Vatican and Italy. These long and at time tedious efforts to link all actors together, keep the relevant information flowing, and allow interlocutors to meet in person, was a key to the subsequent success, because it secured the link between the private initiative and the formal recognition of the international community. This role became essential to bridge the gap between Renamo's desire to speak as a political organization and the request by the Frelimo government not to recognize it as such, but to simply address them as "persons." The Community had the freedom, as a private entity, to interact at both levels simultaneously. This multi-layered approach enabled the Community to play the fundamental role of integrator, catalyzing the orientations that were present but latent in the political arena at that time.

As in the case of Frelimo, the relationship with Renamo was a product of the long-term commitment of the Community to Msgr. Gonçalves, who, as archbishop of Beira had cultivated the dream of a possible political solution to the violence that was ravaging the country. This desire led him to seek contact with some of the representatives of Renamo. The first of these contacts occurred in Lisbon, followed by a series of meetings in Rome in early 1986. It was at that time that the peace process was conceived in its substantive form. Gonçalves came to Rome sharing a desire, a dream that seemed almost an impossibility, and through the interaction with the members of the Community, it became a plan, a reality. The brainstorming sessions in Rome, often in a very informal setting around the table, allowed for the exploration of alternatives and strategies that could move the chances of direct contact between the Frelimo government and Renamo closer. Meetings were held with Giovanni Berlinguer and with Giulio Andreotti in May of 1986. Both of these Italian politicians, one Communist and the other Christian Democrat, supported the idea of reaching out to Renamo and facilitating dialogue. The option of using religious channels was endorsed, and soon after bishops Gonçalves and dos Santos joined forces with other religious leaders, such as Anglican Bishop Singulane, in seeking contact with Renamo. In January of 1988, the Catholic bishops had an informal meeting with President Chissano. It was a turning point, because the president moved away from the *a priori* condemnation, and encouraged the Catholic bishops to seek contacts with Renamo, in order to explore and clarify the thoughts of those who "started killing before talking." While the language was still strident and confrontational, there was a recognition that it was necessary to "understand" Renamo.

In this effort to understand Renamo, Sant'Egidio proved helpful, because some years earlier, using Italian channels, the Community had started following Renamo beyond its scarce appearances in the international media. Knowing that it had to establish a credible connection directly with Alfonso Dhlakama, the Renamo leader in Gorongosa, the Community followed its channels and requested the liberation of a nun in Renamo's hands. On April 25, 1988, Sr. Lucia, a 65-year-old Portuguese nun, was liberated and handed over to a missionary recommended by Sant'Egidio in a pre-arranged place on the border between Malawi and Mozambique. This event demonstrated to the facilitators of Sant'Egidio that the channels were indeed operative, and that the desire to continue the exploration of dialogue was indeed genuine. In addition, the contacts of Gonçalves in Kenya were fruitful with the assistance of Bethwel Kiplagat, Secretary General of the Kenyan Foreign Ministry.

At this point, it became clear that the possibility of direct negotiations was linked to the coordinating work of the Community, which was becoming the point of connection for an increasing number of actors. The group of actors was eclectic, dispersed, and distrustful, all of them expressing interest in the "possibility" together with great reservations. This is why the secretariat function of the Community became essential. The very act of keeping in touch with everyone on a constant basis; the careful verification of each piece of information; the hospitable welcome to anyone who was genuinely interested in the process; the creative use of already established network, all became the infrastructure of an intervention that may be better described as a continuum, rather than a discrete series of meetings or events. At this point, the objective of the Community's intervention was to explore, support and make possible the establishment of direct negotiations between the Frelimo government and Renamo. In order to achieve this goal, it was necessary to invest daily in quality relationships with all relevant actors, accepting their idiosyncrasies and supporting their desire for peace.

During this period, the members of the Community discovered the importance of their role in establishing and maintaining proper constructive relationships. The representative of Renamo, who had successfully conveyed the message requesting the liberation of Sr. Lucia, clearly preferred to speak with Bishop Gonçalves rather than to dos Santos, who was seen as too close to the Frelimo government. Thus, he passed on the opportunity to meet the Cardinal from Maputo, and waited until a meeting with Gonçalves could be arranged. The strategy at this point was to ask Renamo to declare a cease-fire by the time of the Pope's visit, and to "Let Dhlakama talk, make a plan and then present it to Frelimo." The initial meeting between Da Fonseca, the representative from Renamo, and bishop Gonçalves occurred in Lisbon, at the Franciscan monastery on April 29, 1988; and a second meeting occurred in Rome at the convent of the Little Sisters. This time he met both Gonçalves and dos Santos. The Community facilitated both meetings with the goal of achieving direct contact with Dhlakama. His availability was assured for a meeting in a neutral country in Africa, possibly Zaire. Gonçalves accepted the challenge and ostensibly went to

Zaire, but actually met Dhlakama in Gorongosa. He was very well received, and obtained confirmation for a cease-fire during the coming visit of the Pope. Dhlakama knew that "Frelimo is winning diplomatically," and according to the bishop he wanted peace, democracy, and elections. Gonçalves spoke openly about Renamo's massacres and the need to stop the violence. This visit was a fundamental turning point and a great success, in part because the bishop discovered that Dhlakama was of the same tribe, Ndau. They spoke their native tongue and found the quality of communication to be very high. The meeting gave a very useful and rare insider view of Renamo, of its leadership, and of their commitment to possible direct negotiations.

These preliminary contacts continued during the spring and summer of 1989, when a delegation from Frelimo came to Nairobi and "meetings" were held through "third persons" (at that point Kenya and Zimbabwe). Positions were still distant and negotiations were not direct, but at least the principle was established and the framework identified. It was clear during this phase that facilitation was necessary; that the issues to be addressed were numerous and that the work would take time and dedication.

It was at this juncture that the Community decided to extend a private invitation to Dhlakama to visit Italy in April 1989. The invitation was accepted and visas were requested for three more Renamo representatives: Ululu, Domingos and Almirante. However, problems related to the armed struggle forced a postponement, and the visit only happened in February 1990. Once again, this meeting was a turning point. The personal relationship established with bishop Gonçalves was now shared with other members of the Community, who had been following the process since its inception. Mistrust of Frelimo was high, but a growing sense of trust in a process that could assure direct negotiations grew. Preliminary arrangements were made for possible secret meeting, but it had to be aborted. Three months later, it became possible to welcome Raul Domingos to Rome, as Renamo representative, for a meeting with the Frelimo delegation led by Minister Guebuza. Domingos declared "Rome is our symbol of peace."

The Initial Meetings

What should be done when enemies meet? How is it possible to prepare the way to maximize positive results and minimize negative ones? What is the role of the victims and their memories when someone attempts to end a conflict that caused a million deaths and four million displaced people? These were some of the questions that the members of the Community, led by Andrea Riccardi and co-ordinated by Matteo Zuppi, asked themselves when preparing for the first direct talks with Frelimo and Renamo. Many questions related to the specific conflict (What are the parties' positions? What are their interests? What is their leadership style? What is the history of their relationship?). In addition, many questions were raised, because the proposed encounter was a "new thing": it was new for the parties (they had never succeeded in meeting directly), it was new for the international community (Why an NGO? What could be the role of non-state actors in such a high-stakes negotiation? Why in Rome and not elsewhere?), and it was new for the Community of Sant'Egidio. Thus, consideration was required to understand the parameters and to develop the best framework for the talks. Through the two-year engagement, some fundamental orientations were key, and these emerged for the first time during the July 1990 talks in Rome. Among them we can identify:

- emphasis on the parties themselves
- reliance on self-representation and self-determination
- active support of the international community
- effective secretariat function
- faithful and respectful facilitation
- exploration of alternatives
- no closed time frame
- confidentiality of communication but transparency of results
- accountability of outcome

For the Community, this was a new initiative. While active in Rome in many significant areas of service to the poor and areas of public concern, Sant'Egidio had been involved only marginally in political processes. This newness allowed for intense explorations of possibilities, settling for what made sense in the moment, and always open to the direct involvement of the parties in decision making. Thus, from the choice of accommodations to the establishment of two separate headquarters in Rome, from the protocol to the definition of the schedule, all decisions were made through triangulation facilitated by the Community's members. As it probably happened to Burton when he first attempted to operationalize controlled communication and to Kelman with the interactive problem-solving workshops, the *formula* emerged out of the necessity to link ideals with practical constraints. In this case, the assumptions were that both parties were ready to talk; that they had demonstrated a willingness to seek a peaceful solution; that both had established trusting relationships with the Community, but not between themselves; and that Sant'Egidio could provide a safe space for the encounter to happen. The Community had to be respectful of the legitimacy of the government, while reassuring Renamo of the safety and usefulness of the exchange. In terms of approach, the fundamental orientation was, using the words of Pope John XXIII "to seek what unites rather than what divides."

The unity to be sought was not only in the final document or in a public declaration, rather it had to be experienced in all interactions. It was perceived as indispensable that all acts, all words, all elements of the process had somehow to reflect that invitation to unity. Unity, which was indeed a mere dream at that point, had to be experienced as a real possibility. If conditions were right, unity would emerge even among old and bitter enemies. It did not matter if that unity was at the beginning expressed only by what could appear to be small choices. Decisions, such as both parties accepting to come to Rome, having separate headquarters, having a U-shaped table for discussion with four observers, using Portuguese as the language, were made in unity, by both parties with the facilitation of the Community. Sharing these choices strengthened communication among the participants and allowed everyone to get to know the others better. In particular, it helped the Community to get acquainted with the actors whom the leadership of both parties had identified. Armando Guebuza, the head of the Frelimo delegation, was well known for his strong approach. A skilled politician from the South (as much of the Frelimo leadership), he was a refined speaker, able to cajole and confront with great impact. Raul Domingos, fourteen years younger, with no institutional experience, led the Renamo delegation, bringing to the table the military dimension of the conflict as well as the connection with the central areas of the country, as he was from Beira of the Sena tribe. For him and the entire Renamo delegation, the experience in Rome was extraordinarily formative, as it allowed for the transformation of a guerrilla group into a political actor.

The members of the Community directly involved in the talks were two of the four observers: Andrea Riccardi and Matteo Zuppi. However, hundreds more were actively participating through an array of services that transformed the experience profoundly from beginning to end. The arrival of a delegation was prepared in detail, making sure that not only were the delegates properly welcomed at the airport, that security was guaranteed, and that they would be safely accompanied to their accommodations, but also that the latest information about the talks was shared, that the reaction of Italian political circles was presented, and that the close but cool support of the Vatican was explained. Members of the Community embraced the delegates in a warm welcome and accompanied them throughout the process, helping them meet whatever personal needs arose. This integrated approach proved indispensable to understand reactions more precisely, to counteract negative news, to absorb negativities and in general to assist the growth of mutual understanding.

One of the roles of the facilitators was to explain one party to the other, at times just to repeat, with accurate but different words, what the other side was saying. Since the beginning, the tendency of the parties was to not accept the other's position as a legitimate starting point, and yet to welcome the same position if it were presented by the neutral party. This process was not only operative during formal talks, but also in the endless conversations that occurred at breakfast, lunch and dinner, while in the car or shopping. The Community thus provided a communication space that was filled with possibilities, a microcosm revealing what was possible when the parties were seriously committed to dialogue. This led to an awareness among all delegates that direct talks were possible, and this was the first breakthrough. The realization that negotiation was fea-sible and that the responsibility lay with the parties themselves grew over time, and because it was experienced rather than imposed, it became an essential in-gredient of the next two and half years.

Also on the observer team was Mario Raffaelli, who served as chairman, and Jaime Gonçalves, the archbishop of Beira. Sant'Egidio sought the involve-ment of the Italian government, because the Community could not provide the entire range of services and guarantees that the negotiations required. The gov-ernment was instrumental in making it possible for the delegations to be in Italy, provided financial assistance, and secured the institutional backing necessary for success. As a former Under-Secretary for Foreign Affairs, and a long time friend of Mozambique, Raffaelli was able to chair the difficult formal meetings with charm and wit, encouraging the parties not to focus on right and wrong, but rather on making peace possible. Also as a parliamentarian of some experience, Raffaelli brought to the table an ability to navigate the process informed by the functioning of parliamentary democracy. Under his chairmanship, the parties felt that it was possible to express their grievances and proposals freely, and that a fair handling of the conversation was possible. The quiet presence of Jaime Gonçalves inspired trust and hope, while reminding participants of a civil soci-ety that was strongly calling for the cessation of hostilities.

The initial tension between the two delegations was palpable, and was ex-pressed both through the protocol and the content of the meetings. The govern-ment wanted "normalization," that is, the re-establishment of a normal civil and political life in the country, and price it was ready to pay was its presence at the talks. By moving away from its previous positions that considered Renamo as bandits and criminals, the government intended to absorb Renamo into the legal fold. The government expected that Renamo should be grateful for the opportu-nity to meet directly, and should therefore lower their demands and accept the government's positions. Guebuza represented this position very forcefully in meetings with Zuppi and Raffaelli before the formal encounter. He strongly questioned the intention and the mandate of the Renamo delegation, and it was only through an astute response of the observers that he accepted to probe the mandate through the "facts" rather than by Renamo's formal documents. Renamo was even more committed to confront vigorously, and during the talks (as well as in private), its delegation never acknowledged Frelimo as the gov-ernment of Mozambique. To them, Frelimo had usurped the legitimate govern-ment of the country, and therefore no discussion of a cease-fire was expected, nor was a return to the pre-war status quo possible. The legal fold was illegiti-mate and a profound transformation of the state was needed before a real peace process could take place. Furthermore, Renamo demanded that a credible Afri-can country serve as mediator—a position vehemently rejected by the Frelimo government, who viewed the involvement of a third country as a useless addi-tion and an indirect accusation of its inability to solve the internal problems of

Mozambique. In addition, Renamo was determined to address the issues of political liberties, a multiparty system, electoral law and so forth.

During the preliminary talks, the distance between the two delegations regarding the issue of a cease-fire was enormous. For Frelimo, the cessation of hostilities was the first move; for Renamo it was the last point. Thus, it was decided that the first encounter should focus on an exchange of point of views, because stating the different perspectives was seen as the first step towards mutual acknowledgment. This conversation was helped significantly by the decision of the head of the Renamo delegation to address his counterpart with his title of "minister," after being greeted by him at the meeting room door. Another element that created the right environment was the introductory speech by Andrea Riccardi, who said, among other things:

> We are aware that we have in front of us Mozambican patriots, truly Africans, without the presence of foreigners. Each of you have deep roots in the country. Your history is called Mozambique. Your future is called Mozambique. We ourselves are here as hosts of an event that we feel to be totally Mozambican. In this perspective, our presence intends to be forceful where friendship is concerned, but discreet and respectful.[2]

The tone and content of Riccardi's introduction captured the spirit and the form of Sant'Egidio's contribution. It was not a formal, forceful presence that could impose solutions. Rather, it was a committed web of relationships, carefully nourished through personal contacts that were allowing direct, fragile yet hopeful dialogue. The recognition that the process was owned by the Mozambicans themselves was paramount, and the observers, as well as all members of the Community, were only involved insofar as the parties requested. Yet, the expectation of peace was stronger precisely because of the *weakness* of the third party's involvement, which put the responsibility for success or failure on the parties themselves.

In this context, Guebuza's first intervention was very positive. He stressed the "enormous expectations" that the first direct talks had created, and he saluted the Renamo delegation as "os nossos compatriotas" (our own compatriots). His remarks about the agenda and the need for an agreement on location were clear and to the point. In response, Domingos was also positive. Addressing Guebuza as "minister," he stressed the importance of being "face to face" as "brothers" even if in conflict. He agreed on the need to identify an agenda and location of future talks, but it was clear that the formal setting was not conducive to positive and immediate results. For this reason, the meeting was adjourned after a little more than an hour, allowing the two delegations to prepare their initial proposals. The role of the observers became even more crucial and focused on making sure that all formal encounters would be successful exchanges. Thus, all future meetings were very carefully prepared for, with attention to process and format that was consistent with Burton's controlled communication, but was *discovered* through experience in preparing and facilitating the first meeting.

The second meeting focused on the agenda. While the starting positions were very distant, with Frelimo focusing on normalization and Renamo stressing democratization, the parties agreed to merge the two proposals into one draft to work on a joint communiqué as suggested by the facilitators. The text that was produced captures the essence of the initial meetings and the subsequent negotiations (see annex). The points to be emphasized in this successful process and outcome are as follows:

1) The parties recognized and acknowledged each other. Each freely accepted the idea that a genuine peace process was impossible without the other. They framed this self-recognition in terms of belonging to the same "Mozambican family" as "compatriots."

2) They not only accepted, but built on the practice of direct dialogue, constructively bypassing any hurdles in the process. Before entering into the experimental phase of direct dialogue, they had to come to terms with Frelimo's resistance to another government's involvement and with Renamo's request to have active third-party involvement. The solution was to ask the observers to become mediators—a creative response to these two positions that addressed both parties' interests.

3) The commitment to peace was not rhetorical but embedded in an actual process. Both parties agreed to continue that process by owning it and having control over it in both form and substance.

4) The communiqué wisely called for an incremental approach. When enemies who have been fighting each other for more than fourteen years come together and start a process of direct dialogue, no solution can emerge without time, no alternative can be seriously considered without time, no perspective can be valued without time. The incremental approach contained the essential flexibility that allowed the process to continue successfully during the two years in Rome and beyond.

5) The parties recognized after the first direct meeting the need for a future-oriented approach: change had to happen and it had to be reflective of the discussions between the two delegations.

6) Finally, both parties recognized the need to meet again, to experiment further with the potential of direct negotiation, facilitated by the team of observers now as mediators. This final practical step, together with the appreciation expressed to the Community of Sant'Egidio, was a proper conclusion to a momentous meeting that started to close the war and opened the parties to the possibilities of peace.

The Process of Transfer

The results are so far extraordinary: the peace process has been very successful, the level of violence in the country is minimal, and the economic growth has been significant. The pattern of interaction established in the very first contact continued throughout: initial sharing, further elicitation, tentative response, positive feedback, practical implementation, shared evaluation, and open follow up. This sequence became a *de facto* methodology, which without being formally recognized, was applied to many interventions. The transfer of ideas, suggestions, and possibilities did not happen through a sharp divide between a closed laboratory or workshop setting, in which partners could brainstorm and generate ideas, versus an open, highly divided political field in which the same ideas were subsequently introduced. Rather, the ideas were generated in a closed environment in which they were *tried* by actors that did not have the political constraints of the decision makers. It is important that the Community kept episodes like the encounter with Mr. Berlinguer alive in their midst. The "story" of that meeting was kept alive and "revisited" several times among the members of the Community and also with visitors. This had a very important effect on the parties themselves, because it told them how much was possible with little investment, how it was possible to find unexpected allies, how it was necessary to try, how courage was an ingredient of a new solution, and so on. These "lessons" were not explicitly expressed but rather implicitly shared, allowing for a significant self-understanding on the part of the new actors, who would volunteer comments such as "This is interesting, therefore . . . ," "It is good they did this, so now we can . . . ." Keeping the story alive created an environment of expanded possibility, orientating the conversation not towards a mechanic repetition of the previous event, but rather pushed the limits of creativity towards analogous responses to new and unique challenges. During the course of many years, the story became a collective patrimony, a sacrament of success, because it captured a sense of hope that the impossible is possible and the unthinkable is indeed thinkable!

The peace process in Mozambique was made out of many of stories like this, told and retold numerous times. The general collective ethos of the Community prevented the individual appropriation of the story and the consequent bragging. On the contrary, this kept it alive, allowing not only for a "transfer" of an objective piece of content, but as a motivational lever, as a constructive example of a procedural model that informed the entire transformational process. It became an "experience of peace" before peace was achieved.

Because the intervention was not intentionally designed as an ICR exercise, but rather as an impromptu response to a genuine need, the Community of Sant'Egidio's contribution to the peace process in Mozambique did not have the clear dichotomy of some other interventions, where the results must be transferred to the negotiation phase. When the initial interactions took place, there were no negotiations in sight. They were relevant in their own merit, yet they also functioned as the seed of a larger plant, which later developed into a full mediation process to which the Community contributed greatly. More than "transfer," we should therefore speak of a "morphing" process that made it possible for the parties to engage in a successful peace process. The parties were "experiencing" the peace they would "transfer" to Mozambique. The "spirit of Rome" was actually an exposure to stories similar to the encounter of Msgr. Gonçalves and Mr. Berlinguer: a moment of peace in a time of war, an actual opportunity to imagine peace while still embroiled in violence. These moments were essential ingredients of the peace process, because they broke the narrowing of the mindset provoked by violence. The originality of the experience is that it was "the first case of a track-one mediation led by a track-two organization."[3] The creative beginning of the encounter of a bishop with a communist leader was transformed into the much more relevant and ambitious contribution to a lasting peace in Mozambique.

In this process, the Community of Sant'Egidio was not a team of objective, trained, professional consultants, but rather an organic web of committed relationships that helped the parties to address their grievances constructively. While the communication was indeed "controlled" as imagined by Burton, the distinction between the two tracks (unofficial and official) was less pronounced. Even the problem-solving dimension was more a general quality of the effort, as opposed to a specific characteristic of a given encounter. It took more than 10 years and numerous encounters of all kinds to positively resolve the structural and religious freedom issues that created the problem in the first place. Yet, every step of the way a "problem" was solved. The lack of communication, the need to access new ideas, the necessity of new interpretative frameworks, were all problems continuously addressed during a very long process of more than sixteen years. This process transformed a not well known bishop of Beira into a prominent figure in his country, in Africa, and in the Catholic Church. The same can be said for the Community of Sant'Egidio, now certainly better known now than before the peace agreement in Mozambique was signed. Even more striking is the transformation of Renamo and its leadership, now politically relevant in the country and certainly very far away from their military past. Instead of a process of transfer where unofficial representatives participate in small groups led by scholar-practitioners, the successful peace process in Mozambique can be characterized as a gathering process in which ideas, contributions, and solutions were offered by those involved in different forms and formats. What is strikingly similar to more structured methods of ICR is the desire to observe reality objectively and offer creative responses to it. In the case of Mozambique, the effort proved to be strong enough to empower participants to the point that they became the official representatives in the process, which is a strong element of transfer.

There is no doubt that the activities can be described as ICR in the broader sense, especially regarding face-to-face exchange, communication, and problem-solving. Significantly, the human needs that were represented in the process were not only of the parties themselves, but of the many who were suffering because of the conflict. It is my firm belief that this ability to represent the needs, interests, and experiences of the victims has been one of the most significant contributions of the third parties involved in the process, including the Community of Sant'Egidio. Representation of the victims and their needs was also a way to cast the entire process within the realm of international norms. While the Universal Declaration on Human Rights was not frequently quoted, it offered nevertheless a powerful reminder of the standards that any peace agreement had to comply with in order to be successful. This was also a way to imagine a stable set of political benchmarks that the new system emerging from the ashes of colonialism and many years of war had to include. Within this framework, the contribution of the Community can be described as a prolonged ICR intervention that morphed into a successful full-fledged peace process. While the Community has been involved in many other successful attempts to promote collaborative problem-solving among warring parties (Algeria, Guatemala, Kosovo, Albania, Burundi, Congo), never has the morphing process been so successful as in Mozambique. To the credit of the Mozambicans themselves and to their leadership, they were indeed able to capture the potential of a sustained communication effort, guaranteed through impartial third-party involvement over the course of many years. The spirit of those first talks in Rome certainly transferred itself to and is still freely flowing in Mozambique today.

Annex: The Joint Communiqué

From July 8 to 10, 1990, at the headquarters of the Community of Sant'Egidio, Rome, a direct meeting took place between a delegation of the government of the People's Republic of Mozambique, headed by Armando Emilio Guebuza, minister of transport and communications, and a delegation of Renamo, headed by Raul Manuel Domingos, chief of the External Relations Department. Mario Raffaelli, representative of the government of the Italian Republic, Andrea Riccardi and Matteo Zuppi, both of the Community of Sant'Egidio, and Jaime Gonçalves, archbishop of Beira, attended the meeting as observers.

The two delegations, acknowledging themselves to be compatriots and members of the great Mozambican family, expressed satisfaction and pleasure at this direct, open, and frank meeting, the first to take place between the two parties. The two delegations expressed interest and willingness to do everything possible to conduct a constructive search for a lasting peace for their country and their people. Taking into account the higher interests of the Mozambican nation, the two parties agreed that they must set aside what divides them and focus, as a matter of priority, on what unites them in order to establish a common working basis so that, in a spirit of mutual understanding, they can engage in a dialogue in which they discuss their different points of view.

The two delegations affirmed their readiness to dedicate themselves fully, in a spirit of mutual respect and understanding, to the search for a working basis from which to end the war and create the necessary political, economic, and social conditions for building a lasting peace and normalizing the life of all Mozambican citizens. At the close of the meeting, the two delegations decided to meet again in due course at Rome, in the presence of the same observers. They expressed satisfaction and gratitude for the spirit of friendship and the hospitality and support shown them by the Italian government and by all those who helped make this meeting possible.

Done at Sant'Egidio, Rome, on July 10, 1990. For the delegation of the government of the People's Republic of Mozambique: (signed) Armando Emilio Guebuza. For the delegation of Renamo: (signed) Raul Manuel Domingos. Observers: (signed) Mario Raffaelli, Jaime Gonçalves, Andrea Riccardi, Matteo Maria Zuppi.

Notes

1. This chapter is a revised version of a paper presented at the annual meeting of the International Society of Political Psychology in Boston, MA, July 2003.

2. The full text of Andrea Riccardi's introduction is in the archive of the Community of Sant'Egidio. A summary is available from the minutes of the negotiations, one copy of which is in my office.

3. Observation made by Ambassador Jeffrey Davidow, then U.S. Undersecretary of State for African Affairs at the USIP conference in July 1992.

5

Contributions of a Semi-Official Prenegotiation Initiative in South Africa

Afrikaner-ANC Meetings in England, 1987-1990 [1]

Daniel Lieberfeld

The series of prenegotiation meetings between elite Afrikaners (South Africans of mainly Dutch descent) and officials of the African National Congress (ANC) provides a rich example of the contributions that facilitated meetings can make to the settlement of intractable conflicts. The meetings, which took place in England between 1987 and 1990, were the most politically influential initiative involving the exile ANC and those with access to the highest levels of South Africa's government. The initiative was specifically aimed at starting an official negotiation process. The relatively clear lines of transfer from meeting participants to government elites underscore the potential for transfer from interactive meetings to official decision makers of both changed intergroup perceptions and substantive proposals.

Background and Context for the Meetings

During the twentieth century the conflict in South Africa was essentially between those fighting for equal rights for Africans and other groups deprived, on the basis of their racial and ethnic identities, of political, economic, and social

participation, and those fighting for the maintenance of a white supremacist order (*apartheid*) based on dispossession and domination of the black majority. In
the 1940s and 1950s, the ANC abandoned fruitless attempts to mitigate racist
oppression by petitioning the government, and pursued confrontation as a means
of pressing for an end to the white monopoly on political power and for a democratic, non-racial, and unified South Africa. By the late 1980s, the ANC-led
opposition included the legal, but repressed Mass Democratic Movement
(MDM) within the country, along with the ANC, outlawed since 1960, many of
whose leaders were in jail and the rest in exile.

After 1948 the Afrikaner National Party (NP) controlled the government.
Under President P. W. Botha during the 1980s, the decision-making authority of
the defense forces and security services exceeded that of Parliament and the
cabinet. Botha's government adopted a counterrevolutionary strategy that included reforms short of sharing actual political power, violent repression of anti-
apartheid forces, and a divide-and-rule approach toward subordinated ethnic
groups.

The government's superior military power stymied ANC guerrillas' infiltration campaigns from neighboring states. Government propaganda had also de-
monized the ANC in the minds of most whites, and prohibited the press from
quoting any ANC members, or even printing their pictures. Nevertheless, the
ANC was central to any political solution in South Africa due to its wide support
among the black majority. The government sought to circumvent the ANC by
elevating the regional ethnic leader Mangosothu Buthelezi to the status of national representative for Africans. However, this strategy was frustrated by
Buthelezi's refusal to participate in state-sponsored constitutional structures
without the prior release of ANC prisoners, particularly Nelson Mandela.

The ANC also enjoyed diplomatic support and aid from the Communist
East Bloc and from some western European and Third World countries. Western
governments began to establish closer relations with the ANC in response to
anti-apartheid activism within their countries and to the decreasing importance
in the Cold War of regional conflicts after the advent of Soviet President Gorba-
chev in 1985. The trend toward peaceful resolution of such conflicts was mani-
fest in southern Africa by U.S.-Soviet cooperation in the negotiation process that
resolved the conflict in Namibia late in 1988. South Africa's government faced
international isolation and an economically crippling decline in foreign investment due to the political situation. Internally, the government was unable to undermine the ANC's legitimacy or meet the challenges posed by the rapid growth
and urbanization of the black population.

Niël Barnard (1994, interview by author), director of South Africa's National Intelligence Service (NIS), conveyed the government's pessimistic assessment of its medium- and long-range prospects:

> There was a very deep feeling from 1986 to 1989, that we can still continue,
> but for how long? Would it be five years, ten years, fifteen years? The basic

question was where would we be at the end of those ten, fifteen, or twenty years? Would we be in a situation . . . of the country just disintegrating? To negotiate in such a climate would be much more difficult than to negotiate in a situation of relative capacity economically, security-wise, and so forth.

In sum, the more foresighted leaders on each side perceived a stalemate.

Yet when "talks about talks" began in 1987, there was little evidence of the imminent precipice or impending catastrophe that Zartman (1989, p. 6) has described as requisite to conflicts' "ripeness" for resolution. To the contrary, the government's harshly repressive measures, taken under a national State of Emergency, had beaten back the challenge from the ANC's internal allies, the United Democratic Front and the MDM. The ANC had also lost a major base in neighboring Mozambique, and was on the verge of losing its remaining regional sanctuaries. With no realistic expectation of success in either mass insurrection or guerrilla warfare, ANC leaders also faced pressure from its international allies to negotiate. For elements in the government, including the NIS, the sense of relative control and stability, established during the State of Emergency, bought time to negotiate a favorable political solution. As the Afrikaner group noted at the first meeting with the ANC in England in November 1987:

> The (pro-negotiation) position of (the security) apparatus is based on the perception that the mass democratic and armed struggle and the impact of the ANC has been sufficiently controlled so as to reestablish a considerable degree of stability. Given this stability, the state can now act to try to further stabilise the situation by taking steps, which, if properly responded to, can lead to full-scale negotiations. (ANC, 1987a, p. 8)

For their part, ANC leaders opposed negotiations so long as the organization was outlawed and the government held ANC prisoners. Prisoner releases were a fundamental precondition for negotiation. As ANC leader Aziz Pahad (1994) noted, the ANC leadership in exile "couldn't be discussing (negotiations) externally without the leaders in prison being out." These prerequisites were reaffirmed at the ANC's June 1985 National Consultative Conference in Kabwe, Zambia. While adopting a militant tone, the resolutions of the Kabwe conference nonetheless afforded ANC President Oliver Tambo a mandate for contacts with "a wider group of whites than the small minority actively . . . supportive of us," so as to "win them over" (ANC, 1985, p. 4/E9). Later in 1985, Tambo tried to establish contacts with Afrikaners close to the government, through Quaker peacemaker H. W. van der Merwe. Van der Merwe approached Willie Esterhuyse and Sampie Terreblanche, two prominent Afrikaner academics with government ties, who agreed to meet with ANC officials in Zambia. When word of the proposed meeting leaked, President Botha dissuaded the two from going. However, separate groups of English-speaking businessmen, led by the chairman of the giant South African mining conglomerate Anglo-American, and of leading liberal members of parliament, did travel to Zambia in 1985 to meet ANC leaders. A watershed encounter came in mid-1987 with the conference in Dakar, Senegal, at which ANC representatives met with about sixty Afrikaners, most of them dissidents without ties to the ruling NP (Lieberfeld, 2002). Bolstered by the success of the Dakar conference in winning over Afrikaner participants, Tambo and his deputy, Thabo Mbeki, pursued contacts with more politically influential Afrikaners than those at Dakar.

The Third Party's Motives and Approach

Consolidated Goldfields (Consgold), an English-owned mining corporation that, after Anglo-American, was the second largest gold company in South Africa, became the sponsor for the Afrikaner-ANC initiative that Tambo and Mbeki sought. Consgold's corporate image and relations with shareholders had been ruffled by the international anti-apartheid movement's calls for disinvestment from South Africa. Moreover, Consgold hoped to continue profitable operations in South Africa and, as Consgold consultant Fleur de Villiers noted (2002), "If (the country) was going to go up in flames, it wouldn't be possible. They were looking to the security of their investment." Envisioning a potential transition from white rule, Consgold executives asked de Villiers to suggest ways to moderate the South African conflict.

De Villiers, who also worked as a political editor for the Johannesburg *Sunday Times*, had been at Harvard University in 1980 on a journalism fellowship and had taken a conflict resolution course there with Roger Fisher. She dismissed most public discussions and conferences on South Africa as "liberals talking to other liberals." The government generally would not send representatives to a conference when anyone with ANC sympathies was attending. Further, "if one did get people from the liberation movement together with Afrikaner nationalists in a public forum, all you got was public positioning and grandstanding rather than dialogue." De Villiers (2002) suggested that Consgold "could act as midwife to a meeting between Afrikaner nationalists who could influence the government, rather than liberals who couldn't talk back in to the government." De Villiers counseled that any productive dialogue between Afrikaner nationalists and the ANC had to be kept secret in order to occur at all, as well as to diminish the incentives for public position-taking that were inimical to trust building.

When Consgold asked for suggestions regarding Afrikaner participants, de Villiers suggested Willie Esterhuyse, the professor of political philosophy at Stellenbosch University whom Botha had dissuaded from meeting the ANC in 1985. De Villiers had known Esterhuyse for several years as "one of the major instruments of Afrikaner nationalism within the academic community and within the Rapportryers and the Broederbond"—elite and secretive Afrikaner nationalist organizations to which many senior Afrikaner politicians belonged.

Esterhuyse had left the National Party and the Broederbond in the mid-1980s, but, de Villiers (2002) noted, had retained political influence while "remaining totally open to ideas that the government thought heretical." Esterhuyse had been a close political advisor to President Botha and had taught Botha's daughter at Stellenbosch (Esterhuyse, 1998). For the initial Consgold-sponsored meeting in 1987 he recruited two Stellenbosch colleagues with political ties, Sampie Terreblanche and Willie Breytenbach. The latter had worked for the minister of constitutional affairs and had also been secretary to the State Security Council, which, under Botha, was in the upper reaches of the state bureaucracy. Esterhuyse also invited J. P. de Lange, Chairman of the Broederbond who had met informally with Thabo Mbeki in New York in 1985, to be part of an Afrikaner delegation. In the event, concerns over confidentiality caused de Lange to decline, and only the three Stellenbosch professors attended the first meeting with the ANC.

Consgold Chairman Rudolph Agnew had close ties to Britain's governing Conservative party, which was under pressure from the Commonwealth countries to impose sanctions on South Africa. Agnew authorized expenditures of several hundred thousand pounds for the meetings. These were chaired by Consgold's public relations director and strategic advisor, Michael Young, who was the only third party present. In his Consgold position Young had met Tambo, Mbeki, Pahad, and other ANC officials in London in June 1986, at a meeting between ANC leaders and representatives of banks and industrial corporations with major interests in South Africa. Young also helped organize an unfruitful effort to connect ANC leaders and Afrikaners in London. As a former advisor to the Thatcher government on Africa, including the negotiations over the end of white rule in Rhodesia/Zimbabwe, Young had regional expertise and contacts with the South African government.

Young established his bona fides with the ANC four months before the first Consgold sponsored meeting when he arranged a meeting between ANC President Tambo and Linda Chalker, the British foreign affairs minister for Africa. The Tambo-Chalker meeting represented the ANC's first official ministerial-level contact with Britain. Tambo and Mbeki also asked Young to arrange a meeting with politically influential Afrikaners. Thus, an important feature of the initiative is that the intervention request originated with one of the primary parties.

Young's links to the British government, of which the ANC was deeply suspicious, were appreciated by ANC leaders who, as the Cold War waned, sought diplomatic rapprochement with Western governments. According to ANC delegation leader Aziz Pahad (2000):

> We were aware that Michael (Young) would have been discussing this (meeting) with British intelligence. . . . It couldn't be otherwise. But for us there was no problem: . . . It helped us to then get an understanding within the then-

British government that we are not all these "mad Russian agents" interested in
armed seizure of power; we were serious about transformation.

After pursuing the connection with Esterhuyse that de Villiers had fur-
nished, Young oversaw logistical arrangements for the meetings, acted as chair,
and offered his interpretations of the conflict's international political context.
Young (2002) considered his goal "to facilitate two sets of people who in the
public arena were speaking past each other."

In general, neither the ANC nor the government considered intermediary efforts worth the risk of losing control over the timing and substance of talks. In
1984, for example, ANC leaders rebuffed a proposal by British and South African academics for an informal problem-solving workshop with government officials because, according to the ANC, "informal discussions . . . between our-
selves and members of the National Party, in their personal capacities, do not
require any mediation" (ANC, 1984, p. 1). Both the government and the ANC
were averse to involving outside parties, "who would invariably come with their
own agendas" (ANC, 1989a, p. 2). This concern was reinforced by the two
sides' observations of the late-1970s Lancaster House talks on Zimbabwean independence and, more immediately, the talks on the independence of Namibia,
about which an ANC Executive Committee member commented (ANC, 1989b,
p. 15):

> Refer[ing] to the Lancaster House and the Namibian situations . . . we have to
> initiate and set the agenda, and not leave it to others to impose it on us. If nego-
> tiations come . . . we do not want to be prescribed to by forces whose interests
> do not coincide with the interests of our people.

The government team that was meeting with Nelson Mandela likewise told him,
"It is important for South Africans to solve their problems without foreign intervention" (ANC, 1989c, p. 4).

While using track-two meetings to gather information about and even to
pass messages to the ANC, NIS Director Barnard (1994, interview by Waldmeir) resented the interference such meetings represented:

> The more the outside world tried to become involved, the more stubborn we
> became to try not to let them have any kind of involvement. This is why people
> like myself fought tooth and nail to convince [P.W. Botha] that there must be
> no facilitators and no outside involvement. We will talk to [the ANC] on our
> own, direct . . . There was no way that we as a government were going to be
> prescribed to by clerics, academics, and the private sector as to how we should
> conduct the political business of this country.

As Barnard's deputy, Mike Louw (1995), noted, "One of the first things we
[NIS officials] said to Thabo [Mbeki] and company when we met overseas was
'please let's get rid of all these middle men and facilitators and what have you;

we are not going to make any progress with them.'" In Louw's view, which likely represented a consensus in the NIS, ANC officials' meetings with Afri-kaners were part of "a very huge effort, well planned by the ANC, who had these naïve people coming to them in order to drive a wedge in the Afrikaans ranks and to break up the Afrikaner hegemony." In fact, the ANC did consider track-two initiatives to be a means of widening divisions in the enemy camp (ANC, 1987c).[2]

The government and ANC's shared wariness toward intervention precluded a more active third-party role and helps to explain both the low level of third-party intermediary activity in the South African conflict generally, and the es-sentially bilateral cast of the meetings in England. Young's substantive interven-tions during the meetings were largely limited to occasionally pressing parties for specifics, asking, for example, "What do you mean by 'cessation of vio-lence'?" (Young, 2002).[3] Nor was Young usually present for walks in the woods, extended fireside discussions and other informal interactions "when the real business of mutual discovery would take place" (Sparks, 1995, p. 83).

Characteristics of the Meetings and Participants

Meetings were held every four months, on average, between late 1987 and late 1989, with twelve meetings in all through the beginning of formal official talks in mid-1990. Follow-up meetings also continued past the beginning of official negotiation. These "circum-negotiations" (Saunders, 2001) bypassed stalled of-ficial talks and produced an ANC-business leaders agreement on the National Economic Forum in mid-1991 (Esterhuyse, 1994). Each of the meetings in En-gland lasted two to three days, typically over a weekend, with formal sessions on Saturday and Sunday mornings extending to mid-afternoon. After the initial meetings at upscale hotels in Marlow and Kent, most took place at a secluded Consgold mansion and wooded estate in the village of Mells, near Bath.

Since the ANC side was entirely comprised of officials, the meetings may be considered "Track One-and-a-Half," rather than Track Two. However, the groups maintained the fiction that ANC members were there in their personal capacities only. The ANC group was led initially by Pahad, a South African of Indian origin who had been part of the ANC delegation at the Dakar conference roughly two months earlier. Other ANC alumni of the Dakar conference in-cluded Harold Wolpe, a Jewish academic and anti-apartheid activist with close ties to Joe Slovo of the South African Communist Party, and Tony Trew, a white political analyst who worked for Amnesty International and acted as the ANC's recorder at the meetings. As of the second meeting, Mbeki, an experienced ANC diplomatist (and South Africa's current state president), took over leadership of the ANC delegation, while Pahad (currently deputy minister of foreign affairs) continued to coordinate the meetings for the ANC. ANC intelligence leader

Jacob Zuma (currently vice president) attended subsequent meetings. Joe Nhlanhla, also of ANC intelligence, attended later meetings.

Esterhuyse responded to ANC requests that he recruit "Broederbond establishment Afrikaners" to the meetings (de Klerk, 1994), by bringing leaders, all of them men, from the Afrikaans media and the Dutch Reformed Church, policy specialists from academia, and executives of Afrikaner-owned conglomerates.[4] (ANC reports consistently referred to their interlocutors as "Broederbonders"; while most were members, the Broederbond had no official role in the meetings.)

Shortly after preparations began for the first meeting, National Intelligence Service officials contacted Esterhuyse and requested that he report back to them about it. Esterhuyse consented, on condition that he also inform the ANC that he would be reporting to the NIS. Esterhuyse reportedly told Mbeki of the channel to the NIS at the third meeting, in 1988. Since Mbeki and ANC President Tambo sought to explore the possibility of a negotiated settlement, they encouraged Esterhuyse's debriefings with NIS officials, which reached NIS Director Niël Barnard.[5]

As of the third meeting in England in 1988, therefore, two forms of dialogue took place: one involved all the ANC and Afrikaner participants, while a second "meeting-within-a-meeting" involved Esterhuyse, who reported back to the NIS and also relayed NIS chiefs' questions, and Mbeki, who reported to an ANC "President's Committee" composed of about seven senior officials, of whom at least four belonged to the ANC's military and intelligence branches.[6]

Within the larger group, the participants maintained explicitly unofficial roles, but, as Pahad (2000) noted, "both sides understood that the people that we were talking to were listeners, who were reporting back to their home." The other members of Esterhuyse's group remained uninformed of Esterhuyse's contact with the NIS, although Esterhuyse did assure them that the government would not prevent the meetings.

Using the Esterhuyse-Mbeki channel the NIS and ANC later set up a direct clandestine ANC-NIS meeting, apparently the first ever, in Switzerland in September 1989 (Sparks, 1995, p. 113). Following this meeting, the NIS chiefs reported to the new state president, F. W. de Klerk, that official negotiation could begin once the government released political prisoners and legalized the ANC and other opposition groups. According to Pahad (2000):

> Without those meetings (in England) . . . I don't think those quieter meetings with the intelligence communities could have taken place, at the highest level at the end. It couldn't have taken place because those were forerunners to the security-intelligence meeting, which were then forerunners to the . . . actual negotiations.

Substance of the Meetings

From the first meeting the groups focused on how to satisfy each side's preconditions for official talks, as well as what the agenda for such talks would be, and how much "common ground" for an official agreement could be found. Pahad (2000) noted that unlike the recent public Dakar meeting, at which "we were more directly dealing with fears of our white competitors," in the meetings in England "we were dealing more in details of the future." Indeed, the talks were nearly exclusively focused on the country's present situation and its future, with a standing agenda item entitled, "the way forward" (Esterhuyse, 1994). The Afrikaner participants saw themselves as "bridge-builders and go-betweens" and the initial meeting as "a first step in what could become a negotiating process" (ANC, 1987b, pp. 1, 3).

The Afrikaner group informed the ANC delegation that the heads of government security agencies believed they had achieved a desired level of stability in the face of the mid-1980s uprisings inside the country. Now it was up to the ANC to address the particular concerns of the "securocrats" at the center of government decision making. Their concerns, according to the Afrikaner group, were constitutional protections that whites would enjoy in the economic sphere, and guarantees of Afrikaner control over their own cultural and educational policy. The Afrikaner group also inquired whether the ANC might accept devolution of political power to the regional level, and, indelicately, asked whether the ANC would accept political power while leaving the military and the economy in hands of those that currently controlled them (ANC, 1987b, p. 6).

The government, the Afrikaner participants reported, sought to address ANC and international demands for prisoner releases by first releasing Govan Mbeki, Thabo's father, a then-77-year-old with a life sentence. However, government officials worried that the ANC would turn such a release into a "damp squib" by not giving a "positive response," or by "moving the goal posts" and making new demands. Esterhuyse and his colleagues conveyed that if the ANC's response to the elder Mbeki's release proved satisfactory, the government might agree to release Nelson Mandela and even to legalize the ANC (ANC, 1987b, pp. 5-6). In the event, the government released Govan Mbeki three days after the first meeting in England.

In the first meeting the Afrikaner group also raised the question of whether the ANC, in return for its legalization, would suspend its "armed struggle" and end its sanctions campaign—a trade-off that eventually became the basis for the bargain reached at the official level. A main goal of the prenegotiation meetings, according to Esterhuyse (1994), was "trying to get clarity on the different positions." For example, the government in 1989 used the meetings to obtain "elaboration" of the ANC's official Harare Declaration that set out preconditions for official talks.

According to Esterhuyse (1994), the group discussed nearly every issue that eventually became the subject of the official constitutional negotiations.[7] A crucial idea broached at the prenegotiation meetings, apparently at the ANC's suggestion, was the possibility of establishing a Government of National Unity during a prospective transition to a democratically elected government. Mbeki considered such a government desirable "for the sake of international confidence and the revival of the economy." After a unity government had been informally agreed to, the post-apartheid economy became a focus of later meetings, for which Esterhuyse, at the ANC's suggestion, recruited the heads of some of the country's largest Afrikaner-controlled corporations.

By early October 1989, Mbeki could report to members of the ANC executive that the government was preparing to release the remaining imprisoned ANC leaders with life sentences, beginning with Walter Sisulu and ending with Nelson Mandela. This concession made possible the bargain whereby the ANC agreed to renounce armed struggle in return for the ANC's legalization and the release of prisoners—the quid pro quo that allowed the two sides to proceed to official talks.

Report-Backs from the Meetings

The government was encouraged to take the above steps because of reports from the prenegotiation dialogues in England, as well as prenegotiation talks with Mandela in prison, indicating that ANC leaders were not doctrinaire communists, that they were not committed to economic nationalization, that they would promulgate a constitution that protected Afrikaner culture, and would agree to a unity government that seemed to offer the National Party the prospect of retaining enough power to control the pace of political change.

F.W. de Klerk, who succeeded Botha as president in September 1989, had previously learned of the meetings in England, although not the NIS's role, through his elder brother, Willem, who attended and had kept him informed. After the first meeting, the ANC had asked Esterhuyse to bring in new members to help acquaint the ANC with a wider circle of Afrikaner establishment. Willem de Klerk (known as "Wimpie") was recruited as of the third meeting, in December 1988, in part due to his brother, then a relatively hard-line government minister who the ANC was "very worried" might become Botha's successor (de Klerk, 1994).

Willem de Klerk's own political influence recommended him to the ANC as well. De Klerk (1998) recalled,

> I was specifically invited by Thabo—because I was F. W.'s brother to a
> certain extent, and also a political commentator, and I was also a mem-

ber then of the executive council of the Broederbond, so that was a good contact from their point of view.

Willem de Klerk participated in four meetings between December 1988 and F. W. de Klerk's February 1990 address to parliament announcing the ANC's legalization.

Willem de Klerk's reports to the Broederbond and to his brother, the future state president, stressed the ANC's willingness to negotiate, its decreasing commitment to "armed struggle," and its willingness to handle minority (i.e., white) rights with sensitivity. Willem de Klerk (1998) recalled,

> I learned a lot from the ANC. I sensed, number one, from high-ranking people—Thabo (Mbeki), Jacob (Zuma)—that they were very eager to negotiate and that they had already decided to a certain extent that the armed struggle should be suspended. . . . Besides being eager to negotiate and willing to suspend the armed struggle, their vision was that it was necessary to establish a western-oriented democracy to a certain extent in South Africa—that we must be globally acceptable—that was for me a wonderful experience. So I felt very close to them in basic ideas.[8]

Regarding the economy, Willem de Klerk (1998) noted, "I was also very impressed during those meetings that socialism, pure socialism, was not really high on the (ANC) agenda. They referred time and again to a 'mixed economy'."

De Klerk (1998) described the reports he gave, and his brother's response:

> I gave feedback to F.W. He was very cautious. He said "no," he doesn't want to know anything about it. But I gave him written feedback every time—my impression of what's possible and what's not possible, what would be the minefields in the future . . . the willingness for negotiations, that the armed struggle was already something of the past in their minds. That they will handle minority rights very sensitively . . . that (they agreed) we must have in the constitution certain articles that would prevent a majoritarian situation. . . . And I gave him the report that . . . (the ANC) understand that, and that they are focused on bringing South Africa a democracy that will be accepted . . . by the world.

Willem de Klerk (1998) assessed that these reports lowered F. W. de Klerk's perceptions of risk in negotiating with the ANC:

> He was very uncomfortable, because politicians always want to handle everything themselves. They can do it better, and "who am I?" and so forth. He never discussed it with me during that phase, but after his 1990 speech (legalizing the ANC), we had a very in-depth discussion. He said, "I must honor you—I did on the second of February (1990) what you, and others, have tried to tell us." And he referred to the reports on the ANC. He said it helped to clear his mind and the mind of his colleagues that a quantum leap is necessary, and that it's not that—the word is not "dangerous"—that it is not that risky.

Willem de Klerk's reports to the Broederbond executive council also stressed that negotiating with the ANC would not endanger the Afrikaners' existence:

> The essence of my message was "Look boys, everything is okay. We can do business with the ANC. They are not that radical. They are willing to negotiate. They are willing to compromise. They see the Afrikaners as an indigenous part of the South African population. They are not that dangerous." (Sparks, 1995, p. 80)

Gerrit Viljoen, a senior cabinet member and former Broederbond chairman, received reports from Willem de Klerk, and himself met with Nelson Mandela in prison. Viljoen (1994) noted, "The unoffical contacts worked against demonization," in that "the ANC's reasonableness and lack of bitterness came across. It was clear that their priority was not to destroy their opponent."

Owing to the meetings in England, ANC leaders also understood the essential terms of the prenegotiation bargain. Pahad (2000) recalled that F.W. de Klerk's February 1990 announcement of the ANC's legalization and Nelson Mandela's release was not a surprise:

> Because of our interactions, especially [in England] and with the Intelligence, there were already indications—amongst that small group—of what even the speech, the general trend of the speech, would be. Not the details, but the general direction. . . . [From] Willie [Esterhuyse] and Wimpie [de Klerk] and others . . . and then, later, with Niël Barnard and them. You'd have had a sense of what was coming. Those of us who were in the . . . discussions were very . . . in detail informed of even the prisoner releases. In fact, those discussions even helped to refine the thinking of the prisoner releases, et cetera.

Intra-Party Resistance to the Meetings

Despite the utility of the informal dialogue, officials on each side feared that the second-track process might entail loss of official control, and might also embarrass them with their own side's hard-liners, should the talks eventually be disclosed. Willem de Klerk (1998) recalled his brother and Niël Barnard of the NIS discouraging him from participating:

> Barnard [and the NIS] were worried that we were going to spoil [things]. They wanted to push us aside to have full control—that's typical of politicians—full control of discussions and the negotiation situation.
>
> [F. W. was concerned that there would be] too many confusing messages—that was the first thing. And the second was that he was a little bit worried that my connection with him would be a stumbling block in his role later on.

ANC officials who were not specifically informed about the meetings also resented them. Military leader Chris Hani complained that some National Executive Committee members only learned of the meetings via a media report (possibly concerning a different meeting) and were "embarrassed when we have to say to our members that we don't know [about] these things" (ANC, 1989a, p. 1). After the second meeting in England (the first one attended by Thabo Mbeki), Hani told ANC colleagues at a meeting in Lusaka, Zambia:

> It is very disturbing that [Mbeki] leaves to hold discussions with Afrikaner intellectuals without prior consultations. I cannot understand why [we] . . . were not apprised. Anyone who goes to such a meeting should be delegated by the movement. . . . We register our extreme displeasure that Comrade Thabo has unilaterally gone to London without any consultation and without a mandate (ANC, 1988, pp. 1-3).

At the same meeting, ANC intelligence chief Joe Nhlanhla objected that meetings were taking place, "without any consultation let alone coordination. . . . There is a loss of control" (ANC, 1988, pp. 1-3). Nhlanhla's objections were apparently met by including him in subsequent meetings and in the channel to South African intelligence. Jacob Zuma, also an ANC intelligence leader, actively participated in the meetings in England as well.

Another negative political implication of the talks for the ANC, and a major reason for their secrecy, was that the ANC's followers within the country would be harder to mobilize to oppose the government if they learned that the exile leadership was negotiating with the regime's representatives. As Mbeki (1995) noted, "The particular problem (in) the ANC was the impact of the process of negotiations on the level of activism."

Regarding opposition to the talks from those within the ANC leadership who favored insurrectionary strategies, Pahad (1994) commented:

> There was a feeling by some that those who were talking . . . were being co-opted and were selling out. But thank goodness for the then-president [Tambo, who supported] getting the process on the ground. . . . [Opposition] was never a homogenous grouping over a long period of time. . . . They were never powerful enough to say "We now take a decision and this must stop."

Conclusions

Circumstances of the Initiative

Track-two dialogues between white South Africans and the ANC began and intensified in response to the township uprisings of mid-1980s. (This was also the case with Israelis' unofficial dialogues with the Palestine Liberation Organization, which escalated in response to the late-1980s Palestinian uprising or *Intifada*.) The Consgold-sponsored initiative evolved due to ANC President Tambo's longstanding interest in a negotiated settlement, and his and Nelson Mandela's acknowledgment that government forces could not be defeated militarily.

For its part, the South African government was motivated to pursue the possibility of negotiating with the ANC after it had temporarily beaten back ANC attempts to make the country "ungovernable." The security forces believed that they had achieved stability in the near-term sense, but were pessimistic about retaining power over the medium- and longer-term in the absence of a negotiated settlement. As ANC delegates concluded from the assessment of government thinking provided by Esterhuyse's group in England, "It is quite clear that this move (toward negotiation) is taken from what is believed to be a position of strength and in a situation in which it is believed that the ANC has little room for manouevre" (ANC, 1987a, p. 8).

The South African case therefore suggests modifications to the proposition that conflicts become "ripe" for settlement when adversaries perceive themselves at the edge of a precipice or a place "where the 'ins' start to slip and the 'outs' start to surge" (Zartman, 1985, p. 9). The "ins" were not slipping in 1987. Rather, the government had achieved short-term stability, but key elements in the security bureaucracy recognized that the prognosis would only worsen over the longer term.

The untenability of the status quo became more salient due to the NP's declining domestic political prospects as the conflict wore on. Faced with loss of support to the Conservative Party (CP), which completely rejected negotiation, and after the NP's unimpressive showing in the September 1989 elections, de Klerk's government was pushed to adopt the pro-negotiation position of the liberal Democratic Party (DP) in order to preserve its own political majority among white South Africans. It is noteworthy that the DP's founders had all participated in track-two meetings with the ANC, and that negotiations with the ANC were the DP's substantive *raison d'être*.[9]

Participants' Characteristics

A consistent core of participants on each side anchored the two groups. Sustained dialogue permitted participants to progress though discussion of the country's political and economic future. The structure of the meetings was designed to foster joint thinking about the future. The core group on the ANC side was led by Thabo Mbeki, deputy to President Tambo. On the Afrikaner side, the core group contained politically influential intellectuals who retained access to and credibility with the ruling NP through their former official ties, family and personal connections, and membership in elite Afrikaner organizations. The meetings thus produced multiple vectors of influence on the government: reports to future President de Klerk; reports to the Broederbond executive and, through it, to other cabinet members; and reports to the NIS.

Pillar (1990, p. 254) suggests, "The best agent for a peace initiative is one who is known to have access to his government's leaders and can convey their intentions accurately, but who holds no official position and thus can be disavowed if necessary." By using non-officials as a channel to the ANC, government leaders could surmount major obstacles to direct talks, namely fear that prenegotiation meetings would be exposed and exploited politically by the far-right-wing CP in its anti-government attacks. While the ANC side in England held official positions, Afrikaner participants were non-officials who had access to, and were deemed credible by, high-level government decision makers. To better qualify himself as an intermediary, Esterhuyse had divested himself of formal ties to the Broederbond and to governmental structures (Esterhuyse, personal communication). Esterhuyse filled the agent role well since the state president trusted him and the intelligence chiefs considered him reliable. NIS Deputy Director Mike Louw (1998) noted of Esterhuyse:

> We trusted him, his instincts . . . We regarded him not as someone who had a rosy view of a meeting with the ANC . . . He was a trained person in political science and . . . his views were balanced. He could give you quite a clear report on the personalities that he spoke to, what he saw as weak points, strong points, how a person behaved under this or that circumstance.

The report-backs from Esterhuyse to NIS personnel and the inclusion of ANC intelligence personnel in the meetings led to direct contact between the ANC and the government. The participation of security and intelligence personnel permitted the talks to become an official negotiating process.

The Third-Party Role

Forward-looking private-sector initiatives can catalyze political processes leading to conflict settlement, as Consgold's sponsorship of the meetings in England and the Anglo-American organized 1985 meeting in Zambia attest. The contributions of third parties should not, however, be exaggerated in the South African case since Consgold's role was limited to providing a venue, logistical arrangements, and resources. Consgold's Michael Young also acted as chair and as a go-between on pre-meeting agenda formulation. However, the formal agendas mattered little, "with contributions [during the meetings] being made as participants wished" and the actual order of discussions differing from what was originally suggested (ANC, 1987b, p. 1).

Moreover, Young's substantive interventions were minimal, in keeping with a facilitative, rather than a mediatory, role. Young's procedural interventions were mainly limited to occasional requests for clarification. Young was not

a social scientist, and the insights he offered the two sides concerned his interpretations of British government policy on South Africa and the international
environment generally—subjects for which both sides had other sources—rather
than insights concerning social and psychological factors in the conflict. It was
the bilateral meetings between Esterhuyse and Mbeki, which took place without
Young's knowledge, that enabled ANC prisoner releases and, eventually, ANC-
government negotiation. It is possible, however, that the ANC representatives
believed the reports that they assumed Young was giving to British intelligence
were diplomatically useful.

Setting

Scholars have noted the utility of novel settings in overcoming communica-
tion-inhibiting conflict norms and in fostering learning and new ideas (Kelman
and Cohen, 1986, p. 337). The Consgold-sponsored meetings included substantial informal social interaction, with participants dining together and drinking
alcohol—an element of shared South African culture. Informality and equal
status between groups fostered interpersonal trust. According to Esterhuyse
(1994), the setting, an opulent estate in England with possibilities for extended
walks in the woods, "helped us to talk very openly." Any sense of exoticism afforded by the setting may also have enhanced participants' sense of shared
South African identity. The two delegation leaders, Esterhuyse and Mbeki, the
latter an expert at bridging cultural differences, developed a close bond. Esterhuyse (1994) also discovered that he and Pahad had mutual friends in South Africa, and that he and Trew were acquainted from their university days.

Political Transfer Effects

The talks' effects on individual Afrikaner participants were profound. Esterhuyse (1994) noted that after his second meeting with Mbeki,

> I came back and I told (my wife) . . . I am prepared to entrust my life to Mbeki,
> . . . and this fellow was regarded as a terrorist, a Communist . . . The main rea-
> son was . . . the way in which he understood the Afrikaners' predicament. It
> was incredible. You must remember the fellow was out of the country for so
> long, and he was the victim of a lot of things, even an attempt to kill him, in
> Lusaka, and still he was able to understand the feelings. And the second thing
> (was) . . . there was no bitterness.

For key government decision makers and constituents, the meetings decreased perceptions of the threat that the ANC posed, as well as the risks of a
negotiation process leading to a unity government. For President de Klerk, the
meetings lowered the domestic political barrier to reversing the government's

long-standing refusal to negotiate with the ANC by helping to legitimize the negotiation option among Afrikaner elites whose support the government required. Even NIS director Barnard (1994, interview by author), while generally resentful of third-party-sponsored track-two initiatives, conceded that such initiatives "played an important role in psychologically preparing the grassroots of this whole (settlement) process."

Besides fostering support for negotiations from Afrikaner elites and government insiders, the meetings nudged the government toward negotiation by shifting the domestic political terrain as the Democratic Party formed to the left of the NP, spurred by Willem de Klerk's covert meetings, along with liberal parliamentarians' public unofficial meetings with the ANC.

To the extent that the meetings succeeded in procuring the release of imprisoned senior ANC leaders, they supported the positions of Mbeki, Pahad, and other "diplomatists" within the ANC, rather than giving bureaucratic impetus to those directing the ANC's insurrectionary and guerrilla-warfare tracks. Members of this latter group did object to talks, but mounted no cohesive effort to prevent them. Rather, internal objections seem to have been largely met by informing key ANC intelligence leaders about the proceedings or including them in meetings. For their part, NIS leaders feared that talks would be sabotaged by other elements of the security bureaucracy, notably Military Intelligence, and sought to keep such agencies from discovering and sabotaging the talks.

Along with other meetings with white South Africans, those sponsored by Consgold pushed ANC leaders to moderate the organization's negotiating positions—notably on economic nationalization, constitutional protections, and a unity government—in response to questions raised by their Afrikaner interlocutors. As Frene Ginwala, a close advisor to President Tambo, noted (1994), "People from home were asking questions about where do we stand. We couldn't just talk about 'liberation.' We had to start putting content to the future."

Substantive Transfer Effects

Most importantly, the unofficial meetings allowed for clarification and refinement of each side's substantive positions, thereby fulfilling an "exploratory function" in which participants can generate options and test the acceptability of specific proposals. According to the Afrikaner participants, government security chiefs sought "information about how the ANC would react to various possible moves by the state and especially the release of Govan Mbeki and, then, Nelson Mandela—aimed at opening . . . the path to negotiations" (ANC, 1987a, p. 2). Reports on the talks reached government officials with the authority to negotiate with the ANC. These included the state president, senior cabinet members, and the NIS, as well as Afrikaner economic and cultural elites who were the NP's core constituency. Willem de Klerk's reports to F. W. de Klerk and to the executive of the Broederbond stressed the ANC's willingness to negotiate and to address whites' concerns about their protections under a prospective ANC government, as well as its pragmatism and decreased commitment to "armed struggle" (de Klerk, 1998).

Each side thus established that its bottom-line prerequisites for official negotiation would be met: State leaders required assurance that the Afrikaners' national existence would not be threatened, that their cultural rights and economic power would be protected, and that a sufficient degree of political control could prospectively be maintained during and after a democratic transition. The ANC side needed to be able to declare victory to its supporters through the regime's releasing ANC prisoners, granting amnesties, legalizing the ANC, ending political executions and the State of Emergency legislation, and allowing the ANC to organize and to contest elections. These government concessions also met the ANC's need for a return from exile in order to assert its direct control over internal opposition groups.

The meetings also served a "verification function" in which each side checks the consistency of the other's positions (Rouhana, 2000, p. 313). The government tested the positions taken by external ANC leaders against those Mandela took in his prison talks with the government committee headed by Barnard. The government's prospects for exploiting schisms in the ANC wilted as it failed to discover substantive differences between Mandela and the exile leadership, thus making a negotiated settlement seem inevitable. The ANC also viewed track-two meetings strategically, as a means of undermining the regime's support.

Procedural Transfer Effects

The very occurrence of prenegotiation contacts involving those at the centers of power indicates that elements of each side's leadership are interested in the possibility of exploring common ground. Kelman (1996a, pp. 12-13) considers unofficial initiatives successful insofar as they contribute to changes in the political cultures on each side in ways that make the parties more receptive to negotiation. The meetings in England did, as Kelman suggests, contribute directly to "the emergence of a sense of possibility," "belief that at least some elements on the other side are interested in a peaceful solution," "greater awareness of the other's perspective," "initiation of mutually reassuring actions," "a shared vision of a desirable future," "exploration of ideas for the overall shape of a solution to the conflict," and "exploration of ideas for moving the negotiations forward." During the meetings, the Afrikaner side provided the ANC delegation with reasoned explanations of both government securocrats' motivations for reaching agreement and government leaders' political constraints. At the first meeting, for example, the Afrikaners conveyed that "What is at issue now is for the regime to find a way of releasing prisoners without losing face, without stoking white fears about violence, and without giving the CP the opportunity to make capital out of the release." In a later meeting, the Afrikaner participants explained that "De Klerk was compelled to be ambiguous because of the impending (September 1989) elections, not because he was not committed to genuine change . . . When de Klerk says he must be given time he is serious and genuine. He had hurdles to overcome (e.g., the police)" (ANC, 1989a, p. 2). In response to the Afrikaner participants' complaints about ANC bombings in South Africa at Ellis Park and Hyde Park, Mbeki explained the occasionally loose nature of ANC command and control procedures and promised to monitor guerrilla units so that civilian targets would be avoided in the future (Young, in Harvey, 2001, pp. 149-151). Understanding why the other side is motivated to reach agreement, and understanding its political and organizational constraints, are essential to the development of "working trust" among adversaries (Kelman, 1996b).

Procedurally, the intelligence bureaucracies used the channel between Esterhuyse and Mbeki to set up secret track-one talks. Participation in multiple meetings in England also helped develop a "cadre" of ANC officials adept at interactions with influential Afrikaners. These track-two veterans—notably Mbeki, Zuma, and Pahad—subsequently transferred their substantive and procedural track-two experiences to official talks. Pahad (2000) assessed that due to the meetings in England:

> You didn't come to the table starting from position of "them and us." . . . And a lot of the issues—about whether you can have a qualified franchise and how you first develop the economy, then you have a political transformation but in the meantime you have certain minor concessions, whether you can release some prisoners and not other prisoners—all those matters had been discussed in those other meetings, the Henley (England) and the Mells Park meetings, and . . . those plus the meetings with the Intelligence were much more . . . detailed (and) concrete.

In sum, the Consgold-sponsored meetings differed markedly from other track-two initiatives involving the ANC in that it was a sustained dialogue; it focused on concrete, detailed, and pragmatic steps to political accommodation; and its proceedings were fully and directly transferred into the centers of government decision making. The initiative fulfilled certain of the participants' expectations: It enabled them to gain information about the other side and to test the other side's responses to specific proposals. It also enabled the government to check the consistency of the positions of the ANC's exile leadership with those of Nelson Mandela in prison. Elements on each side may also have justifiably anticipated that the meetings could help to fortify pragmatists and undermine opponents of negotiation on each side.

Several effects of the initiative, however, were unexpected. Psychologically, members of the Afrikaner delegation did not anticipate the degree to which they would identify with ANC members, their relations with whom would become more trusting, and their perceptions of threat would diminish. The two sides developed a shared vision of the future and a stronger sense of the possibilities that negotiation offered for peaceful conflict resolution. Politically, the meetings lowered the political obstacles to the ANC's legalization. The meetings also gave impetus to the formation of the Democratic Party, which provided the NP with electoral incentives to negotiate with the ANC. Procedurally, the talks led to a direct ANC-NIS channel and also gave the NIS an unanticipated bureaucratic stake in negotiations with the ANC. Substantively, the Afrikaner side did not anticipate the ANC's offer of power-sharing during the transition and the ANC did not anticipate that they would be pressed to liberalize their constitutional and economic policies. The meetings also catalyzed mutually reassuring actions, such as the government's release of ANC prisoners, and the ANC's 1989 Harare declaration setting out detailed and reasonable preconditions to official talks. Overall, the initiative is notable for its private-sector sponsorship, while also highlighting the role of the security and intelligence bureaucracies in the process of transfer, and illustrating how track-two dialogues may fit into each side's larger strategic intentions.

Notes

1. A United States Institute of Peace grant (SG 112-97) provided generous support for this research. I would also like to thank Rupert Taylor, Patti Waldmeir, and the staff of the Mayibuye Centre archive at the University of the Western Cape for their valuable assistance.

2. Even the ANC-allied South African Communist Party endorsed the strategy of using track-two contacts for dividing white ranks, declaring apropos of the Dakar conference, "No achievement of the liberation movement has been more important than the splitting of Afrikanerdom" ("The Dakar Get-Together," *African Communist,* 1987, p. 10). Some of the Afrikaners who participated in track-two contacts may have been aware of the ANC's strategic intentions, while nevertheless electing to participate in service of the goal of eliminating *apartheid.*

3. Young commissioned an anecdotal account (Harvey, 2001) that highlights his own role.

4. Media figures included Ebbe Domisse, editor of the leading government Afrikaans newspaper, Gert Marais, editor of a leading Afrikaans business journal, and Willem de Klerk. Dutch Reformed cleric Ernst Lombard attended a later meeting. Policy experts included Marinus Weichers, a constitutional law professor at the University of South Africa whose students included Nelson Mandela (via a correspondence course from prison), as well as Esterhuyse, Breytenbach, and Sampie Terreblanche. Business leaders included insurance executives Willem Pretorius, Marinus Daling, and Attie du Plessis (brother of finance Minister Barend du Plessis), as well as Louis Kriel and Mof Terreblanche, a confidant of F. W. de Klerk. Government Minister Dawie de Villiers attended a meeting after February 1990.

5. Barnard also held secret, overlapping talks with Nelson Mandela as of May 1988. While Tambo and Mbeki were aware of the parallel talks, Mandela apparently was not.

6. These included Joe Nhlanhla and Jacob Zuma of ANC intelligence and Joe Modise and Steve Tshwete of the ANC's military arm, Umkhonto we Sizwe.

7. During the Conference on Democracy in South Africa (known as Codesa).

8. The length of the transition period remained a point of contention, however, with the ANC favoring only a short period of co-governance before general elections were held, and the regime holding out for a relatively long period.

9. The DP's founders were Zac de Beer who met ANC leaders in Zambia with the Anglo-American-led group in 1985; Dennis Worrall who met in Zimbabwe in 1987; Waynand Malan, who met in Frankfurt in 1988; and Willem de Klerk. Israel's liberal Meretz party, whose founders also participated in track-two negotiations with Palestine Liberation Organization representatives, played an analogous role in the process that led the Labor party to negotiate with the PLO (Lieberfeld 1999a and 1999b).

6

Sustained Dialogue in Tajikistan

Transferring Learning from the Public to the Official Peace Process [1]

Harold H. Saunders

The Character of the Conflict in Tajikistan

The former Soviet republic of Tajikistan declared its independence of the Soviet Union in September 1991 and within a year was in the throes of what became a vicious internal conflict. It was essentially a struggle for power to fill the void left by the sudden dissolution of the Soviet Union in which regional centers vied for control of the government to protect their own interests. Underlying that central struggle was a multidimensional complex of conflictual relationships involving regional and clan-based groups, different ethnicities and nationalities, a range of ideologies from militant Islam to moderate democrat and communist and a variety of intergroup grievances. These complex needs and interests of these multiple parties gradually surfaced in the blunt interactions in the dialogue particularly in the first three meetings and then well beyond as situations as issues evolved.

In the spring of 1992, a coalition government was formed in the wake of mass protests to incorporate democratic and Islamic elements into the post-Soviet government. The coalition government was unworkable, and the president was forced to resign in September. In November, at a session of the parliament a new government was formed that reflected the growing military strength in the southern region, the Kulyab. Emomali Rakhmonov from the Kulyab became the acting head of government. While efforts to stop the fighting went on as Rakhmonov consolidated his regime, the continuing dispute over principles of power-sharing blocked agreement, and local vengeance fueled vicious fighting which the U.N. High Commission for Refugees estimated led at least one-tenth of the people to flee their homes. This was the situation when the intervention described in this chapter began in March 1993. To our knowledge, there was no systematic channel of communication at that time between the government and the fragmented opposition forces. It was not until April 1994 that U.N.-mediated peace negotiations began.

Although this internal conflict turned into one of the most vicious conflicts that broke out on the territory of the former Soviet Union, it received minimal public international attention in the West because there was little television coverage and no Tajikistani diaspora outside of Central Asia, the Commonwealth of Independent States, and Afghanistan. Unlike the conflicts in Georgia and around Nagorno Karabakh, the combatants were not fighting to dismantle the country in battles for secession. Nevertheless, Tajikistan's position on the border of Afghanistan, surrounded by countries speaking Turkish-based languages while itself grounded in a Persian-based culture, and constituting a southern security border of the Commonwealth of Independent States made its conflict seem a potential threat to stability in much of Central Asia and the nearby Middle East. A threat to the interest of the United States in stability, and a potential arena for destabilizing interaction between Russia and the United States sharpened international concern. In that context, the concern of regional governments and of the United Nations mounted.

The Roots and Conceptual Framework for Sustained Dialogue

As background for discussion of the intervention that began in March 1993 and came to be called the "Inter-Tajik Dialogue within the Framework of the Dartmouth Conference," we must go back for a moment to trace its roots. The vehicle for this intervention is the process we call Sustained Dialogue.

The "management team" that initiated the Dialogue came from the Dartmouth Conference Regional Conflicts Task Force. The Dartmouth Conference is the longest continuous dialogue among Soviet, now Russian, and U.S. citizens. It first met in October 1960 at Dartmouth College in the U.S. state of New Hampshire—hence its name. It continued in the form of plenary sessions on the average of every eighteen to twenty-four months—with some longer periods between meetings—until 1990. In 1981, two task forces were formed to probe areas in the central Soviet-U.S. relationship where détente had foundered—arms deployments and arms control in one task force and, in the other, regional conflicts where the superpowers competed through proxies such as in Central America, Angola, the Arab-Israeli arena, Afghanistan, Southeast Asia, and the

Korean peninsula. The primary purpose was always to probe the deeper interests of the superpowers and the dynamics of the overall Soviet-U.S. relationship.

The founding co-chairs of the Regional Conflicts Task Force in 1982 were Evgeny Primakov, who later became foreign minister and prime minister of Russia, and Harold Saunders, former U.S. Assistant Secretary of State for Near Eastern and South Asian Affairs. By the time the Soviet Union dissolved, the Task Force had held semi-annual meetings for a decade. As one meeting followed another, participants asked how they should manage and develop a continuing series of focused meetings. At one point, Primakov said, "We will begin the next meeting where the last one ended." This made possible developing a cumulative agenda, building a common body of knowledge that participants could test between meetings, and learning to talk and work analytically together. By 1989 participants were developing scenarios together to analyze how regional conflicts might evolve and how the superpowers might respond to avoid direct confrontation.

In 1992, participants asked themselves what they should do following the dissolution of the Soviet Union. They decided to continue work (1) now focusing on the new Russian-U.S. relationship, (2) conceptualizing the process of sustained dialogue that they had learned together through the 1980s, and (3) applying that process together to one of the conflicts that had broken out on the territory of the former Soviet Union. They chose Tajikistan because few others were paying serious attention to peacemaking there; because the conflict threatened to involve the interests of Russia and the United States as well as China and the regional countries; and because two Russian members of the Task Force had close academic connections there that would permit them to explore the interest of individuals from different factions in the civil war in coming together in dialogue. This may have been the first joint Russian-U.S. citizens' peacemaking mission. Throughout the Dartmouth Conference, participants had felt that engaging in common work in the common interest of developing a more constructive relationship might serve as a confidence-building measure, but always they suggested projects for the two governments. Now, perhaps heralding the new era in the relationship, citizens outside government set themselves to that task.

Also in the spring of 1993, the co-chairs of the Task Force—Gennady Chufrin had succeeded Primakov—published an article conceptualizing the process that they now called "Sustained Dialogue" which American and Soviet participants had developed together over a decade as a five-stage process (Chufrin and Saunders, 1993). These five stages were not an artificial construct but rather a conceptualization of literally hundreds of hours in non-official dialogue between Americans and Soviets as well as, in Saunders' experience, among Israelis and Palestinians in the 1980s.

The five-stage framework is not intended as a rigid template but rather as an analytical and working framework to permit moderators and participants alike to understand the progression of relationships in their work together.

Those stages are:

- *Stage One*: Either people on different sides of a conflict decide to reach out to each other, or a third party creates a space for dialogue and invites conflicting parties to come together there. People decide to engage in dialogue—often with great difficulty—because they feel a compelling need to build or change a relationship to resolve problems that hurt or could hurt their interests intolerably. These participants are themselves a microcosm of their communities.
- *Stage Two*: They come together to talk—to map and name the elements of those problems and the relationships responsible for creating and dealing with them. In early meetings, they vent their grievances and anger with each other in a scattershot way. This venting provides both the ingredients for crystallizing an ultimate agenda and an opportunity for moderators to analyze and "map" the interactions—to understand the dynamics of the relationships. This stage ends—at least for a time—when someone says: "What we really need to focus on is . . . ." With the use of "we," the character of the exchange changes palpably from confrontation to an ability to talk analytically about the problem they have identified as affecting them all.
- *Stage Three*: In much more disciplined exchanges, participants probe specific problems to uncover the dynamics of underlying relationships with these aims: (1) to define the most pressing problems; (2) to probe the dynamics of the relationships underlying these problems; (3) to lay out broadly possible ways into those relationships to change them; (4) to weigh those choices and to come to a sense of direction to guide next steps; (5) to weigh the consequences of moving in that direction against the consequences of doing nothing; and (6) to decide whether to try designing such change.
- *Stage Four*: Together, they design a scenario of interacting steps to be taken in the political arena to change troublesome relationships and to precipitate practical steps. They ask four questions: What are the obstacles to moving in the direction we have chosen? What steps could overcome those obstacles? Who could take those steps? How could we sequence those steps so that they interact—one building on another—to generate momentum behind the plan for acting and to draw larger numbers into implementing that plan?
- *Stage Five*: They devise ways to put that scenario into the hands of those who can act on it (Saunders, 2001).

In this process of Sustained Dialogue, there is always a dual focus: Participants, of course, focus on concrete grievances and issues, but always the moderators and participants are searching for the dynamics of the relationships that cause the problems and must be changed if the problems are to be resolved.

In this process, a concept of relationship is essential. We have defined relationship rigorously in terms of five components—five arenas of interaction in constantly changing combinations within and between the parties interacting: (1) *identity*, defined in human as well as in physical characteristics—the life experience that has brought a person or group to the present; (2) *interests,* both concrete and psychological—what people care about—that bring people into the same space and into a sense of their dependence on one another—*interdependence*—to achieve their goals; (3) *power,* defined not necessarily as control over superior resources and the actions of others but as the capacity of citizens acting together to influence the course of events often without great material resources; (4) *perceptions, misperceptions, and stereotypes*; and (5) the *patterns of interaction*—distant and close—among those involved, including respect for certain *limits on behavior* in dealing with others.

Power is, of course, an important component of a relationship, but much of the time other components are more likely to determine how a person or group acts to shape the character of an interaction. Power must be defined much more broadly than it has been. Instead of defining it as control, I define it as the capacity to influence the course of events. This capacity is most often seen when citizens act in concert with others.

The concept of relationship can be both a diagnostic and an operational tool. One can analyze a relationship through this prism, and then one can actually get inside any of these components through Sustained Dialogue to enhance understanding or to change an interaction—and hence to change a relationship. In dialogue, identity can be understood and can grow as one sees oneself through interaction with others. A person can be humanized as misperceptions and stereotypes give way to realistic pictures. Common interests can be discovered. In that light, patterns of interaction can change from confrontational to cooperative. As respect for another's identity grows, individuals impose limits on their behavior toward the other to reflect that respect. Those changes also introduce new elements into the equation of power. As one understands that dynamic process of continuous interaction, one learns that power in part may emerge from careful and sensitive conduct of the process, rather than only from wielding material resources.

The Multilevel Peace Process: the Rationale for Transfer

The framework for analyzing and assessing the transfer of ideas and actions from Sustained Dialogue to the larger polity is the concept of a multilevel peace process. It rests on two ideas.

First is the establishment of a political paradigm for use in dealing with the deep-rooted human conflicts so prevalent today for which the so-called "realist paradigm" is inadequate. That traditional paradigm focuses on states' and governments' manipulation of resources to maximize power defined as the ability to coerce or control. The conflicts that dominate the stage today often involve nonstate actors, are beyond the reach of governments, reflect the power generated by citizens' capacity to work together, and focus on relationships as defined above.

The paradigm I find more helpful in working with these conflicts—I call it the *relational paradigm*—can be stated as follows: *Politics is about relationships among significant clusters of citizens in a cumulative, multilevel, and open-ended process of continuous interaction over time in whole bodies politic across permeable borders, either within or between countries.* The concept of relationship provides one framework for analyzing and working with this process of continuous, multilevel interaction.

Second is the concept of the *multilevel peace process.* It is rooted in my intensive involvement in the Arab-Israeli peace process after the 1973 Arab-Israeli war—the Kissinger shuttles and the Camp David accords. We began calling what we were doing the "negotiating process." We began with the purpose of mediating a series of interim agreements as stepping-stones toward an ultimate peace agreement. We quickly recognized that each interim agreement changed the political environment, enhancing citizens' sense of the possibility of a changed relationship. That sense of possibility translated, at least in democratic Israel, into citizens' "permission" for the government to explore a formal peace agreement with Egypt. To capture that larger picture of what we were doing, we coined the phrase "peace process."

From their experience, participants in the Inter-Tajik Dialogue in October 1996 coined the phrase "multilevel peace process." In their joint memorandum following their seventeenth meeting they wrote: "It is necessary to broaden public participation in the efforts to achieve peace by developing a multilevel peace process in order to assure the widest possible involvement in achieving and implementing a peace agreement" (Chufrin et al, 1997, p. 98). They recognized the importance of the official peace process—the formal negotiations at the top of the political pyramid. They were deeply engrossed in their own "public peace process" involving members of the policy-influencing community, mostly outside government, at the upper middle level of the body politic. But they also recognized the work in civil society where much of the fighting in the civil war took place. The key for them was the interaction among all those levels.

The formulation, "multilevel peace process," emerged from an exchange in the Dialogue in which one participant recounted the following experience: He had served with a joint opposition-government commission to negotiate a cease-fire in a region where fighting had cut a critical east-west road. When he had finished his account of negotiations involving field commanders, municipal officials, local elders, and other community interests, another Dialogue participant said: "The reason our cease-fires rarely hold is that they have been negotiated between the president and the leader of the opposition without any reference to the people on the ground with interests at stake and with guns. What we need is a multilevel peace process that connects the local people with the top-level negotiators through working groups."[2]

The rationale for transfer, therefore, is rooted in the relational paradigm and the multilevel peace process. It does not focus exclusively on influencing policy—although that is certainly one interest. It focuses on transforming relationships and political practices at all levels of the polity to build a society where differences can be dealt with peacefully.

The Inter-Tajik Dialogue

In early 1993, two Russian members of the management group from the Dartmouth Regional Conflicts Task Force spoke in Tajikistan with more than a hundred individuals from the main factions in the civil war to explain the work of the Dartmouth Conference Regional Conflicts Task Force and to ascertain their interest in coming into a space for dialogue created by the Task Force.

Of the convening experience, the two Russian colleagues said: "They could not have accepted an invitation from Russians or Americans. They seemed comfortable in accepting an invitation from an international movement—the Dartmouth Conference." The idea was not mediation but providing an "international" space in which enemies might talk safely. The purpose of the conveners is also important to note. In our first grant proposal for this dialogue, we did not say we intended to mediate an agreement. We said rather: "We want to see whether a group can form within the conflict that is able to design a peace process for their own country." The rationale from the start was that only participants within the conflict could transform conflictual relationships and design and transform the relationships and practices necessary to develop the capacity to resolve their differences peacefully.

In March, nine individuals gathered in a conference room in Moscow for an "experimental meeting" to explore whether they might engage in dialogue on an ongoing basis. The civil war was at its peak. The original participants were from the second or third level of their organizations. We avoided top people on grounds that participants at slightly lower levels could reflect the views of their group with authenticity, would be listened to by their leaders, but would be freer than top leaders to suspend judgment in listening and to explore new perspectives. In the early meetings it was difficult to include a good Islamic voice, but that gap has been well filled. The number of participants steadily increased—first to an average of a dozen, now 15-17. By mid-2003, two participants have consistently attended since 1993 and early 1994 and more than half had attended more than half of the thirty-five meetings.

After two meetings in the conference room in a Moscow institute where participants went at night to a hotel and separately to meals, the Dialogue has always met at a conference center outside Moscow or St. Petersburg and twice in Dushanbe, the capital of Tajikistan. Moving to places where everyone lived, met, ate under the same roof and could walk together in a supportive natural environment markedly improved interactions. The early meetings had to take place outside Tajikistan because many of the opposition were in exile. Each meeting has normally lasted three days.

The meetings were co-moderated by the co-chairs of the Dartmouth Conference Regional Conflicts Task Force—Gennady Chufrin and Harold Saunders. They worked within the five-stage framework described above, moving back and forth across the stages as required. As the group settled down the following pattern for meetings evolved: Until lunch the first day, participants review events in Tajikistan since the last meeting. Before lunch a co-moderator often poses questions to be discussed informally—questions designed to help participants focus on particular problems they have identified. The afternoon discussions continue discursively around fewer problems. Before dinner, specific questions are posed by a co-moderator as overnight "homework." By the second morning, the exchange normally changes character markedly and becomes much more disciplined and deeper. By mid-afternoon the group appoints a subgroup to draft a joint memorandum. They work in informal consultation with others during the evening and early morning, bring the draft for group discussion, and revise the memo. Then they use the remaining time to discuss matters not included in their main focus.

Whereas at the beginning, the management team selected the participants, the Tajiks have now largely taken over that role. Whereas the early memos were drafted in the mode used at Camp David in 1978 with the co-moderators writing what they felt they had heard for group discussion and revision, the participants took over that role about 1997. As described below, the management team's relationship with participants changed to one of mentors and even co-workers when the Dialogue in February 2000 created its own NGO—the Public Committee for Democratic Processes.

By mid-2003, the Inter-Tajik Dialogue within the Framework of the Dartmouth Conference, as the participants came to call themselves, had met thirty-five times and celebrated their tenth anniversary. One can describe this experience as evolving through four phases:

From March 1993 through March 1994, the group met six times during which participants moved from being barely able to look at each other to playing a significant role together in paving the way for government and opposition decisions in early 1994 to engage in formal peace negotiations under a U.N. mediator. In March 1994, just before negotiations began, they produced their first joint memorandum, "Memorandum on the Negotiating Process of Tajikistan" (Chufrin et al, 1997).

From April 1994 through June 1997, three Dialogue participants served as members of the two negotiating teams in the U.N.-mediated Inter-Tajik Negotiations. One of them served throughout that period and is now the deputy foreign minister of Tajikistan. Another is minister of industry. The third was a vice-chair of the Uzbek Association in Tajikistan, who served on the government team. This period ended with the signing of a peace agreement.

From July 1997 through February 2000, five participants in the Dialogue served in the Commission on National Reconciliation, which was established in the peace agreement of June 1997 to oversee implementation of the provisions of that agreement. Other Commission members joined the Dialogue when the Commission's work ended in early 2000.

From March 2000 to the present, members of the Dialogue and other Tajikistani citizens formally registered their own nongovernmental organization, the Public Committee for Promoting Democratic Processes in Tajikistan. Their strategy is one of peacebuilding. They are working on four tracks: (1) creating a complex of dialogue groups in six regions of the country; (2) holding public forums on major national issues such as drugs, education, and poverty in major regions of the country; (3) experimenting with three—soon to become six—Economic Development Committees in towns particularly torn apart during the civil strife where deliberative practices are being used to address economic problems in those communities—their own elaboration of building "social capital"; and (4) workshops over two and a half years in collaboration with the Ministry of Education and three professors from each of eight universities to develop curricula, a text, teaching materials, and courses in peacebuilding.[3]

Early in each of these four phases, participants in the Dialogue stated and then restated their objectives. In August 1993, they said, "What we need to work on is starting a negotiation between the government and the opposition on creating conditions so refugees can go home." After negotiations began in April 1994, they asked themselves whether they should continue the Dialogue. Their answer was emphatic: "Yes. We helped to get negotiations started. Now we have to assure that they succeed. Our objective now is to design a political process of national reconciliation in Tajikistan." At this point the management team assured the government of Tajikistan that the Dialogue would not interfere with the work of the negotiators but would rather think beyond the negotiations and concentrate on ways of preparing the citizens of Tajikistan to implement whatever agreements came from the negotiations. To be sure, Dialogue participants did address key issues in the negotiation but always in terms of options for addressing them. Some key ideas actually found their ways into formal agreements. After the peace agreement was signed in June 1997, they stated their purpose as establishing the elements of democracy in a "united, democratic, secular, peaceful Tajikistan." After the end in February 2000 of the formal transition period defined by the peace agreement, their further refined objective of removing obstacles to democracy is captured in the four-track program of the Public Committee described above.

Transfer from the Inter-Tajik Dialogue to Official Levels

As stated above, we see the question of "transfer" in the context of the multilevel peace process including the official peace process, the public peace process—the Sustained Dialogue—and the civil society. In the spirit of this study, I focus primarily on the transfer from the public to the official peace process.

The transfer of thinking and learning from the Inter-Tajik Dialogue to the Inter-Tajik Negotiations, to the Commission on National Reconciliation, and now to the government of Tajikistan has taken three forms. The explicit principle that governed these interactions was the recognition that there are some things that only governments can do such as negotiating, funding, and enforcing binding agreements; but there are some things only citizens outside government can do such as transforming conflictual human relationships, modifying human behavior, and changing political culture. This recognition in 1994 took the form of assurance to the government of Tajikistan that the Dialogue would be guided by the principle of complementing, not duplicating or second-guessing, the work on official levels (Saunders, 1999a). This did not mean that the Dialogue refrained from addressing issues that were being addressed at official levels. It did mean that participants in the Dialogue recognized that they had no authority to negotiate, so they cast their reflections on issues in terms of options to be considered. Those *three lines of transfer* have been the following:

After twenty-four of their thirty-five (as of this writing) meetings, participants have written a *joint memorandum* reflecting their deliberations. On the occasion of their twentieth meeting of their Dialogue in 1997, they published the memoranda that then existed. *Dialogue Participants* took these joint memoranda and the broader learning from their Dialogue (1) into the Inter-Tajik Negotiations and (2) into the Commission on National Reconciliation where some were participants. Others also briefed government and opposition leaders separately on the substance of the Dialogue. Today, they take these reflections into the government and political parties where they work. They have frequently published and appeared on television.

The U.S. moderator after each meeting wrote an *analytical memo* of ten to fifteen pages for internal reasons, but he also shared those memos with the U.S. State Department and United Nations headquarters in New York, which often shared them with the U.N. mediating team.

Discussion of transfer would be incomplete if it did not call attention to participants' own testimony that experience over time in the Dialogue enhanced their capacity to play an effective role as they carried skills and practices learned in the Dialogue to the official level. One example illustrates the point: a participant who joined the Dialogue as a professor of Persian philology and vice chair of the Democratic Party has become deputy foreign minister and remains in the Dialogue because he values it as a vehicle for personal and professional growth.

To repeat, the guiding principle was to maintain complementarity to the formal mediation and governmental processes. That this effort succeeded is reflected in a comment in an informal talk by U.N. Undersecretary for Political Affairs, Marrack Goulding, when he referred to the Inter-Tajik Dialogue as the most significant unofficial peacemaking effort at that time complementing formal U.N.-mediated negotiations. In 2001, Vladimir Goryayev, a staff member of the U.N. mediating team, commented in a published article: "U.N. mediators also maintained liaison with the "second track" dialogue initiated by Ambassador Saunders of the Kettering Foundation. Despite the apparent complexity of international interventions in the Tajik conflict, clear mandates and effective coordination prevented duplication and "competition of initiatives"—thus facilitating the comparatively rapid achievement of a peace agreement and helping to alleviate the suffering of those affected by the war" (Goryayev, 2001). The editors of *Accord* wrote more broadly, "Thus the Dialogue provided a unique bridge between the official peace process and civil society and complemented the more overtly political approaches to ending the war" (Abdullaev and Barnes, 2001).

Evaluation

In turning to the question of evaluation, my bottom line is that building a habit of ongoing self-evaluation into the process of dialogue is far superior to the necessarily unrooted comments of an outside evaluator. There is no judgment more authentic than that of the people whose lives are at stake, and the moderators must necessarily evaluate repeatedly what the process is achieving and what more it might achieve. The purpose of the U.S. moderator's analytical memo after each meeting was to engage in this reflection.

In turning to the question of evaluation it is necessary to redirect attention to the relational paradigm within which Sustained Dialogue takes place and to the framework of the multilevel peace process.[4] Within these, the act of evaluation operates on two levels: First is the continuing self-evaluation by a group engaged in the peace process; second is the self-evaluation of those continuously managing the Inter-Tajik Dialogue. Documenting the first are the twenty-four joint memoranda from the Dialogue as well as reflective articles by participants published in Tajikistani newspapers and other media. Ultimately, there has been the formation of the Public Committee for Democratic Processes and its progress on the four tracks it designed for its programs. Documenting the second process are the thirty-five analytical memoranda written by the U.S. moderator after each dialogue taking stock of what happened and what needed to happen next. Further, near-verbatim notes have been written on each meeting.

A further precept guiding thinking about evaluating such a process is the recognition that in any complex political process, the cause-and-effect relationship between one actor and any outcome in the larger political process is unknowable with any precision. Interactions can be documented, but the dynamics of decision-making and mediating/negotiating processes are complex and often mysterious—even to the participants themselves. Two examples:

First: In August 1993, participants in the Dialogue's third meeting decided to focus on how to start a negotiation between the government and the opposition. In the fourth meeting, they discussed in detail how that might be done. They identified as a major obstacle the fact that the opposition was physically fragmented, ideologically diffuse, and geographically dispersed. Pro-government participants asked: "Who from the opposition would join a negotiation? How would we find you to invite you?" Within a month, opposition factions met in Tehran, Iran, wrote a joint platform, and created an opposition coordinating center in Moscow. Two participants in the Dialogue signed that platform and brought it back to the fifth meeting of the Dialogue. They submitted to two days of questioning by pro-government participants; their answers were written down. The pro-government participants left the meeting saying: "We believe the foundations for negotiation now exist. We will report to our government."[5] A month later, the government accepted the invitation from a U.N. emissary to join U.N.-mediated peace talks.

Did the Dialogue play a role in paving the way for negotiation? Yes, certainly. At the very least, as a senior government official later made the point, it was impossible any longer to argue that talks between the government and the opposition were impossible. The Dialogue helped change the environment in which the government decided. Can the Dialogue claim exclusive credit for starting negotiations? No, of course not. Individuals in government and in opposition circles were already struggling with the question of how to end the violence, and a U.N. emissary was pressing on behalf of the U.N. Secretary General to begin negotiation. The work of the Dialogue was one factor in contributing to conditions in which a decision to negotiate was made.

Second: In June 1995, the peace negotiations were stymied over the question of how to create an institution to oversee national reconciliation. The opposition for some time had proposed a Commission on National Reconciliation to be created as a supra-governmental organization in lieu of a coalition government, which the government had rejected. The Dialogue produced a joint memorandum containing three options. In one, they suggested positioning a National Reconciliation Commission *under* the authority of the negotiations to oversee the implementation of the peace accord through four sub-commissions (Chufrin et al, 1997). Their very first joint memorandum, "Memorandum on the Negotiating Process for Tajikistan," had recommended in March 1993 that the negotiating teams establish four sub-commissions to deal with such issues as returning refugees, demilitarizing armed elements, economic rehabilitation, and constitutional reform (Chufrin et al, 1997). The purpose was for the negotiators in dealing with these specific problems to initiate actual work that would begin bringing together elements of the bureaucracy and the civil society. That was the pattern which the National Reconciliation Commission ultimately adopted. Can the Dialogue claim credit for designing the Commission on National Reconciliation as ultimately established by the peace agreement? No, the idea had been in the air for some time, although participants in the Dialogue feel that the ideas of positioning the Commission under the authority of the negotiating teams and of perceiving the Commission as initiating and overseeing a complex of political processes originated in the Dialogue itself. They certainly thought persistently in terms of the multilevel peace process.

Understanding the role played by non-official dialogue—the public peace process—in peacemaking will depend heavily on what question is asked.[6] I see at least two possible approaches. The normal evaluator's question might go something like this: Can you demonstrate what impact your intervention had on producing a peace treaty? Our answer is that the Dialogue played a significant role but others probably played a more significant role. It is certainly possible, as one of the long-time participants has done,[7] to document the interplay of ideas between the Dialogue and negotiators or members of the Commission on National Reconciliation, but exactly who gets how much credit for what is unknowable. I was at Camp David with Presidents Carter and Sadat and Prime Minister Begin in 1978; one of my roles was to produce each of twenty-three successive drafts of the Camp David accords. I could not know, and I believe President Carter could not know exactly who was responsible for each formulation and reformulation in that intense mediating process in which conversations took place around the tennis courts, over meals, and during walks in the woods—as well as around various working tables.

Another way of posing a question can be found, to repeat, in the first grant proposal the U.S. team wrote to a U.S. foundation[8] at the beginning of the Inter-Tajik Dialogue: "We want to *see whether* a group can form from within a conflict to design a peace process for its own country." Implicit in this approach has been the notion of continuous self-evaluation—evaluation as part of an unfolding, cumulative, open-ended political process. Neither participants nor the moderators have waited for outside evaluation to determine how they were progressing. At each stage participants in the Dialogue have reviewed their progress and stated a new objective for themselves. They have moved from being barely able to look at each other in the first meeting to producing twenty-four joint memoranda in thirty-five meetings. Then together without any initiative from the Russian-U.S. management team, they have formed their own Public Committee for Democratic Processes. They have developed their own strategy for peacebuilding.

There is no doubt in my mind that this group is pursuing the most coherent strategy for peacebuilding in the country and is taking solid and even measurable steps it has designed for itself. The more important point is that this has been an open-ended political process with new steps being defined that could not in any way have been envisioned at the beginning of the process. Posing an objective that could have been foreseen at the outset for evaluators' judgment would have been much too restrictive and could have closed the door on the opportunity for participants to make continuous mid-course corrections and move beyond premature definitions of success.

Another framework for judging the success of the Dialogue itself lies in the five-stage process laid out by the management team. In the first six meetings, the Dialogue participants clearly moved through all five stages of Sustained Dialogue as they learned to think and talk together and then actually to produce a joint memorandum together which laid out a design for the negotiations they had helped begin. After that, as noted above, we learned that a well-established dialogue group will in each meeting work its way through at least the last two or three stages of a Sustained Dialogue as they come together, talk about the situation in their country since the last meeting, probe one or two of the most important issues in depth, and produce a joint memorandum about it. This provides the opportunity for judging success at each meeting.

While the impact of this work in producing specific outcomes may be unknowable, perhaps that should not be our primary interest. Has a group formed from within a civil war with the capacity to design a peace process *and* a peacebuilding strategy for their country? Yes, beyond question—and beyond a level that no one would have dared imagine in 1993. Think what would not have been possible if evaluators had told funders along the way that the Dialogue was "just talk without measurable outcomes." Even when the whole story is told, the judgment of the Inter-Tajik Dialogue's role will necessarily be partly subjective. The ultimate statement of accomplishment is to say, as we often do, that the Inter-Tajik Dialogue has become "a mind at work in the middle of a country making itself."

Notes

1. An earlier version of this chapter was presented at the International Studies Association Annual Meeting, New Orleans, March 24, 2002.

2. This quotation from the dialogue is from my notes on the meeting. It is agreed practice not to attribute quotations to any participant. Some of the Dialogue participants had been introduced in a related series of meetings on the field of conflict resolution to John Paul Lederach's triangle describing a whole body politic with the official negotiators and governments at the top, with nonofficial groups—"middle-range leadership"—in the center, and with citizens' groups—"grassroots leadership"—at the bottom. For a full discussion, please see John Paul Lederach, *Building Peace: Sustainable Reconciliation in Divided Societies* (Washington, DC: United States Institute of Peace Press, 1997), Chapter 4, especially pp. 37-55.

3. This description of the four periods through which the Inter-Tajik Dialogue unfolded was first published in Kettering Foundation, *Connections* (Vol. XIII, Issue 1, June 2002), pp. 16-17.

4. For a full discussion of evaluation using the Inter-Tajik Dialogue as an example, please see Saunders, "Evaluating Sustained Dialogue," in *A Public Peace Process: Sustained Dialogue to Transform Racial and Ethnic Conflicts*, Chapter 10.

5. All quotes are from my notes on the meeting.

6. A useful exchange between a practitioner and a social scientist/practitioner articulates differences in approach to evaluation. Please see: Nadim Rouhana, "Interactive

Conflict Resolution: Issues in Theory, Methodology, and Evaluation," Chapter 8 and Harold H. Saunders et al., "Interactive Conflict Resolution: A View for Policy Makers on Making and Building Peace," Chapter 7, especially pp. 263-267 in Commission on Behavioral and Social Sciences and Education, National Research Council, Committee on International Conflict Resolution, Paul C. Stern and Daniel Druckman, eds., *International Conflict Resolution after the Cold War* (Washington, DC: National Academy Press, 2000). Each author refers to the other's chapter, so the two chapters include a minidialogue on the subject.

7. Abdunabi Sattorzoda in an as yet unpublished manuscript. He cites a late-2001 book by opposition leader Said Abdullo Nuri published in Tajiki which also describes this interaction.

8. Memorandum from my files. The William and Flora Hewlett Foundation has demonstrated its understanding that fundamental change requires commitment to a process sustained over time through an unprecedented series of four grants over what will be a total of eleven years. The Charles Stewart Mott Foundation supported the project for six years. The Charles F. Kettering Foundation has supported the lead U.S. members of the management team, hosted international fellows and workshop participants from Tajikistan, and supported research in the context of the project throughout.

7

Second Track Conflict Resolution Processes in the Moldova Conflict, 1993-2000

Problems and Possibilities

Andrew Williams

Introduction

"Is He the Most Dangerous Man You Know?"

The above comment by a United Nations official in a workshop organized by London-based nongovernmental organization International Alert could be said to sum up the problems involved in academics getting involved in organizing Second Track problem-solving workshops when there is already an established First Track. In this case, the question was asked of an official of the then Conference on Security and Cooperation in Europe in 1994 in relation to myself. Could there be any fruitful and mutually satisfactory relationship between two parallel tracks in a real-life conflict without the process itself becoming damaged and with the consequent human risk that this might entail? In this case, the reply was in the negative, but it is easy to see how that might not be so. Do not diplomats and politicians engaged in a conflict automatically view with concern and alarm the presence of unofficial, and therefore unaccountable, bit-part players when they are engaged in delicate and difficult maneuvers in a real conflict? Are not these unofficial interveners "dangerous," or what might be referred to as "loose cannons"? In contrast, I hope that I can show that first- and second-track collaboration is not only possible, but also even desirable as the methodologies used by both types of actor are compatible and the results productive for all concerned.[1]

My main aim is to show through a series of snapshots how the relationship between the tracks in this process has developed over time, in the context of a second-track process in Moldova, in which I have been involved with a number of colleagues, with the main period of activity being between November 1993 and March 2000. I will draw on the discussion that took place in the above-mentioned workshop in 1994, the details of which have been published (Bristol and Cohen, 1995), and in the workshop that I attended in Kiev in 2000 where I helped to chair a large problem-solving (hereafter PS) workshop. This workshop led to a publicly announced joint press release by the OSCE, the parties to the Moldova conflict and the Ukrainian and Russian mediators. I will also touch on some of the workshops that took place around those dates, but in a much more general way as they were subject to strict rules of confidentiality. I will only mention names when those individuals have themselves been already identified in print, with their permission. I will also assume that the readers of this chapter do not need to have explained to them the differences between "official" mediation and informal PS methodology.

I will precede that with an outlining of the main actors in the conflict, the parties themselves and the international First Track mediators as well as my colleagues in the Centre for Conflict Analysis (CCA) and the Foundation for International Security (FSI) with whom we have worked in close cooperation since 1998. CCA was not the only group working in Moldova towards a settlement of the problem there, and other groups will be identified in the text.[2]

The Moldova/Transdniester Conflict

In the aftermath of the break-up of the Soviet Union, a number of what can be termed "generic" problems emerged, often identified as the need to redefine the identity of the parts of the former Soviet Union (FSU) which gained their independence, the need to redefine the borders of those new entities with their neighbors, and a linked need to redefine their political, social and economic orientations in the light of the major changes in these areas. In some cases (such as in the Baltic states and Kazakhstan), the transition to independence was relatively peaceful, and has led to the establishment of solidly established governments. In others, of which the main obvious examples are Georgia/Abkhazia, Armenia/Azerbaijan and Tajikistan, there has been civil war, economic decline and other problems (Birgerson, 2002; International Crisis Group, 2001, 2002).

Moldova is arguably a case more within the second unhappy group. Before 1991 Moldova was the scene of many changes of political sovereignty, with the most notable change coming in 1940 with the implementation of the "Molotov-Ribbentrop" Pact between Nazi Germany and Soviet Russia. This saw the annexation of the Romanian province of "Bessarabia," which is now the right bank of the internationally recognized state of Moldova. However, it would also be true to say that until 1918 this whole area was a province of the Tsarist Empire, so "ownership" is a murky historical conundrum. In 1940 Stalin decreed the formation of the Moldavian Soviet Socialist Republic, which was its official name until 1991. The other key act that formed the MSSR was the annexation to this body of sections of the Ukraine, which geographically corresponds to the Left Bank of present day Moldova.

When the state of Moldova was officially formed in August 1991, upon the partial break-up of the Soviet Union, some of the inhabitants of the above-mentioned section of the left bank of the Dniester river (hence "Transdniester") that divides Moldova, decided to create what was in effect a separate "state," the Transdniestrian Moldovan Republic (TMR). Elements within the official Moldovan government reacted by sending police-type forces over the river to bring what they saw as renegades into line. A brief war ensued with the garrison of the previously Soviet Army based in Tiraspol siding with the TMR and driving the official forces back across the river. The cease-fire declared on July 17, 1992 has held ever since with Russian and Ukrainian peacekeeping forces deployed along a line of control along the river.

There are of course different versions of how the breakaway happened, and its logic, as well as many differing accounts of who was to "blame" for the subsequent escalation into war and the standoff that ensued. These are the normal stuff of conflict and the main "meat" that is discussed in any PS workshop.

Internal Actors

The main protagonists in the conflict are the government of Moldova and the government of the breakaway Transdniestrian Moldovan Republic. At the time of the last official, Soviet era, census of 1989, Moldova as a whole had an ethnic makeup of 64 percent Moldovan (Romanian speakers), 13.8 percent Ukrainian, 13 percent Russians, 2 percent Bulgarians and 1.5 percent Jewish. The area of the TMR has a more Slavic complexion made up of a 40 percent Moldovan, 25 percent Ukrainian and 23 percent Russian population.[3] It has been asserted that this is an ethnic dispute in the style of the former Yugoslavia, but it would be more accurate to say that while there are evident linguistic cleavages, the main differences of opinion among the elites and populations of both banks of the Dniester are on what kind of economic, social and political system they want. The TMR broadly speaking wishes to retain Soviet-style institutions and looks "East" for its inspiration, the state of Moldova has aspirations to join the European Union and already has close partnerships with other "Western" institutions.[4] Since 1991, it has in effect been a "state within a state" with the full panoply of institutions (economic, financial, security, etc.) that states have.[5]

The nature of such a conflict has naturally polarized opinion about the aspirations and goals of the internal parties. The elites in the TMR have in particular been accused by a number of commentators of being more interested in criminal activity than political progress (e.g., King, 2001). It would be truer to say, as does the current OSCE ambassador at the time of writing, William Hill, that "there are powerful economic interests on both sides" (Hill, 2001, p. 30). The elites on both sides of the river had (and have) a very similar background, given their emergence from the Soviet-era Communist elites. Only now are younger and less traditional elites beginning to emerge, the results of which are difficult to predict.

Experts appointed by the TMR and the government of Moldova have met regularly, nearly always in the company of the official mediators (see next section). These meetings have on occasion been stormy, but the relationship between the experts has also not been totally hostile, as has also been the case between the majority of the two populations.[6] In the PS workshops there was also not much evidence of any disparity of esteem being accorded by either side to the other. On occasion there were naturally outbursts of anger, but the relationship in the Second Track discussions that I observed was always characterized by an almost old-fashioned courtesy. There was none of the "band-standing" that could be observed in more public fora, such as the 1998 conference that I attended in Kishinev (see below) or in First Track discussions. There was also no real evidence of a disparity of power being deployed by the representatives in the Second Track, and this greatly helped the open and often generous interaction that occurred.

External Actors

In 1993 the Conference for Security and Co-operation in Europe (CSCE), later called after the end of 1995 the Organisation for Security and Co-operation in Europe (OSCE), was asked to help organize local discussions between these two main parties, which they have done ever since in a variety of geometries.[7] There have been a number of OSCE ambassadors in post, usually for a period of about 18 months, although the most recent ambassador, William Hill, has been in post twice for a cumulative period of over four years. The establishment of the OSCE mission is rarely more than about twenty in total, with a mixture of political, administrative and military personnel, the latter of which spend most of their time observing the cease-fire line and checking that the arms that it has been agreed should return to Russia are in fact leaving.

Since the war of 1992 Russian Presidents Yeltsin and Putin have sent their personal representatives to participate in negotiations over the future of Moldova, all of whom have played a significant role in the discussion between the parties. Likewise the president of Ukraine has had a similar personal representative in place since 1994. These two governments have strong national interests in the conflict. Both have significant ethnic minority populations living in Moldova. Ukraine shares a border with Moldova and has an arguably strong claim to certain sections of Moldovan territory. Nevertheless, both also act as "mediators" in the conflict. It should noted that Romania has a very strong interest in Moldova as it believes that the entirety of the Moldovan Republic on the right bank of the Dniester was wrongly expropriated by means of the 1939 Molotov-Ribbentrop Pact whereby, as we have seen, the Soviet Union and Nazi Germany divided up large sections of Eastern Europe, including what the Romanians call "Bessarabia," for their own ends. Romania has nonetheless tried to stay aloof from the conflict, no doubt rightly understanding that to get involved would not only jeopardize its entry into the European Union, but also create tensions with powerful neighbors. There remains a strong nationalist feeling within Romania, and to a certain extent a pan-Romanian movement within Moldova, that one day a "reunification" of the old Romania will be possible. This unofficial articulation is one of the main reasons quoted by the TMR for not wishing to be entirely part of Moldova, as they fear that may take them entirely into a part of Europe with which they have no desire to be associated.

The Second Track Interventions by CCA/FIS

The Second Track that I was involved with was made up of academics and a number of others who had academic backgrounds. We were hence all used to the atmosphere of the academic seminar and also used to listening carefully to what others had to say. While a few of us had had experience of negotiation in international organizations (myself for example), none of us saw the workshops in such a light. We were all reasonably well versed in PS methodology and therefore attempted at all times to lead the sessions with patience and without wishing to arrive at any particular outcome. Our role as we saw it was to give a forum for the parties to express their hopes and fears, and to bring in positive feedback as well as to provide expert input should it be required on issues as they arose or as they developed. We did not take sides and were content, if the parties were, to leave issues aside and move onto others. In this way we hoped to reduce negative feelings of stalemate or intractability. In all our cases we did not see an ideal "end-game," but rather wanted to create a sense of process.

Three Stages of Contact

1993-1996:

In November 1993 I went, with an Irish colleague, to Tiraspol and Kishinev in Moldova to explore the possibility of my network of colleagues in the CCA becoming involved in a Second Track PS process.[8] We spoke to a number of high-ranking officials in the two centers and were asked subsequently if we would host an informal problem-solving workshop in my hometown of Canterbury, England to explore ways of moving towards a resolution of the conflict. This resulted in a workshop being held in July 1994 in Canterbury, the first of three held there. The others were in 1995 and 1996, so at the rate of about one a year. There were always five or six members of the two parties represented, always at a high level, as well as a PS team of five or six. The participants included advisors to the leadership, parliamentarians, members of the negotiating teams on constitutional and economic issues, and other officials in unofficial capacity. Each delegation tended to be led by one or two higher ranking personalities. The PS team also had two elder statesmen who tended to take the lead in the workshop discussions, with the "younger" members (such as myself) playing a subsidiary role in discussion with the parties informally. I was usually the only one who spoke Russian (and not brilliantly!), and this came in useful in acting as an informal translator and social organizer. We always had a skilled interpreter from Moldova present who played a significant facilitation role. Simultaneous translation in Russian and English was also provided in these workshops. They were always of about five days' duration.

In terms of issues discussed in the workshops, Williams (2002) draws on the First Track to identify the primary concern:

> As the OSCE official account has it, "the definition of the status of the Transdniestrian region has remained the most important and challenging task for the Mission." It was also one of the areas that has proved most painful for the parties to discuss in public, involving as it does the problems of how the "division of competencies" between the parties in Moldova should be devised and what "guarantees" by which guarantors should be provided.

In addition, the primary issues which surfaced included the following, as identified by Williams (2002):

- Education—what should the curriculum contain; should all three languages (Russian, Romanian, Ukrainian) be used in the education system?
- Language—should the new Moldovan state have one official language or more?
- Currency—should there be one currency? Banknotes, for example, were printed in Russian under the USSR; the new "Kupons" in MD (1993) were printed only in Moldovan, and those of the PMR (also 1993) in three languages.

The nature of the discussion in the PS workshops was, mainly to, firstly, allow the parties to "ventilate" their feelings about the other side and issues that they held dear, followed by a primary analysis by the PS team. We would then ask the two sides to analyze (usually in the form of "homework") what they could achieve in meeting any goals identified either alone; together; or with outside guarantees. This was done by the simple expedient of using yellow "stickies" and asking each person to fill out six of each on each question. The responses where then collated by us.

Ground rules were also simple. We all agreed at the outset of each workshop that there was an implicit commitment of both sides to treat the other with respect and esteem, and not to interrupt the other when they had the floor except on occasion for clarification. There was also an agreement that there would be no publicity for the meetings, except in the most general sense and no point scoring upon the return to Moldova. The proceedings were, and still are, confidential except in their broad outlines, which are now quite well known.

I have heard this stage of the intervention work called the "Canterbury Process," after the informal, academic setting where the workshops were held at the University of Canterbury at Kent in the U.K. The main aim of these meetings was to establish the basis of the conflict and to explore ways that it might be resolved. Other third parties were not present for the first two of these, but for the third there was observer participation by the OSCE and the Ukrainian and Russian mediators. It should be noted, as does Nan (1999), that during this period there were also meetings held at the grassroots level, organized by the newly (1995) formed Moldova Initiative Committee of Management (MICOM), a steering committee that has helped a broadly based group of Moldovan and TMR NGOs and also participated in community-building activities. The main organizing body for these NGOs is known as the Joint Committee for Democratization and Conciliation (JCDC). MICOM and the JCDC have held a number of workshops within and outside Moldova over the past few years, especially in Nitra, Slovakia (I attended the 1994 one myself) and latterly in Albena, Bulgaria (Hall, 1999; Nan, 1999).

An initial general observation might be made about this first phase. One of the key elements of any PS process is the establishment of trust with the parties. In the first two workshops this was not a problem, and it was thought useful to include the mediators for the third workshop. This did not prove to be as fruitful as had first been hoped, mainly because the expectations of the OSCE for expediting negotiations exceeded the parameters of what is expected in a PS workshop. The session started to turn into a "negotiation," and the informal and exploratory tone of the first two workshops was lost. To those who believe in the PS approach this was no surprise. It has often been said that the two approaches of Track One and Track Two are incompatible as their methodologies are so different. They are certainly incompatible if one tries to do them at the same time, but we found that when the First Track was in effect "blocked" for whatever domestic or other reason, it was useful to go back to a more informal Second Track to try and generate ideas that could "un-block" that situation.

Hence, a second broad generalization about this first phase might be that it was increasingly observed that the discussions that were taking place in Canterbury were generating broad thinking on how the conflict might be approached in the First Track by the official mediators. In other words, the workshop generates results that can be used in the First Track. They are not binding, they are suggestive. They take the parties out of the hothouse and give them an opportunity to think laterally. This was the context that the remark at the start of this chapter was heard, about me (or us) being "dangerous." An OSCE representative was able to say that we were not, and that the discussions were actually quite useful. The parties also indicated the same feelings.

1998-2000

After the unfortunate experience of the 1996 Canterbury workshop, there was a difference of opinion about how to proceed, with a group in MICOM undertaking a number of confidence-building workshops of the "grassroots" in Moldova in which CCA was not involved. These very interesting events are chronicled by Nan (1999). I and my CCA colleagues took the view (maybe mistaken but strongly held) that it is not possible to participate in NGO and community-building processes while at the same time holding high-level leadership sessions. The reason for this is quite simple: it is felt by us to be impossible to have a "Chinese" (i.e., imaginary) wall between the activities that NGOs pursue and the absolute neutrality necessary in a PS workshop. Some of the Moldovan NGOs were, for example, set up to make representation to the Moldovan and Russian governments about Moldovans who had been unjustly deported to Siberia in Soviet times, many of whom never came back. This is a clearly contentious issue for the TMR, which holds its Russian links to be very important, and for the Moldovan state, which could be held liable for compensation. It is also we felt bound to lead to embarrassing overlap between current political issues, which change, and long-term issues, which do not.

Hence, in a second phase of CCA involvement, from 1998 to 2000, we teamed up with the Foundation for International Security (FIS) for another series of three workshops, held in a secluded English village setting north of London. If anything these sessions (of which there were four in total) were more relaxed and intended to be so. A variety of issues were discussed, and in particular the putting of flesh on the bones of what had become a key theoretical concept during the talks from 1994 on, that of the "Common State." This is not the place to explore such concepts in much detail, although I have tried to do so in a recent article (Williams, in press). In that article, I quote a press release of 2000 saying it is: "the existence of two distinct and coequal states in a contractual relationship, each of them with its own arms, security apparatus, border, customs and other state attributes" but under an umbrella of a Constitutional structure that guarantees rights for all parties within "one Moldova."

In this phase the collaboration between CCA/FIS and the OSCE was much closer. Although the 1996 workshop had not been satisfactory for the above-cited reasons, it was felt that the idea of developing the Common State concept was not without some hope. A mutual contribution between the tracks could be made to work if a different kind of accommodation could be developed. This hope was realized when the expression was used in the 1997 Memorandum signed in Moscow by the parties and the OSCE. The document was not ratified but it had entered popular parlance where its main defenders ever since have been the Russian government, the OSCE and many within the main parties themselves.[9] This, I would argue is one of the key demonstrations of the "transfer effect" between the two tracks.

These four workshops involved three facilitators and one translator from the FIS/CCA team along with a senior OSCE official. As with the Canterbury workshops until 1996, each party sent the same number of delegates, in this case usually four from each. The Russian and Ukrainian mediators were not present, but I understand that they were kept informed of any progress. The subject matter of these workshops was often more technical than in Canterbury, one being on Customs for example, in an attempt to give concrete substance to the process of analysis. Thus, one or two experts were brought in who gave mini-presentations on various aspects of an issue in play in Moldova itself. These workshops were distinguished by their good nature and the close working relationship developed by the parties and the OSCE, in conjunction with the PS team. The reason why these sessions worked so well, in answer to the research questions of this book, has to be that everyone had become acculturated to the PS methodology, and there was genuine sharing of thoughts and exploration of possibilities for resolution in a way not seen in 1996. This was discussion among equals and it worked.

Kiev 2000

Perhaps the best proof that the PS intervention worked was the organization in March 2000 of a meeting in Kiev that was sponsored by the OSCE, the Russian and Ukrainian mediators, and hosted by the Ukrainian Foreign Ministry in Kiev. The two parties to the conflict sent their normal quota of about six participants, all at high level. The rest of the membership of the meeting was on a much larger scale than I have ever seen for a PS workshop, with about fifty scholar delegates from the Ukraine and Russia, as well as a smaller group of seven scholars from Britain, other European countries and the United States.

The setting was a sanatorium not far from Kiev, but isolated from the rest of the area. The availability of a large area of private ground meant that informal discussions were possible and a huge amount of informal discussion did indeed take place. The idea was presumably to find if a wider variety of analysts could generate a wider variety of ideas and inputs for the First Track, who were all physically present. The meeting continued for nearly a week and was very intensive and wide-ranging in its scope. It resulted in a document that was in effect a constitution for Moldova based on the idea of the "Common State," produced here as an annex. I believe that I am right in saying that this is reproduced in annex for the first time outside the official channels.

The actual process of the document's production had more in common with a First Track negotiation than a PS workshop. Apart from the two members of

CCA present, most of the key members of the parties and the official mediators who were now familiar with PS workshops, there were many participants who were not. The sheer number of those present made discussion in the cosy "fireside" tradition developed in the U.K. virtually impossible. There was an overwhelming feeling that a document *had* to be arrived at, which imparted a certain artificiality to the discussions. All concerned were aware that we were designing an outcome from the outset and that is in direct contradiction to PS methodology, no matter how worthy an aim it may have been for the official mediators and others present.

And yet there was much significant discussion. In my view, this was an attempt to draw together the best elements of a PS workshop AND a fusion of First and Second Track agendas and concerns in a broader PS format. The creativity of the PS workshop, it was hoped, would stimulate the production of a document that could be used by the First Track in a more concrete way than in any of the PS workshops held in the U.K. It was certainly a bold attempt at creating a new way of looking at both PS and Track One in harmony and not at odds with one another. A detailed analysis of the annexed document cannot be attempted in the short space available in this paper, although I have attempted to do this elsewhere (Williams, in press).

Some Findings and Conclusions

Mechanisms

The innovative nature of the mechanisms employed in the workshops conducted by CCA and then by FIS/CCA is probably not great at first glance. After all, discussions about the nature of the state and constitutional divisions of competency are not unusual in such fora and they happen all the time in international conferences. What was new was the ability of delegates and academics to think through these processes in away that was very off-the-record and yet was intended to be fed into the more precise thinking and action that was necessary in the First Track.

The main mechanism can be compared to a "club sandwich" with one layer being bitten into after another. When the First Track was faltering the Second Track swung into operation. This enabled new thinking to be generated, new trust to be forged and a breathing space to be developed, one that was not filled with the possibility of violence.

Transfer Effects

It is notoriously difficult to trace cause and effect in such matters. It might be said that the "Federal" constitution now (early 2004) being discussed in Moldova is not called that of the "Common State," as discussed in Kiev in March 2000, and that it does not at present seem to be acceptable to the main internal parties, even if the OSCE and the external mediators are keen to see it implemented. But it should also be said that before the PS workshops had taken place there was no real dialogue (or communication) at all between the parties, or only out of the barrel of a gun. The discussions that took place quietly in 1994-1996 are now fairly common knowledge in the salons of Kishinev and Tiraspol. They are also widely discussed, sometimes with more heat than light admittedly, in the streets and fields of the country. It would be too grandiose to suggest that the Second Track has empowered a debate in civil society about the conflict and the future of Moldova, on both its banks, but I think it can be reasonably suggested that this is the case. Of course, this has also been helped by the activities of NGOs in the region and by such activities as those of MICOM.

The targets of the transfer between the tracks were obviously the parties themselves, but also it was hoped that a wider public would be influenced. This might be said to have included the legislatures and the decision makers as well as the mediators themselves. We believe that the PS approach is one way of improving the conduct of international relations in the broad sense. In this respect the above-stated disagreements with MICOM were more ones of tactics than of goal. Any attempt at PS has as its main overriding goal the improvement of relationships, indeed their transformation, from one of debilitating conflict to one of communication, leading to cooperation, even if that cooperation ends in "divorce." We were hoping to influence the debate by making it clearer, more rational and ultimately more productive of peaceful outcomes.

However, it would be wrong to say that the relationship between the tracks was always happy. This was illustrated to me when I went to a conference in Kishinev in May 1998 as part of the delegation of a working group organized by the Royal Institute of International Affairs. This immediately preceded our second period of involvement described above. I was there in a purely personal capacity as one of the few British academics interested in Moldova. This culminated in a semi-public, two day meeting in Kishinev that saw the presence of the parties at the highest level, the official mediators and the OSCE. I was asked to comment on the state of the talks. In discussions with some First Track representatives, I realized that all concerned did not greet the role played by unofficial third parties in the conflict with unequivocal joy. It would be fair to say that, at that time, the OSCE was keen not to have involvement by outside organizations that did not share its "values." These are the basic values of the international community, and involve the notion that self-determination must not be allowed to mean "secession." The OSCE, and indeed all other national and international players in this and other post-Cold War conflicts do not wish to see states breaking up. If they are to do so, it must be with common consent. This had not been granted by anyone to the TMR. A PS approach, on the other hand, can conceivably involve any solution that meets the interest and "values" of the parties. If a divorce was to be brokered by a PS workshop, then that would be seen as detrimental to the "values" of the wider international community (Williams, in press). Therefore the only way that a viable resolution of a conflict such as that in Moldova can be realistically achieved is to seek a harmonizing of a series of sets of views—those of the parties and those of the key First Track players—in this case the mediators described above.

One transfer effect that seems to me evident is the production of the Kiev document, which is reproduced in the annex. It gives a blueprint that might be useful in other similar conflicts. But it has to be said, as mentioned above, that the parties themselves did not ultimately take it up wholesale, even if there are certain generic similarities to the present document. The "federal" constitution now on the table and being sponsored by the official First Track players, especially Russia, is not the same as the one elaborated in Kiev in 2000. The one now in play was (confusingly!) drawn up, as far as I am aware, by the mediators acting alone and without the parties or a Second Track representative present at another meeting in Kiev in July 2002. When this new proposed constitutional framework was made public, it suggested that both sides of the Dneister would be allowed their own legislatures and constitutions and a great degree of autonomy, in line with the common state idea. Equally we could say that the concept had been there in essence since its first public statement in the 1997 Memorandum signed but not ratified by the parties until Kiev in 2000 (Kuzio, 2003). It has thus been a central idea in the two tracks of discussions between the parties and mediators, seeing its most clear statement in Kiev in 2000 as described above, but hovering like Banquo's Ghost even when not used in such exact terms.

The new "federal" description has not proved entirely popular in Moldova, as it embodies a solution favorable to the TMR and which certain observers see as one dominated by Russia. There were mass demonstrations against it in the Moldovan capital in November 2003.[10] Others have taken a more sanguine view (e.g., International Crisis Group, 2003). But these outcomes should not be seen as a failure of the transfer effect. The idea of a common state was fully discussed in the Second Track PS workshops, elaborated over a number of years in both tracks, and is now in the public domain. But it must be emphasised that it is a creative "problem-solved" idea, which was the product not just of the PS process but of the parties themselves. The PS teams that I was involved with were the midwives of the process, not its parents.

Moldova is one of the poorest countries in Europe. A resolution of the Transdniestrian conflict has to be found or it will get poorer. In the long run, I believe that a form of the common state will be essential, as the only alternative is a return to an unproductive stalemate or a more open war. The PS team(s) with which I had the privilege to be associated over the past years and the mediators in the First Track are all concerned to work towards a resolution of this conflict.

There is perhaps a lesson in this case study to show that the two tracks can productively work together with the elites of two warring "states" to find a common solution to a series of common problems. If a process that leads to a transformation of the parties' perception of each other can be found, then that is ultimately the goal for which all should be aiming. There are many other parts of the former Soviet Union where such conflicts exist. Any solution to these conflicts will meet with some distrust and even dislike from one or more sections of all the parties involved. I cannot think that there is any other method of approaching them that stands a better chance of upsetting the least number of people and interests than a combination of First Track authority and Second Track patience and complementary attempts to include as many of these people and interests as possible.

Annex

Kiev, March 2000

The following document was the result of an extended problem-solving workshop organized by the OSCE and the Russian and Ukrainian Foreign Ministries at which I was present. It has not been previously published and should be taken as unofficial.

I. THE COMMON STATE

(i) PREAMBLE

The common state realizes a common political, economic, legal, social and defence area (based on the territorial integrity of the borders of the M.S.S.R. as of January 1, 1990). The common state is based on the principles of unity and diversity. The unity of the peoples is articulated through the institution of the common state, and the diversity of the people is articulated through the institution of the entities.

(ii) PRINCIPLES

The normative principles upon which the CS will be based are as follows:

- The respect for human rights and the protection of persons belonging to minorities in accordance with the Universal Declaration of Human Rights and the European Convention of Human Rights
- A respect for international commitments and OSCE principles as laid down by the Helsinki Final Act, the Copenhagen Document, The Charter of Paris and all other OSCE documents, and mutual commitments of the parties.
- A respect for the principles of democracy
- A respect for the principle of non-discrimination
- A respect for the principle of the separation of powers
- A respect for the Rule of Law
- A respect for the Constitution of the CS
- A respect for the principle of parity of esteem and loyal cooperation between the entities
- A respect for the principle of the non-use of force
- A respect for the common legal, economic and social space
- A respect for the principle of social protection
- A respect for the environment
- Stage by stage implementation of state-legal relations

(iii) STRUCTURE AND INSTITUTIONS OF THE COMMON STATE

The *principles* that underpin the common state are those of legitimacy and efficiency (after W. Bagehot).

Citizenship will be in the common state.

The structure of the CS might eventually resemble, after a period to be decided by the parties, the following characteristics: (this was followed by a suggestive diagram)
     The *institutions* of the common state are divided into three branches—legislative, executive, and judicial—with a system of checks and balances between the three branches.
     The *legislative branch* will have a parliament of two chambers: a senate and a house of representatives.
     The *powers of the Senate*: the Senate can advise, delay, and redraft legislation presented by the lower house. With respect to constitutional change, it can block (as specified below), and it will have the power to ratify certain appointments.
     The *powers of the House of Representatives*: the House has legislative capacity with respect to the exclusive and shared competencies of the common state. The lower chamber also decides on the national budget and ratifies international treaties.
     Composition of the Senate will be fifty-fifty (50/50) representation from the two entities. The House of Representatives will be elected on the basis of uni-

versal suffrage. At least half (50 percent) of the House shall be elected from multimember constituencies.

Constitutional change can be made by a two-thirds' vote in the House of Representatives and a simple majority in the Senate, followed by ratification by the entities.

The *executive branch* consists of two institutions: the presidency, and the government (the prime minister and cabinet ministers). The electoral system and process to be decided for the president shall assure that the president and vice-president shall come from different entities.

There will be an independent *central bank.*

The *judicial branch* of the common state will be a single system. There will be a constitutional court dealing with the interpretation of the constitution, electoral conflicts, conflicts of laws between the common state and the entities, conflicts of competences between the entities, between the common state and the entities, and among organs of the common state, control of legality, and protection of human rights. There will be a supreme court, as a high court of appeal on civil, criminal, and administrative matters.

(iv) STATUS OF THE ENTITIES

The constitutions of the entities must not contradict the constitutional document of the common state. Each entity shall be comprised of three branches of government—legislative, executive, and judicial—with the separation of powers among them. These institutions will be decided by each of the entities within the overall framework of the constitutional document of the common state.

(v) DISTRIBUTION OF POWERS AND OF COMPETENCES

There will be three categories of powers and competences: those exclusive to the common state, those shared between the common state and the entities, and matters reserved to the entities. By shared competences in the field of legislation is meant that the common state adopts basic laws, while the entities adopt laws that elaborate the basic laws. There are also shared competences in the field of administration as defined by law of the common state. In the field of foreign policy, certain international agreements may require the ratification by both the common state and the entities or an entity.

(1) Prominent examples of powers and competences *exclusive* to the common authorities are:

Foreign policy in general; defence and external security; citizenship; monetary policy (and the Central Bank regime); customs; the national court system; national administrative system; national finances and budget of the common state; national electoral system; national transport policy; national environmental protection; meteorological service; intellectual property rights; amnesty and commutation; state medals and honors; immigration and asylum.

(2) Prominent examples of powers and competences that will be shared between the common state and the entities are:

Foreign policy as it affects the competences of the entities; police and internal security; language policy; electoral policy; social policy; property rights; the system of local administration.

(3) All matters not specified in the exclusive or shared jurisdictions will be reserved to the entities unless otherwise agreed. Prominent examples of powers and competences that will be in the jurisdiction of the entities are:

Regional transport; education; culture; regional environmental questions; regional courts; regional administrative system; regional finance; regional transport; regional elections.

II. TRANSITIONAL STAGES

We consider that the following stages might be advisable:

- A continuing harmonization of the constitutional structure and the laws of the entities and continuing cooperation between the entities
- A Constitutional Commission should draw up a document acceptable to both sides
- This should then be approved as a constitutional document by the parliaments of both entities and submitted to a popular referendum by both entities
- This should lead to reform of the parties' constitutions and the setting up of the institutions of the common state
- This should occur simultaneously with the transfer of functions from the entities to the common state

III. GUARANTEES

Recommendations of measures likely to give reassurance to the population of the common state and the international community:

These recommendations should be read as occurring in conjunction with the transitional stage.

(1) Economic Incentives
    We suggest that the guarantors should commit themselves to seeking the following:

- Debt forgiveness (by their major creditors)
- Reconstruction assistance (again by external actors)
- Financial aid should be given to the entirety of the common state

(2) Political and Juridical Reassurances

- The guarantors should be regularly available to assist in resolving political disputes over fulfillment of the Agreement.
- Conciliation commissions with representatives of the entities, the common state, and the guarantors to implement agreed policies should be set up.
- If disputes relevant to the post-conflict period cannot be resolved by these mechanisms, they may be referred to the OSCE Court of Arbitration and Conciliation.
- We expect both parties to agree to a general amnesty for acts connected in the context of the conflict.

(3) Military Guarantees

- Any eventual peacekeeping force, whatever its composition, should be with the agreement of the internal entities.

Notes

1. This chapter is a reflection on my personal experiences as a member of different problem-solving teams in the Moldova conflict between 1993 and the present. It should be stressed that the opinions expressed are purely my own and do not engage my colleagues, the parties or the mediators in any way. I would like to state at the outset, however, that I am grateful for their input, conscious or unconscious, on what is to follow, and that I have tried to make sure that what I have written is as objective and clear as possible without embarrassing or endangering those I have had the pleasure of working with over the past few years both in the field and in other contexts.

2. There have been a few attempts to address the technical aspects of conflict resolution and even the complementarily of the different "tracks" in the Moldova case, notably by Susan Allen Nan in *Coordination and Complementarity of Multiple Conflict Resolution Efforts in the Conflicts over Abkhazia, South Ossetia and Transdniestria*, Doctoral Dissertation, George Mason University, Fairfax, Virginia, 1999. It is also more than

worth mentioning the literature which has emerged addressing the particular detail of the discussions that have taken place in the various tracks, some of which have published documents relevant to the conflict in annexes. For example: European Centre for Minority Issues, *From Ethno-political Conflict to Inter-Ethnic Accord in Moldova*, Flensburg, ECMI, 1998), p. 47, and Bruno Coppetiers and Michael Emerson, "Conflict Resolution for Moldova and Transdniestria through Federalisation?" *CEPS Policy Brief*, No 25, August 2002. See also Andrew Williams, "Conflict Resolution after the Cold War: The Case of Moldova," *Review of International Studies*, March 1999.

3. Figures drawn from Vladimir Kolosov, and John O'Loughlin, "Pseudo-states as Harbingers of a Post-Modern Politics: The Example of the Trans-Dniester Moldovan Republic, (TMR)," presented to the Political Science Association, London, March, 2000, pp. 38. My thanks to Asher Pirt of the University of Kent for pointing out these figures to me.

4. A good source for the political and other structures of the TMR can be found in Dov Lynch, *Managing Separatist States: A Eurasian Case Study*, Paris, Institute for Security Studies, November 2001, http://www.iss-eu.org/occasion/occ32.pdf

5. The reasons why the TMR feels it has a claim to statehood is not the subject of this paper. Good accounts of these reasons and the unfolding of the conflict can be found in published work on the subject. What needs to be known is that the conflict in Moldova has pitted two sections of the country against each other from 1991 until the present and has now been widely written about. Apart from my own account, it has attracted the attention of a number of scholars and practitioners from Europe and beyond. See, for example: Andrew Williams, "Conflict Resolution after the Cold War: The Case of Moldova," *Review of International Studies*, March 1999; M. F. Hamm, "Introduction" to "Moldova: The Forgotten Republic," *Nationalities Papers*, Vol. 26, No. 1, March 1998; Charles King, *The Moldovans: Romania, Russia and the Politics of Culture*, Stanford: Hoover Institution Press, 2000, and John Lowenhardt, Ronald J. Hill and Margot Light, "A Wider Europe: The View from Minsk and Chisinau" *International Affairs*, 77, 2001, pp. 605-620.

6. This is confirmed by Nan, 1999, p. 237.

7. For a good overview of the OSCE's activities in conflict management and resolution in the former Soviet Union see Maria Raquel Freire, *Conflict and Security in the Former Soviet Union*, Ashgate, 2003.

8. One version of this is recounted in Michael Hall, *Conflict Resolution: The Missing Element in the Northern Ireland Peace Process*, Belfast, Island Pamphlets, 1999

9. For the full text of this document see the official OSCE website, which contains copies of many of the key official documents: See: http://www.osce.org/moldova/overview.htm

10. See for example, Vladimir Socor, of the Institute for Advanced Strategic and Political Studies, Washington D.C., IASPS Policy Briefings no. 41, 26 November 2003 where he says this constitution "will turn Moldova into a Russian-supervised federation."

8

Track One-and-a-Half Diplomacy

Contributions to Georgian-South Ossetian Peacemaking

Susan Allen Nan

Introduction

This chapter examines how high-level unofficial conflict resolution efforts directly contributed to peacemaking by impacting the official negotiations in the Georgian-South Ossetian peace process. The high-level unofficial interventions considered here form a specific type of conflict resolution approach. The interveners are unofficial NGOs, yet official negotiators or other influential officials from one or the other side of the conflict are core participants. This type of initiative is a unique combination of aspects of the traditional types of track-one diplomacy (official diplomacy) and track-two diplomacy (unofficial diplomacy), and is thus referred to as Track One-and-a-Half diplomacy (Nan, 1999, p. 202; Nan, 2004).

Track One-and-a-Half diplomacy represents an unusually direct way for unofficial activities to contribute to official peacemaking. Track One-and-a-Half diplomacy brings a strength of track-one diplomacy, the direct engagement of senior official representatives of the conflict parties, together with a strength of track-two diplomacy, informal off-the-record workshops on conflict resolution. Track One-and-a-Half diplomacy can develop a core group of official negotiators from both sides of a conflict that share improved conflict analysis and negotiation skills, share some personal understanding of and relationship with each other, and share substantive insights into the conflict issues that divide them.

This combination of factors would be difficult for either Track One or Track Two to develop on their own. Traditional track-one diplomacy lacks the relationship-building, informal exploratory substantive discussions, and conflict analysis and negotiation skills training components that unofficial workshops can bring. Traditional track-two diplomacy usually lacks direct involvement of official negotiators representing the conflict parties. The Track One-and-a-Half diplomacy initiatives described here leveraged their direct engagement with official negotiators and their unofficial relationship-building, skills-building, and creative thinking capacities to contribute to the Georgian-South Ossetian peace process.

In order to explain this example of Track One-and-a-Half Diplomacy, a brief analysis of the Georgian-South Ossetian conflict follows this introduction. Then, the unofficial parts of the peace process are overviewed. The focus here is on the Track One-and-a-Half diplomacy initiatives, and their direct impact on the official negotiations process. The main initiative discussed was led by Conflict Management Group (CMG) in cooperation with the Norwegian Refugee Council (NRC), and is referred to as the CMG workshops. In addition, several smaller initiatives by Vertic, and its successor organization Caucasus Links, are highlighted as also providing some direct impact on the official negotiations.

Most of the information for this case study comes from primary sources, including interviews with many of those involved in unofficial and official conflict resolution initiatives addressing the conflict over South Ossetia. These participants, facilitators, and analysts discussed their understanding of relevant conflict resolution initiatives and the peace process as a whole. Interviewees included relevant senior officials on both sides of the conflict, official mediators, and leaders of relevant unofficial conflict resolution activities. Self-reports by official negotiators of the peacemaking contributions of unofficial workshops based on their personal experience formed the core of the data. These self-reports were triangulated with the observations of official and unofficial mediators who observed the same peacemaking contributions through shifts in the peace process. I conducted twenty-seven interviews between 1998-1999, and the initial results have been reported elsewhere, as this case study is one of three in a larger focused comparison study (Nan, 1999).[1] In addition, I conducted twenty-four follow-up interviews, roughly half of which were with individuals included in the original twenty-seven interviewees, in 2000 (Nan, 2000).

Analytical Introduction to the Conflict over South Ossetia

A brief analysis of the Georgian-South Ossetian conflict provides more context in which to understand the significance of the Track One-and-a-Half initiatives and their contributions to peacemaking.

The Georgian-South Ossetian conflict centers on two parties, Georgia and South Ossetia, and their competing and seemingly irreconcilable claims for

Georgian territorial integrity and South Ossetian independence or self-determination. Each of the two parties in this sovereignty conflict has remained remarkably cohesive in their approaches, despite shifts in the leadership on both sides. The central issues of territorial integrity and self-determination emerge from Georgian and South Ossetian needs for security, identity recognition, and participation in governance. Georgians and South Ossetians are separated along ethnic, linguistic, and, to a lesser extent, religious lines, with most Georgians identifying themselves as Christians, and some South Ossetians identifying themselves as Muslims. Each party brings a power dynamic to their negotiations; Georgia is an internationally recognized state which includes the territory claimed by South Ossetia, yet South Ossetia holds de facto control over the territory.

The Georgian-South Ossetian conflict emerged during the break up of the former Soviet Union (Nan, 1999 and Nan, 2004). Under the Soviet Union, South Ossetia was an Autonomous Oblast of the Georgian Soviet Socialist Republics. In 1989, some South Ossetians advocated South Ossetian unification with North Ossetia, and spoke in support of Abkhaz ambitions for independence. Increasing tensions led Georgia to abolish South Ossetia's autonomy and South Ossetia to declare itself an independent Soviet Republic. A full-scale armed conflict broke out in December 1990, killing over one thousand people (Mukomel, 1997). In January 1991, intervention by Soviet Internal Affairs forces marked the end of the fighting.

The Georgian-South Ossetian conflict escalated to warfare and then quickly de-escalated to an unsteady cease-fire. External intervention has prevented a return to warfare since 1991, with a formal cease-fire in place since 1992. In summer 1992, a tripartite Russian-Georgian-Ossetian peacekeeping force replaced the Soviet troops. In 1994, a quadripartite team consisting of Russian, Georgian, North Ossetian and South Ossetian leaders met to seek a comprehensive political settlement of the conflict over South Ossetia. The parties reached agreement that Russian peacekeepers would maintain a cease-fire while peace negotiations continued. Since then, South Ossetia continues to insist on its independence, and Georgia continues to restore its territorial integrity. Nevertheless, with peacekeeping troops separating the two sides since 1991, a cease-fire has held.

Beyond military separation of the two sides, external mediators have also sought to assist the negotiation process. The Organization for Security and Cooperation in Europe (OSCE) and Russian-mediated negotiations began in 1995. These official negotiations have resulted in reduced peacekeeping forces in the area, reduced tensions, and agreements in areas such as economic development. However, agreement on the political status of South Ossetia has remained elusive. Over the course of more than a decade of post-war interactions and negotiations, there has been little promise of significant movement on the central issues of territorial integrity and self-determination. These issues must somehow be addressed prior to a full resolution of the conflict. Meanwhile, the conflict's frozen state continues to adversely affect the lives of people living in the relatively isolated and depressed economy of South Ossetia and those Georgians who fled South Ossetia, many of whom have yet to return to their homes. Perhaps a hurting stalemate (Zartman, 1985) is in place, but if so, the stalemate is not yet hurting the leadership of either side enough to overcome the resistance to a settlement. South Ossetian authorities are no doubt under pressure from the authorities in Abkhazia, another area of sovereignty conflict in Georgia, to continue seeking full independence. Both Abkhazia and South Ossetia have been seen to have support from their northern neighbor Russia in their resistance to Georgian rule.

Despite the forces complicating movement towards resolution, the parties have been open to both official and unofficial mediation attempts, and other peacebuilding and development initiatives. Georgians and South Ossetians have cooperated on confidence building measures such as reducing armed forces in the areas, conducting joint patrols, and also engaging in mutually beneficial development initiatives.

The Georgian-South Ossetian Peace Process

The peace process surrounding the Georgian-South Ossetian conflict includes both official (track-one) and unofficial (track-two) activities. After a brief acknowledgment of the official and unofficial activities, this chapter turns to more detailed consideration of the particular type of unofficial activities characterized by Track One-and-a-Half activities.

The official activities include both official negotiations between the Georgian and South Ossetian leadership and also confidence building measures supported by the official mediators. Russia and the OSCE serve as mediators of the official negotiations. These official negotiations take place in the context of high-level summits, regular meetings of the working-level Joint Control Commission (JCC) where day-to-day matters of Georgian-South Ossetian interaction and details of agreement implementation were worked out, and related working groups addressing practical issues of joint interest such as economic development. The high-level summits address the central issues of the conflict as well as practical matters. More frequently, through the almost weekly meetings of the JCC and periodic working group meetings, the official discussions focus on practical concerns that may build confidence between the parties.

Official mediators can also encourage unofficial NGO-based confidence building. This is evidenced by the OSCE's support of many NGO-based confidence-building measures engaging the Georgian-South Ossetian conflict. For example, the OSCE has been involved with a migration conference organized by Norwegian Refugee Council and a journalists meeting organized by Helsinki Citizens' Assembly, both in 1997. The OSCE also held two scholarly meetings on economic rehabilitation and democratization and another journalists meeting in 1997. The OSCE supported the establishment of a Georgian-Ossetian joint information center following the journalists meeting. Interviewees unanimously agreed that the joint journalist initiatives helped increase the availability of reliable information throughout the region.

Unofficial initiatives led by NGOs also form an important part of the peace process, and work with high-level leadership, mid-range leadership, and grassroots representatives. Quoting from the summary in Nan (1999, p. 187), the immediate goals of these unofficial interventions include:

- Building conflict resolution skills, knowledge, and local capacities for peace;
- Confidence building measures;
- Strengthening cross-conflict linkages through NGO special interests;
- Building regional identity and addressing regional issues;
- Psycho-social rehabilitation;
- Humanitarian assistance;
- Democracy and civil society building; and
- Unofficial facilitated dialogues amongst negotiators.

The last of these, the unofficial facilitated dialogues amongst negotiators, are the focus of this chapter. The Track One-and-a-Half interventions involved unofficial conveners that brought together officials from both sides of the conflict. These interventions made the most direct contributions to official peacemaking from the unofficial context.

Track One-and-a-Half Diplomacy

In the conflict resolution context, Track One-and-a-Half Diplomacy is defined as diplomatic initiatives that are facilitated by unofficial bodies, but directly involve officials from the conflict in question.

Two groups stand out for their work with unofficial high-level interventions in efforts that fit this definition of Track One-and-a-Half Diplomacy. These groups are first, Vertic and its successor organization Caucasus Links, and, second, a partnership between Conflict Management Group (CMG) and Norwegian Refugee Council (NRC). For each of these groups, some of their work involved unofficial conflict resolution initiatives that included some of the official negotiators and high-level official representatives from both sides of the conflict.

Vertic and Caucasus Links

Vertic first led this process of unofficial facilitation with officials in the Georgian-South Ossetian conflict. Caucasus Links picked up the work of its predecessor organization, the British-based NGO Vertic. Vertic and Caucasus Links focused largely on parliamentary-based aspects of the larger peace process, as well as the potential contributions of younger politicians. Some of their work brought substantive inputs to the negotiators. For example, Caucasus Links brought the South Ossetian Speaker of the Parliament and the State Advisor of the president of South Ossetia to the United Kingdom to study devolution in Scotland. The visitors talked to officials and scholars, learning about models and processes for devolution of power.

The earlier Vertic work focused on opening up dialogue between the two sides, working with younger influentials from both sides. According to a South Ossetian adviser to the President, Vertic organized the adviser's first trip to Georgia after the war. The adviser went to Batumi in the summer of 1994 for a meeting of young people from Georgia and South Ossetia. The adviser characterized this as the first post-war NGO activity between Tskhinval(i)[2] and Tbilisi, and said it was significant in that it opened up contact again. The Vertic Batumi meetings were helpful because they led to contact and a clarification that there are people on both sides who do not want war. This in turn helped older politicians open to contacts. According to this younger politician, the older politicians are more careful with contact. He explained that when the young parliamentarians from Georgia and Ossetia met unofficially, they showed older politicians that talking with each other is acceptable.

Vertic played a significant role in jump-starting stalling negotiations after a fall 1996 decline in the intensity of negotiations. Several interviewees recounted Vertic's bringing the Speaker of the South Ossetian parliament to Tbilisi to meet with the Speaker of the Georgian parliament in a surprise move that broke a long period of post-election lack of negotiating activity. Most other conflict resolution practitioners involved in the peace process had no prior knowledge of Vertic's plans for the initiative, and some might have advised against the risky move if they had been consulted prior to the visit. However, the visit was successful, and the surprise move led to more Georgian-South Ossetian contact, and a thawing of the relationship. This was credited by an official mediator as useful in producing contacts that had not existed before, and also useful in injecting a new energy into the official negotiations.

Conflict Management Group and the Norwegian Refugee Council

The other major group involved in Track One-and-a-Half Diplomacy is Conflict Management Group (CMG). CMG sponsored a project called The Hague Initiative, which brought high-level leaders from conflict regions in the former Soviet Union, including South Ossetia, together to consider conflict resolution approaches. But more direct contributions to the Georgian-South Ossetian peace process came from the longer term workshop series that CMG undertook in cooperation with the Norwegian Refugee Council (NRC).

CMG and NRC worked together from 1995-2000 to facilitate a successful series of unofficial dialogues between high-level Georgians and South Ossetians. The team was well suited to make a positive impact. NRC was well respected by both South Ossetians and Georgians, and NRC brought the team a local on-the-ground presence in the conflict region, through the work of NRC's project coordinator, Lara Olson, who acted daily as local coordinator for the work and provided an ongoing project presence. The CMG team was predominantly westerners, Roger Fisher and Diana Chigas and assistant facilitators, but also included an Armenian, Arthur Martirosyan, who knows the Caucasus well, had lived in Georgia, and communicated in fluent Russian with the Georgians and South Ossetians. His close knowledge of the region allowed him to play some aspects of the insider-partial role, providing locally-informed analysis of the conflict. Roger Fisher and Diana Chigas brought process knowledge to the team, along with expertise in teaching skills for conflict analysis and negotiation.

Institutionally, NRC and CMG managed to engage in relatively successful inter-organizational collaboration which made it possible to bring together the many strengths represented on the team and by the two organizations. Each organization brought different strengths, they had clearly defined roles in the initiative, and they were able to communicate fairly regularly with each other. The partnership represented a rare example of inter-organizational collaboration in conflict resolution. As the field has recognized the need for increased intervention coordination (Nan, 2003), it has seemed easier to begin with communication (information sharing and shared analysis), then coordination (planning together for increased complementarity of separate efforts), and finally cooperation (resource sharing; separate work on related projects). But collaboration (joint work on a shared project) is a more intensive form of cooperation.[3] In the case of CMG and NRC's work, the collaborative effort contributed substantially to the Georgian-South Ossetian peace process.

The CMG and NRC team began work on the workshop series at a time that the official negotiations process was stalled, but the cease-fire continued to hold. In this sense, the timing was appropriate for an unofficial intervention. The intervention could not easily detract from any productive official process, as that was largely nonexistent, but instead paved the way for and then supported a more productive official negotiations process. By reviewing the few unofficial peacebuilding efforts addressing the Georgian-South Ossetian conflict, the CMG and NRC team determined that their work would not duplicate the efforts of others. As an unofficial team, they could offer unofficial new energy to the stalled official negotiations process by building relationships, building skills, and facilitating participants in developing new ideas.

Georgian President Eduard Shevardnadze invited CMG to focus on the conflict over South Ossetia based on the advice of an international diplomat who had studied at Harvard, where CMG is based. The initial CMG analysis suggested that South Ossetia might be a promising area for intervention because the war had ended and the parties had been close before the war. In response to the presidential invitation, NRC made local arrangements for a CMG delegation to visit the region and analyze the conflict and prospects for the peace process.

Reaction in the region to this initial visit was positive. Georgians looked positively on the visit by a group that had been invited by their president. South Ossetians looked positively on the group because of their association with NRC, and because of their highly symbolic itinerary which brought them to spend the night in Tskhinval(i) on their first night in the region. Most westerners avoided staying the night in the less secure and less comfortable South Ossetian region, but made brief day trips from Tbilisi. After meetings in Tskhinval(i) (South Ossetia) and then Tbilisi (Georgia), CMG offered to convene a workshop in Oslo in January 1996, which would bring together influential (some official and some unofficial) Georgians and South Ossetians to explore areas of joint interest. This launched a series of four workshops:

- January 1996 in Norway
- May 1996 in Norway
- June 1997 in Massachusetts, U. S.
- July 1998 in Barcelona, Spain

These workshops were then followed by steering committee meetings in Bulgaria, Armenia, and Georgia/South Ossetia. Individuals who participated through two or more workshops noted that through long-term involvement in the initiative they gained more and more in terms of better relationships with people on the other side of the conflict, better understanding of constructive negotiation processes, and increased understanding of others' views on the substantive issues. Thus, while each workshop and each stage of the project will be described separately below, the initiative should be seen as a long-term whole that built stronger and stronger contributions to the official negotiations process over time.

The first three workshops can be considered as the initial stage of the project, as the nature of the workshops shifted afterward. These first three workshops focused on facilitated brainstorming sessions and negotiations training for joint groups of influential Georgians and South Ossetians. The workshops aimed to build relationships, teach constructive negotiating processes, and develop substantive ideas that might contribute to the official negotiation process. The January and May 1996 and the June 1997 meetings included approximately twelve participants each, all of whom were either senior government officials or influential unofficial individuals. As the process progressed from January 1996 to June 1997, more and more officials participated in the workshops, so that by the third meeting all participants had an official connection to the peace process. At the same time, new leaders on each side of the conflict were involved as power shifts brought new officials into the negotiations process. The participants in all the workshops participated in their personal capacities; they did not represent their official roles or wear their official hats and they could make commitments only of a personal nature. The five-day meeting agendas included exercises and skills building in negotiation, brainstorming ideas related to the Georgian-South Ossetian negotiation process, and both formal and informal time for relationship-building.

At the first workshop, the agenda allowed time for sharing perceptions of each other. The political status of South Ossetia was specifically excluded from discussion. Cultural and economic ties, refugees, and joint interests formed the focus of discussions. The press statement the groups drafted at the end of the workshop thanked the sponsors and said simply that the groups met and talked.

Between the first and second workshops in January and May 1996, NRC maintained a local presence in Tbilisi and Tskhinval(i), and CMG came to do another assessment. The second workshop in May 1996 involved more official negotiators and included consideration of the status question. The meeting generated a variety of interesting ideas relating to the status question and served as an informal substitute for the stalled official negotiations process.

Elections and political changes in the region delayed additional workshops until June 1997, when CMG held another workshop in Massachusetts. Participants in this workshop were all personally and directly connected to the official negotiations. Participants included ministers (of industry, security, and refugees and migration), parliamentarians, and presidential representatives.

The second stage of the workshop series introduced opportunities to focus more directly on the substantive issues of the conflict through joint learning. CMG and NRC brought participants to a July 1998 meeting in Barcelona, Spain to study the autonomy relations between the center and periphery in Spain. CMG determined that the first stage of three meetings had built significant relationships and constructive negotiation skills, and thus the substantive input of joint learning from Spanish experience was an appropriate next step. At the same time, political uncertainty in Russia meant that the conflict was unlikely to be settled at that time, and thus the negotiators should focus on learning to prepare them for future negotiations rather than attempting to craft a settlement immediately. The Georgian and South Ossetian participants together heard presentations on Basque aspirations and the Catalonian constitution. Although the focus of this second stage was on shared learning, CMG also facilitated some brainstorming on conflict issues and allowed additional time for relationship building, as had been the focus of the first stage.

The third stage of the workshop series was made up entirely of steering committee meetings. A core group of Georgian and South Ossetian participants, each high-level officials involved in the official negotiations, agreed to hold meetings together in the Caucasus and Black Sea region after the Barcelona meeting. In the face of decreased project funding, this model would allow more frequent meetings while decreasing travel costs. The steering committee meetings, with less intensive facilitation from CMG or NRC, allowed official high-level negotiators to meet in an unofficial capacity to reflect on their ongoing negotiations.

Unfortunately, a lack of funding cut the project short, and the third stage, the steering committee phase, formally finished in 2000. However, the initiative left in place solid relationships of mutual understanding amongst key negotiators on each side of the conflict.

Contributions to Peacemaking

Both the Vertic and Caucasus Links and the CMG and NRC teams saw their work as complementary to the official negotiations process. Both sought to provide alternative processes that would help the official process move forward. The Track One-and-a-Half initiatives attempted to move the official process forward very directly by involving senior official negotiators from each side in the unofficial workshops and meetings. In the case of the CMG workshop series, the workshops took place with the explicit blessing of the leadership of both sides.

CMG's Track One-and-a-Half diplomacy complemented the official negotiation process with subjective, procedural, and objective impacts (Nan, 1999, p. 217, and Nan, 2004). The workshop series improved *relationships* (addressing subjective elements of the conflict), improved the negotiation *process* (addressing procedural elements of the conflict), and introduced *substantive ideas* into the official dialogue (addressing objective areas of the conflict). These impacts thus range from shifts in the interpersonal relationships of official negotiators, to shifts in the manner of official negotiations, to concrete ideas and proposals that transferred to the official dialogue from the unofficial workshop series.

By working outside of the official process, but with direct participation by many of the key individuals in that process, the CMG workshop series directly contributed to official peacemaking. Individual participants experienced personal changes in their relationships with each other, their comfort level with constructive dialogue processes, and their understanding of each other and the conflict issues. These individuals then carried these changes directly back to the official negotiations process. Over five years, the effect of the four workshops and subsequent Steering Committee meetings has been remarkable. Participants and observers attribute this effect in part to the five-year duration of the program, which allowed relationships and process skills to develop to the point that substantive contributions could be made.

Official mediators, who were not present at the workshops, observed marked changes in the tone of the official negotiations following the onset of the workshop series and each subsequent workshop, and the official mediators attributed these changes to the relationships built at the workshops. Through the informal workshop experiences, participants found more and more personal ties to share before and after formal meetings, or over cigarette breaks, and they grew to understand and trust each other more.

Workshop participants also brought back specific negotiations processes when they returned from the workshops. The most blatant shift might be that official negotiators on both sides began calling each other personally as particular issues warranted direct discussion between meetings. This introduced a previously missing element of direct communication on an as-needed basis. The direct communication by phone, possible only with some level of relationship and trust, allowed negotiators to address issues early, before they could escalate. Even more dramatic, the Vertic-facilitated meeting of the South Ossetian Speaker of Parliament and the Georgian Speaker of Parliament opened up direct communication where none had existed at all.

The actual process of face-to-face negotiations also changed. For example, the official mediators noticed suddenly that the negotiators were considering positions and interests, not simply arguing for their positions, after the first Oslo workshop. Two participants later brought in an analytical framework discussed at a workshop and used it as a basis for structuring discussion of particular conflict issues. These participants felt they and their colleagues on the negotiating teams understood each other better when using a framework that clarified the issues, causes of the issues, possible options, and the realm of potentially constructive choices. This shift to using frameworks to structure discussion also reinforced the idea that there might be win-win outcomes to some discussions.

The shifts in relationships and negotiations processes were also accompanied by direct Track One-and-a-Half Diplomacy contributions to the substance of the official negotiations. For example, a Georgian participant made a high-profile speech abroad and used language from a draft joint statement he had developed during an exercise with a South Ossetian colleague at a workshop. This official statement, which utilized language sensitive to South Ossetian concerns, helped smooth difficult relations at a time of difficulties around refugee return. In addition, the significant Georgian-South Ossetian cooperation on economic development emerged from intensive discussions at the early Norway workshops, where the framework for the May 1996 official memorandum and the March 1997 economic development agreement were also discussed. Participants and facilitators attributed these direct substantive contributions to the informal exploratory discussions at the workshops, where participation in a personal capacity meant participants felt free to creatively explore new ideas from amongst a broad range of brainstormed possibilities. In addition, workshop exercises helped participants develop deeper understanding of each other's perspectives and thus be better prepared to construct workable substantive proposals in future discussions. It is interesting to note that these impressions, shared by facilitators and participants, were also confirmed by the official mediators interviewed, who noted that new ideas had emerged from the CMG workshops, although the official mediators were not so clear about how such substantive contributions had developed in the workshops.

Track One-and-a-Half Diplomacy's Contributions to Peacemaking

The experience of the CMG workshops series, as well as Vertic's work with the parliament speakers, shows that unofficial facilitators can bring positive contributions to official negotiations. These contributions can bring to the official negotiations improved relationships, improved processes, and new substantive inputs. These contributions are very direct in the case of Track One-and-a-Half Diplomacy, because official negotiators themselves experience unofficially facilitated initiatives and take their learning back to the official negotiations.

The CMG workshop series had a lasting impact on the official negotiations. This success can be attributed to a range of programmatic strengths: long term involvement; an intervention team that mixed local knowledge, local representation, and process expertise with the successful inter-organizational collaboration; a balanced focus on relationships, process skills, and substantive ideas; and a carefully selected participant group that brought both openness to the unofficial process and also high-level influence on the official negotiation process.

Finally, it should be clear that the positive impacts that the Track One-and-a-Half diplomacy efforts brought to the official negotiations did not occur in a vacuum. At the same time as these unofficial high-level initiatives, other unofficial efforts were building grassroots support for a peaceful settlement process. The grassroots work most likely shaped the politically possible range of alternatives on both sides and the larger peace process context. These various less direct contributions that unofficial conflict resolution initiatives brought to the official negotiations even without directly involving negotiators as participants are documented in Nan (1999).

Notes

1. The case study presented here builds on the 1999 focused comparison by focusing more directly on the specific contributions of high-level unofficial conflict resolution initiatives to the official Georgian-South Ossetian negotiations. Readers who want more information about the conflict history, the other types of interventions directed at the conflict, coordination between the various interveners, or how this case compares with others in Eurasia, should refer to the more detailed 1999 report (Nan, 1999).

2. Georgians refer to the city as Tskhinvali, and South Ossetians refer to it as Tskhinval, thus I have adopted the unusual Tskhinval(i) in an effort to respect both parties.

3. I developed the communication-coordination-cooperation-collaboration labels for this spectrum of coordination modes in a collaborative discussion with Andrea Strimling. See Nan and Strimling, 2004 for more discussion of cooperation in conflict resolution.

9

The Peru-Ecuador Peace Process

The Contribution of Track-Two Diplomacy [1]

Edy Kaufman and Saúl Sosnowski

Introduction

The peace treaty signed by Ecuador and Peru in October 1998 was not only the culmination of a successful and, at times, difficult diplomatic process; it was a faithful reflection of the transformation of society in both countries that shored up official diplomacy in order to achieve a bi-national consensus for peace. By this means, the longest-standing border conflict in the Western Hemisphere reached its end with a culture of peace, hopefully difficult to derail, and likely to become the norm between the two nations.

A dialogue between society and diplomacy, vital to diplomatic negotiations, came about as a result of parallel interactions between civil society leaders from both countries. This track-two diplomacy had its roots in the University of Maryland, College Park, where academics, professionals and businesspeople from both nations formed "Grupo Maryland." Thus, in 1997, the project "Ecuador-Peru: Towards a Democratic and Cooperative Conflict Resolution Initiative" was launched as part of the University's program "A Culture for Democracy in Latin America." [2] Through an analysis of four unofficial workshops, this chapter will concentrate on the official leadership's transactions and the parallel ways in which track-two diplomacy peacebuilding functioned during the different stages of the process. The chapter will begin with a short background of the history and the methodology adapted to the negotiations; it also has a concluding section examining the strengths and weaknesses of citizen's diplomacy in this particular case.[3]

Brief History of the Conflict

Ecuador and Peru share much more than their geographic proximity with some of the deepest ethnic and cultural bonds in the Americas. Their communities can be traced back to the pre-Incaic era; afterwards, both experienced the destiny of the Inca empire and, as a consequence of its defeat, formed part of the same Spanish viceroyalty for nearly three centuries. At the time, the existence of borders was irrelevant. The border conflict began, in fact, during the period of transition from colonial domination to independence.[4]

Following independence, borders were based on the demarcations of colonial jurisdictions (viceroyalties and *audiencias*). Spain had governed the territory of both countries without clearly defining their perimeters. As a result, there were insufficient records to determine the location of definitive boundaries. One historical problem was the successive governing of the territory itself by Ecuador, the Viceroyalty of Peru, and the sphere of influence controlled by Bogota. When independence was declared in 1824, Ecuador formed part of Gran Colombia (1824-1830). This ambiguity in the historical interpretation of territory, inherited from colonial times, unleashed the border dispute shortly after independence (1829).

From the beginning, the new republics of Ecuador and Peru dedicated their energies to obtaining the necessary conditions for domestic governance. In order to achieve a consensus in the midst of continual domestic disputes, coups between *caudillos*, and ongoing political instability, it became commonplace to appeal to a real or fabricated sense of threat of foreign invasion. As each *caudillo* had his literate secretaries, allegations and litigation sustaining these pretensions were not long in coming. These generated disputes that, in some cases, were no more than baseless fictions and cleverly manipulated legal arguments reflected in a vast body of literature consisting of innumerable pamphlets and flyers. But over the years, these arguments became dogmas that, poorly understood and grossly misused, fed into a false patriotism which, in some cases, preempted any serious analysis of historical reality. The consequences were a mutual distrust and rancor that continued into the late twentieth century.

The border question has been frequently trotted out for domestic consumption by dictators and governing demagogues. This practice has been facilitated by the rough and barren terrain found along much of the border area—specifically, the section under dispute until 1998—and by the lack of understanding that persists in both countries regarding their geography and environment.

In 1887, both countries agreed to submit the dispute to international arbitrage under the King of Spain without discarding the possibility of reaching a negotiated solution on their own. This friendly spirit, however, was short-lived. In April 1910, as the arbiter prepared to issue his ruling and clear up the controversy, armies mobilized towards both sides of the border in anticipation of a decision that would be adverse to their interests. Unwilling to trigger a war, the arbiter resigned.

Ecuador and Peru were unable to reach an agreement on their own. During the past century, additional efforts failed and military tensions flared periodically. In 1941, hostilities escalated into an armed conflict, culminating with military victory for Peru and the signing of the Rio de Janeiro Protocol. The objective of this international treaty was to establish norms for a definitive solution to the bi-national conflict. Argentina, Brazil, Chile, and the United States agreed to act as guarantors to ensure its fulfillment.

While the Protocol contains a relatively exhaustive framework of normative provisions on the items and procedures necessary to establish permanent boundaries, it seems to have failed in at least two respects. First, it apparently contains a geographic imprecision: the existence of a *divortium aquarum* between the Zamora and Santiago rivers, considered in Article 8 to be a reference point in drawing the border. Nevertheless, the Protocol offered a conceptual and dynamic framework far too narrow to achieve effective resolution of the bi-national conflict. The context in which it was adopted forced the losing side to accept conditions that its citizens have later considered to be excessively damaging. At the same time, it did not include provisions that would lead to transforming mutual feelings of hatred, rivalry and ill will.

It comes as no surprise, therefore, that these elements—in addition to political and military factors in both countries—gave rise to renewed armed conflicts in 1981 and again in 1995. While Peru managed to impose its military superiority during the 1981 conflict, Ecuador prevailed in 1995. There are no published estimates of the human and economic costs of these wars, but it is not difficult to surmise their immense impact in terms of the precarious social and economic structures of both nations.

The most recent confrontation with Ecuador led to an intense process of diplomatic negotiations, which concluded with the signing of the peace treaty in Brasilia on October 26, 1998.

Track-Two Diplomacy: The CIDCM approach

Alongside traditional diplomatic channels, track-two diplomacy is required not only to stimulate solutions that lead to peace agreements, but also to construct and cement a lasting peace based on reconciliation between the parties. This is accomplished by generating new ideas outside the box of official negotiations that civil society can follow and sustain because, in the end, it is people, and not political institutions, who find their basic identities affected by these conflicts.

The peace process between Ecuador and Peru was reinforced through citizen diplomacy fomented by "Grupo Maryland,"[5] drawing from the method known as "Innovative Problem Solving Workshops" (IPSW) developed at Maryland's Center for International Development and Conflict Management (CIDCM).[6] In a nutshell, this approach is based on the following four elements: 1) The selection of the project/workshop participants as "Partners in Conflict," namely, participants from across the conflict's divide who nonetheless share traits of a common identity (profession, gender, age, location, etc.); 2) guided by the pioneering work of CIDCM founder Edward Azar, a needs-based approach that endeavors to understand the underlying needs and motivations behind opposing positions; 3) a problem-solving process leading the workshop to seek common ground among participants through written consensus; and 4) the overall objective, which is conflict transformation of the participants via their personal adoption of new skills, and the intra- and intergroup formation of an epistemic community, which has developed a shared understanding of the roots of the conflict and ways to address them.

The decision to accompany peace negotiations with track-two diplomacy is justified, in our view, for the following reasons:

1. The confidentiality and informality allow participants to freely express opinions that, through the use of brainstorming methods, provide a creative dimension that supports the diplomatic process.
2. The selection of participants prominent in civil society—some of them in contact with circles involved in official, track-one diplomacy—provided these workshops with a public and private impact of major significance. Participants attended of their own volition and not as representatives of their respective institutions.
3. CIDCM had already experimented with track-two diplomacy methodology in ethnopolitical conflicts in Sri Lanka and Lebanon and involving groups from the Middle East, Israel/Palestinian Territories, Bolivia, and Kazakhstan and the Caucuses; as well as between states in the case of the Malvinas/Falkland Islands. Therefore, it could be adapted to the Ecuador-Peru case.

The IPSW process is based on four stages: a) an initial trust building, in which informality and personal friendships are encouraged through "Partners" getting to know each other, the program's dynamics and ground rules, and the role of co-facilitators; b) a training stage that builds relevant individual and group skills through different exercises (interpersonal communication, stereotype reduction, de-escalation, creativity, cooperation, etc.); c) the third and most important stage, searching for common ground; and d) reentry, in which a sense of commitment is developed with Partners in order to implement shared ideas in a concrete way through a jointly-developed action plan. Of the different strategies provided by IPSWs, the consensus-building method we used during our first workshop was an adaptation of the ARIA framework (Antagonism, Resonance, Invention, and Action), originally developed by Jay Rothman (1997).[7]

The First Workshop (College Park, Maryland): August 4-9, 1997

Background

The undeclared war, with military confrontations developing in January and February of 1995, is the most serious of the three violent episodes sustained between the two countries since 1941. During skirmishes in Alto Cenepa in 1995, Ecuador demonstrated its great offensive capacity to Peru, returning a strategic military balance to the conflict between the two countries. This new situation, as well as pressure from the guarantor countries, led Ecuador to modify the position it had held in previous decades, accepting the viability of the Rio de Janeiro Protocol signed on January 29, 1941.

Over the past three decades, Ecuador's diplomatic position with regards to the border conflict had been based on repudiating the treaty, arguing that it had been signed under the threat of force and military occupation. On the other hand, Peru recognized the existence of a border dispute that it had previously denied and, therefore, the need to embark on joint negotiations, taking into consideration Ecuador's points of view.

Once again, the ABC countries—Argentina, Brazil, and Chile, the largest in South America—and the United States—as global and regional superpower—agreed to intervene as guarantors to ensure the success of the peace process. It is important to stress the stature of this third party, which greatly influenced the outcome and ensured the implementation of the peace process through positive inducements. Members of the third party took it upon themselves to bring closure to a long-standing dispute with the assumption that it was doable and that it would stimulate the resolution of many other latent border disputes in Latin America. Their mediating role was handled with professionalism. Hence, the negotiation process took on noteworthy intensity and consistency, thanks to the participation of the Four Guarantor Countries from the Rio de Janeiro Protocol that established, under the coordination of Brazil, the Mission of Military Observers (MOMEP) for the separation of forces, demobilization, and verification of military agreements. They have also presided over diplomatic negotiations, urging both countries to reach a definitive solution to their confrontation.

The diplomatic phase began in Brasilia during the most recent armed confrontation. The Itamaraty Declaration, signed by Vice Chancellors and representatives of the guarantor countries on February 17, 1995, called for a cease-fire, a separation of forces, and the beginning of negotiations. Paragraph Six of the

Itamaraty Declaration notes the commitment of both parties to initiating talks within the framework established by the Protocol in order to resolve existing impasses.

The meeting of foreign ministers from Ecuador, Peru, and the guarantor countries in Santiago, Chile, on October 29, 1996 constituted a major advance by establishing the need to take into consideration impasses presented by both countries. The Santiago Accord established that if the parties were unable to reach an agreement, the guarantors would offer their suggestions, and so on and so forth until a negotiated solution acceptable to all parties had been reached.

Track-Two Process

Keeping in mind the above-mentioned "Partners in Conflict" criteria, it was vital to ensure that participants from both sides share a common identity (professional, ethnic, religious, etc.) capable of transcending the limits of the dispute that separated them. In this way, trust building could be accelerated through shared language and idiosyncrasies; ingredients that, in turn, facilitate the search for common solutions. In this case, we requested that our primary co-sponsors, the United States Information Service (USIS) offices in Quito and Lima, propose candidates with diverse political ideas in the following fields: environment, human rights, economy and commerce, academia, and the media. We initially selected these areas because we considered them to be ideal in terms of increased civil society participation regarding specific aspects of the conflict and its repercussions in both countries. At first, we considered the possible incorporation of certain retired members of the Armed Forces, but we opted to postpone their participation to a later stage. Ten people from each country were selected for the first workshop held from August 4-9, 1997, on the College Park campus.

Compared to methods used in other conflict resolution workshops covering much more violent and prolonged disputes, the "ice breakers" used here worked quickly and efficiently. Relationships of trust were created almost immediately. Given that the participants were leaders or spokespersons from different sectors of society, their initial attitude was, with rare exceptions, fundamentally one of conciliation. It is important to recall that at this time, two years had passed since the war and the negotiation process was already underway. In this case, given the favorable predisposition of nearly all participants, the first stage of trust building was relatively short.

We then moved to a skills building stage, experimenting with methods that would be used in the track-two process, generating greater understanding on both sides and, in general, avoiding a "premature breakdown." Training in nonviolent communication, active listening, the de-humanization of the "image of the other" and prejudice reduction were included. The main exercise of this stage consisted of elaborating "a shared vision." The participants were asked to reflect on what would be the ideal situation for both countries within the next thirty years. Beyond specific expressions of their wishes, some asked if it wouldn't be necessary to rethink nineteenth-century nation-state projects that are no longer viable, highlighting the urgent need to reconsider political and economic integration of the region in order to somehow counteract the will for domination prevalent among the intellectual elite of the previous century. From this perspective, they spoke of building bridges across civil societies in Ecuador and Peru by creating lasting networks between business, cultural, and education groups, among others. In this vein, and considering the deep cultural ties between both countries, it was suggested that clinging to the few existing differences was a way of expressing each nation's identity and individuality. On the other hand, while desiring a change in mass mentality is a utopian enterprise, it was considered that the economic integration of the region would help mitigate differential characteristics, changing perspectives concerning confrontation as well as historic relations between both countries.

Considerations of the worst-case scenario highlighted the possible continuation of the conflict and its impact on the economy of both countries. Under the pretext of the "common good" or "national interests," political sectors that had already lost their prestige might be able to make use of the conflict and exacerbate it in order to gain positions and influence, thus wresting legitimacy from any attempt to advance in the peace talks. This would strengthen the military, undermining democracy and civil participation and perhaps even leading to the suspension of institutional guarantees.

The ARIA process began with a rather confrontational review of historic relations between the two countries. Participants formed a working group to explore the role of civil society within the wider framework of negotiations between Ecuador and Peru. On the second day, the "adversarial stage" began, with the objective of having participants discuss the official positions of their respective nations, explain and defend them clearly enough to have their opponents understand them as fully and deeply as possible. To this end, two exercises were carried out. During the first, each of the two parties expressed the official or "hard" position of their countries without having it necessarily reflect their own personal positions. In the second, roles were reversed and each participant presented the position of the opposite side.

In the debriefing, thoughts centered on the contributions civil society could make towards the peacebuilding process and their capacity to formulate creative proposals within a framework of intergovernmental discussions. Participants indicated that the border conflict issue reappeared whenever there were frictions between civil and military sectors, or when a sharp turn in the course of political life was imminent; that the real causes of the conflict should be sought in the changes that had occurred in both countries, especially in terms of civic-military relations and the socioeconomic context; that the conflict was used in an opportunistic fashion by the political class during election time or other similar events and highlighted attitudes taught from early childhood by warmongering education in both societies. This diagnosis was intended to generate ideas for a central task defined in tandem with the participants. The goal was to develop concrete ways to resolve disputes within the context of a democratic culture, despite potential exacerbations reflecting the interests of a government or political class.

Upon concluding the role play, facilitators and "Partners" evaluated the exercise. The differences in use of terminology were noted. These indicated that each side's interpretation of the same Protocol was so different that they seemed to be referring to two completely different versions of the same document; reading materials and studies carried out in both countries reflected opposing interpretations. It was noted that as they made their arguments, their positions gradually became polarized and that within this environment, no concessions could be made or common ground found. When the discussion began, the rational tone established at first was gradually lost, to the point of actually defending the use of force as an option established by international law. It was demonstrated that each side accused the other of being expansionist, military, bellicose, imperialist, etc.

It was also shown that arguments on each side were nurtured both by the national and international media. During the discussion, positions were supported by Protocol articles as well as by historical, moral, and other arguments. Facilitators characterized this stage as unproductive, comparing it to a "dialogue between the deaf" in which the same arguments were repeated several times using different details and inflections that ranged from legal to economic, political, military, and even anthropological and geographic. Both sides had dug themselves into intransigent positions.

As the workshop moved towards discovering the needs behind these positions, the following questions were posed: What are the underlying interests at stake in the conflict? What does each side need? Why is legitimacy given by the public to the declared objectives of each side? What are the alternatives for both sides if no solution is found? At that point the participants focused on: How can a realistic and functional compromise be achieved? How can relations be consolidated, if not cemented, through negotiations? Once the preparation of an Ecuador-Peru conflict agenda was underway, a working group was selected to prepare the specific agenda on which to focus brainstorming meetings for the entire group. One of the participants, who had experience with this method, was in charge of preparing and leading this stage. The main focus was to generate ideas so that civil society from both countries could more efficiently support the peace process.

The "Partners" were then divided into five working groups dealing with their specific areas of expertise. The two questions that served as a foundation for their deliberations were: What are the contributions of civil society to the peace process? How can we support these contributions? The participants drafted the following list of proposals during the final two sessions of the workshop. All proposals were approved by consensus. While the main focus of the working groups was directed towards civil society tasks in Ecuador and Peru,

proposals by consensus

ideas were set forth and exchanged regarding the outlook generated by the ongoing process in Brasilia. The groups focused on environmental problems in the conflict region; the role of the press and mass media in public opinion; the role of education in promoting mutual understanding and the role of businesspeople in advancing local economic development.

The fifth group came up with a list of possible civil society contributions to track-one diplomacy, indicating the need for the governments to reiterate their commitment to maintaining peaceful channels for conflict resolution and discarding the use of force. In order to reinforce the negotiations themselves, they suggested:

1. Nourishing the current process of intergovernmental discussions with information on public opinion trends; using appropriate methods to analyze negotiation results.
2. Establishing contacts with other agencies dedicated to promoting peace.
3. Reinforcing and/or providing incentives for accords that limit and control the purchase of weapons.
4. Seeking the necessary international technical cooperation to clear minefields in the conflict region.

Furthermore, the participants agreed to join forces as a "Research Group for Ecuadorian-Peruvian Peace and Cooperation"—a name that would later be changed to "Grupo Maryland" as previously mentioned—and draft a series of projects based on reciprocal concession formulas that would generate, as a result, mutually beneficial options leading to peace.

Towards the end of the workshop, official visits were made to the Ecuadorian and Peruvian embassies in Washington, D.C. to present the proposals and to encourage the governmental representatives to move forward with the peace negotiations. Advancing towards this level of visibility drew wide press coverage and contributed towards reinforcing Grupo Maryland initiatives to take on a more active role; this, in turn, made it increasingly representative of civil society.

The Second Workshop (Pontificia Universidad Católica del Ecuador—PUCE): March 2-5, 1998

Background

The first round of talks, held in Rio de Janeiro and Brasilia starting on November 24, 1996, allowed for the presentation of impasses. Of these, the most significant included the "partial unfeasibility" of the Rio de Janeiro Protocol given that, according to Ecuador, the geographic landmarks shown there did not exist (particularly the *divortium aquarum* between the Zamora and Santiago rivers); this was in addition to Ecuador's aspirations to obtain the free and sovereign right to navigate the Amazon River, as well as other issues derived from the implementation of the Protocol that had yet to be resolved.

Under intense pressure from the guarantors, an agreement was reached in Rio de Janeiro on January 19, 1998, regarding a set of procedural issues (timeline, list of impasses, etc.) in order to reach a definitive solution to the conflict through the so-called Peace Accord of Itamaraty, which clearly defined topics that still needed to be addressed (the remaining impasses). The main topics included determining the border along a 78-kilometer stretch where, according to Ecuador, the geographic landmarks mentioned in the Protocol did not exist; the discussion of a bi-national Amazon program built on a novel concept of "shared authority"; a process of integration and development; and a regimen of military security and mutual trust.

The discrepancies to be resolved through special commissions formed by citizens from both countries would be expressed through four treaties: "Commerce and Navigation," "Border Integration," "Establishment of a Common Border," and the creation of a "Bi-national Commission for the Development of Measures of Mutual Trust and Security." Each commission would be coordinated by a representative from the guarantor countries. Deliberations took place from February to May 1998, and culminated with drafts for accords in the second and fourth commissions, which had met in Washington, D.C. and Santiago, Chile, respectively.

The Commissions' work was assisted by the input of "Technical Groups," especially for issues related to the "Treaty of Commerce and Navigation in the Amazon," based in Buenos Aires, and "Establishment of a Common Border," based in Brasilia. The Technical Groups were to offer non-binding "opinions" on the most pressing issues of the border debate.

However, negotiations encountered obstacles in the first and third Commissions, highlighting the difficulties posed by the corresponding impasses. The underlying elements of the old dispute and those that had surfaced during the most recent armed confrontation fed into the traits of a long-term culture of conflict that, with its complex web of symbols and meanings, greatly strained hopes for the negotiations' diplomatic phase.

Within the moratorium period established by diplomatic precedent, once the points of the potential accords were leaked to public opinion, the foreign ministries faced varying and complex pressures from their respective societies. Peruvian populations on the Amazonian border found it hard to understand concessions to Ecuador ensuring their right to free and perpetual navigation on the Amazon, while for the Ecuadorians it was difficult to cede on geographic positions such as the military outpost at Tiwintza, which had become a symbol of national pride.

The breakdown in negotiations threatened to return the conflict to its initial stage. Military confrontations manifested themselves through border skirmishes during July and August of the same year, placing the armed forces, once again, as major protagonists. After diplomatic and technical alternatives had been exhausted, the issue continued to await political definition, that is, the outcome of conversations held at top presidential levels. Hope returned with the renewal of these conversations, backed by the inauguration of President Jamil Mahuad in Ecuador. The Mahuad-Fujimori presidential meetings in Asunción and Panamá during August 1998 revealed that both had analyzed different possibilities to reach an understanding, including variations on a cross-border park within the most volatile zone of Alto Cenepa—a proposal also largely drafted at the Grupo Maryland's first meeting in College Park. Above all, the gesture held the possibility of "mutual concessions" vital to any negotiations and contemplated, moreover, by the Rio de Janeiro Protocol itself. In practical terms, above all, the cross-border park had a symbolic value that would fulfill the need to defend the "national honor" of both nations. Likewise, it represented an efficient alternative in terms of managing environmental resources, the conservation of which would have been affected by the fragmentation caused by an artificial border and separate administrations. But the true economic and social importance lay in the "Commerce and Navigation Treaty" accords and beyond these, in the border integration treaties that would doubtless become a key to opening the borders to commerce and integrating the two countries, linking the rich southern zone of the Ecuadorian coast with northern Peru. It was evident, however, that political negotiations between the two countries had to be preceded by real negotiations between the governments and their respective societies; therein the importance of the citizens' mission. It is not surprising, therefore, that the Mahuad administration embarked on a policy of internal negotiations with Ecuadorian society in mid-1998. In Peru, both the proposal for the cross-border park and the "Commerce and Navigation Treaty" received surprisingly unfavorable reactions from significant public opinion sectors.

Different factors concur in explaining these reactions, beginning with deep psychological variables that have not yet been fully explored and are linked to a history of continuous military defeats suffered by Peru, in comparison to which the conflict with Ecuador tends to be perceived as the only moment of triumph and, therefore, as a unique opportunity to affirm a victorious national identity. The internal climate of political polarization, reinforced by the authoritarian nature of President Alberto Fujimori's administration, drove some unofficial sectors to take on radical positions that appealed to very basic nationalistic sentiments. Another weighty factor must be considered: the lack of horizontal channels of communication between Ecuadorians and Peruvians to facilitate mutual understanding and the exchange of opinions without middlemen or censorship. This vacuum contributed to creating a fertile ground to propagate prejudices and aggressive attitudes sustained by disinformation.

The Track-Two Process

The second workshop—which originally was to have been held in Chile—
took place in Cashapamba, near Quito, on the premises of the Pontificia Universidad Católica of Ecuador, from March 2-5, 1998. For this workshop we incorporated indigenous leaders and Church representatives who lived in the conflict
area. As four members of the first team (one Peruvian and three Ecuadorians)
had become negotiators or consultants to official diplomatic negotiations, new
members covered their areas of interest and professions.

The peace process had advanced quickly (allowing us to meet in one of the
two engaged countries instead of under a guarantor's hospitality), and there was
clearly optimism, despite the fact that serious territorial and fluvial impasses remained. Because of the change in venue for the second workshop, a commitment was made to hold the third in Peru. Our facilitating team decided to
streamline the meeting so that on the second day of the workshop, participants
would take on the responsibility of leading the sessions, and different work
groups would prepare public declarations, designing plans—preferably joint activities—for the future. In contrast with the first workshop, during which the
embassies of Peru and Ecuador would only receive their respective nationals,
both the foreign minister of Ecuador, José Ayala Lasso, and the ambassador of
Peru in Quito, Alberto Montagne, participated in the inaugural ceremony. At the
end of the deliberations many practical suggestions were produced and promptly
shared in visits to the Ecuadorian foreign minister and with the Peruvian ambassador.

The agenda began with a dynamic mutual introduction among all members
of the Group, both those who participated in the first meeting as well as indigenous and Church representatives who joined the team during this second encounter. The organizers had only invited participants from both capitals to the
first workshop at College Park, without involving the real stakeholders of the
border area between the two countries; this omission was corrected in the second
workshop to the benefit of all, since the representatives of the region in conflict
brought both a practical knowledge of the ground situation as well as a very
strong motivation to find viable solutions.

The methodology was shaped by the advances made at the level of official
diplomacy. Both countries assured the guarantors that negotiations would be
conducted via four commissions aimed at generating a "Treaty of Free Navigation in the Amazon"; a "Treaty of Integration"; a third to address "Territorial
Delineation of the Shared Border" and "Measures of Mutual Trust and Security." In terms of this last field, the specific role of the Group would be to support the process with steps towards gaining citizens' trust. The agenda included
the following phases:

- *Summary:* Initially, the participants reviewed goals proposed by Grupo Maryland in the first workshop and their effective fulfillment, conditioned by the self-same circumstances of the reentry processes of each member to their social and professional life. Particular attention was paid to the effective implementation of ideas generated in the previous workshop.

- *Activities in Ecuador:* a) Upon its return, the Group carried out a visit to the Foreign Ministry and presented the results of the meeting in College Park; b) several newspapers across the country began to publish articles favorable to the peace process; c) at the Group's request, the Chamber of Commerce informed public opinion of the need to improve the environment for peace negotiations. Above all, this organization asked that everyone reflect on the scope of a free navigation treaty in the Amazon. A major factor was the acceptance by the Ecuadorian military of civil society as a new interlocutor in conflict resolution; at any rate, the Group did not encounter any opposition to this proposal; d) in the field of education, student exchanges were initiated. The Pontificia Universidad Católica del Ecuador (PUCE) had had experience of this kind through the International Association of Economics Students (AIESEC). In 1997, young Ecuadorian and Peruvian university students interacted during a week-long visit. The Group considered that these encounters should continue with the support of educational institutions in both countries. Likewise, an "Agreement of Academic Cooperation" was signed by PUCE and the Universidad Católica de Lima. The formation of an Organizing Committee to design a work plan remained pending.

- *Activities in Peru:* a) Several meetings were held among private businesses and, as in Ecuador, various opinion articles were published in the media; b) the Group detected among certain military officials positions that were not very favorable to reaching a peaceful solution to the conflict. On the other hand, they indicated that this was not the official position of the Peruvian government or the Armed Forces as an institution; c) Meetings were held about specific issues involving women and the environment. Members of the Group supported the National Institute of Natural Resources in generating environmental development proposals. The results of these actions translated into high-impact sustainable development activities.

- *Reflexive phase:* This part involved the presentation of issues compatible with the potential creation of a "bi-national" definition in Group action areas. The term "bi-national" corresponds to a geographic and conceptual area recognized by the governments, in which actions regarding common themes or problems are carried out with cross-border criteria in order to favor a climate of trust among the citizenry of both countries. This was intended to support the measures of mutual trust already established by the governments or to be established in more formal and institutional aspects. The specific theme of this encounter was chosen: "Citizen-participation to generate degrees of trust between Peru and Ecuador." The theme, new within track-two methodology, was a real challenge and an invitation to jointly elaborate new ways to understand issues that basically refer to the field of security and center on military aspects.

The "measures of mutual trust" are, theoretically, focused, concrete actions that seek to reduce tensions, prevent confrontations and make it less likely for conflicts triggered by erroneous interpretations of adversarial intentions to emerge. In the military field, these actions, as well as the institutional commitments that sustain them, are clearly and rigorously designed and established. However, it is possible to reflect that the situations triggered by a "culture of conflict" also refer to other multiple factors and directly involve citizens. Moreover, the establishment of measures of trust among citizens legitimizes official understandings, making them more viable.

Along these lines, the Group was of the opinion that in order to construct the right environment for understanding, it is necessary to identify common interests that can turn conflict situations into opportunities for cooperation. Some of these themes affect communities independently of their separation by borders. Such is the case of health, the situation of cultural groups with shared historical and genetic roots (indigenous peoples along the border), and environmental issues. A special session presented the problem and prospects for working across the border, given the transnational aspects of many of the issues. Before continuing, the facilitators believed it was necessary and feasible for sessions to be conducted by participants from the actual region. They proceeded accordingly following a brief training on how to exercise the facilitator role.

- *Integrative Phase:* This part entailed translating shared creative ideas into specific action projects. In keeping with the nature of the first exercise in Maryland, a series of ideas were launched without considering their feasibility. At that time, the ideas were meant to evolve into proposals that were limited in number, but realistic, with the potential of being carried out through personal or institutional commitments. The participants decided to focus on the two following issues:

1. The role of indigenous peoples: Members of the Group linked to the Church and indigenous communities from both countries participated actively in the analysis of the border situation, adding a direct perspective of the conflict zone. On one hand, the commonalities across the divide are numerous.[8] The position of Coordinator of Indigenous Communities of the Amazon Basin (COICA) had been created to salvage the cultural unity of indigenous peoples and as a mechanism to facilitate the joint discussion of shared problems in order to find a solution. Along the southern border of Ecuador there is no guerrilla activity, drug cultivation, etc. It is practically free of violence, due to the vigilance of the indigenous peoples themselves.

Some urban border communities, however, continued to resist any steps towards conflict resolution. For example, in Loreto (Peru), in the months prior to the date of the Second Workshop, there had been at least five mass mobilizations caused by the fear that the Peruvian government would cede navigation rights to Ecuador.

2. Cenepa diversity: The rich diversity of the heights of the eastern Andes has been endangered by colonization and economic problems within the communities. Therefore, Grupo Maryland highlighted the importance of conservation. In College Park, the Group

discussed implementing a bi-national park that could act as a launch pad for cross-border projects.[9] Taking up this idea once again, the step was taken to consider the development of a "bi-national conservation" project that, among other things, would seek "territorial organization" according to management areas, use of renewable and nonrenewable resources, as well as joint management of tourist areas. An important conclusion drawn from these discussions was that the traditional concept of sovereignty, with strictly territorial connotations and jurisdictions, had become outdated. Likewise, wide areas of the border zone were considered "no man's land," where the inhabitants lacked the necessary infrastructure, undesirable or illegal activities took place, and there was an inclination towards the misuse of natural resources.

During the second day, facilitation exercises were introduced in order to train participants to conduct sessions. The voluntary facilitators established two subgroups. Discussions were to take into account the following parameters:

a) Deliberations should be centered on the role of citizens in a peace process as supportive of diplomatic negotiations (Track One). However, this is not a parallel process, given that diplomacy follows its own logic, framed within the formal relations between States. At the same time, given that logic, citizens do not have direct access to information on the progress of negotiations. Their role, therefore, should be oriented towards creating conditions that facilitate formal processes by generating and broadcasting public opinion favorable to the peace talks. Peace becomes a goal in and of itself, indispensable to the harmonic development of peoples.

b) The contribution of citizens goes beyond merely circumstantial conditions. It is a long-term process that transcends formal treaties between States given that, by nature, conflicts tend to persist and reactivate social conditions of violence and confrontation. The constant and joint action of citizens will have the capacity to gradually deactivate the factors of mistrust that consolidate into long-standing behaviors that shape "cultures of conflict." As a result, the Group's considerations did not necessarily have to contribute ideas that feed back into "Track-One" negotiations. These should aid the consolidation of relations between peoples and communities of both countries and, especially, between those groups that are most involved in the conflict, by advancing compatible ideas without neglecting the formal framework of negotiations.

One group evolved around representatives of indigenous peoples and the Church, given that they lived and worked in the border zone and knew it well. It was proposed that an "integrated vision" be gained of the current situation of these populations, mostly indigenous, that have been affected by the consequences of the territorial dispute.

The second group, called "citizens' initiatives," generated a long list of recommendations, some to be implemented by the "Partners" themselves.[10] These included the evident need to gain a more complete and precise view of the zone; being able to rely on an inventory of all existing projects, studying their viability and feasibility and determining which resources are available or can be obtained through international or governmental institutions. An interdisciplinary, meaningful project centering on economic, anthropological and cultural issues was taken under consideration by Grupo Maryland. However, such a project would require a judicial order providing security for any investments carried out within the zone.

During the final stage of the Quito workshop, the Group analyzed in a plenary session the proposals of both subgroups with the goal of reaching a consensus regarding specific proposals that, given their viability, could be implemented or fomented over the following months. As a first order of business, the conclusions of the working groups in the first workshop were reviewed in order to evaluate whether their objectives had been met, whether they should be maintained or withdrawn temporarily or permanently.

Subsequently, new recommendations were drawn from the brainstorming sessions held by previously established working groups: The Communications/Media Working Group, the Citizen's Education and Participation Working Group, and the Business Working Group. Original proposals were revised for future implementation.

During the final session of the second workshop, the Group prepared two documents—reviewed, revised and accepted by all members during the final plenary session—that were presented to the Ecuadorian foreign minister and the ambassador from Peru ("Cashapamba Declaration" and "Grupo Maryland"), as well as a press bulletin that was sent to media in both countries.

A "Technical Secretariat" was created, based in the Latin American Studies Center of the University of Maryland, College Park. This would not be a decision-making body, but would be in charge of maintaining ties between members of the group and serve as an information center through a web page. Likewise, the Grupo Maryland recommended that as part of the participants' reentry, they announce and promote in their daily activities the ideas and concepts that had emerged during this second meeting.

The Third Workshop (El Pueblo, Peru): August 12-16, 1999

Background

In October 1998, the two foreign ministries reached a consensus regarding nearly all the disputed issues, including those related to the Commerce and Navigation Treaty. This was not the case, however, with regards to drawing a common border, which turned out to be the most sensitive issue, not only in terms of the relations between both countries, but also between each president and his respective constituencies. Following intense personal negotiations, they decided to place the final formula in the hands of the guarantors. In practical terms, the borderline proposed by the Bras Días de Aguiar Decree of 1947 was ratified. They also decided to create a demilitarized environmental reserve in the area where the most recent conflict had taken place and to recognize the symbolic value of Tiwintza in Ecuador, awarding public domain (permanent property rights)—but not sovereignty—over one square kilometer. This opened the way for the signing of the Peace Accord. The priority for both the Ecuadorian and Peruvian foreign ministries then became to ensure that an estimated three billion USD of support from international donors, promised as an incentive during the negotiating process, would become a real source of economic and social development.

The Track-Two Process

The third workshop was held at El Pueblo, a conference village center not far from Peru's capital. It was aimed at reinforcing the new Peace Treaty drafted by track-one diplomats and decision-makers through civil-society peacebuilding efforts, and the implementation of some of the ideas by the participants themselves. A few months after the signing of the Peace Agreement, the Ecuadorian government requested that a senior diplomat in charge of the implementation of the accords and bi-national ventures join the Group. The facilitators approached the Peruvian government, which expressed a similar interest. Hence, the "Grupo Maryland" became what is known as a Track "One-and-a-Half" process. Before agreeing to these new "Partners," it was requested that both foreign ministries share with us the agreed upon instructions, requesting them to affirm that their presence was to be on a personal and not a representative basis (which could have pressured the other nationals in the workshop into adopting a "united" front). This interesting development is another example of the fluidity that Track Two can generate, comparable to the previous workshop, in which the "Grupo Maryland" temporarily lost four members for the benefit of Track One. Three of these individuals came back, joining the group with insights from the various bi-national commissions.

Among the problematic reactions brought back by the participants were the following: a sense of rejection by large segments of the population of Iquitos (Peru) of the peace accords; the feeling of an "open wound" felt by some members of the Peruvian armed forces; the lack of official activities to celebrate the peace accords.

Particular attention was given to the concrete actions that members of the Group—as citizen leaders—could take given their respective professional and personal positions. Therefore, the facilitators decided not to strictly follow the ARIA method used in Maryland, but to maintain its basic fundamentals. In particular, the same brainstorming to originate new ideas was implemented and the results recorded in a detailed action plan for reentry. In the plan, the individuals present, as well as their organizations, undertook specific responsibilities and agreed on which recommendations would be made to their respective governments. As part of the workshop, partners were designated to suggest concrete steps in each of the following areas: media, cultural and educational, civic and public activities. Examples of the many proposed include:

> 1. Media: to publish *joint* articles in both countries to celebrate the first anniversary of the peace accord; to disseminate the new maps that resulted from the peace accords; to promote knowledge of the bi-national indigenous traditions; to emphasize shared historical heroes through films and texts.
> 2. Cultural and educational activities: review of school textbooks, particularly in geography and history, to account for the new realities; the establishment of a joint award, "Premio Pareja-Denegri," to individuals who promote understanding and friendship, initially among these two nations; holding joint meetings of university rectors from northern Peru and southern Ecuador; joint dance festivals and bi-national cultural events in the border region.
> 3. Civic activities: celebrations of peace in the main squares of capitals and provincial areas; organization of bi-national tourism (including ecotourism); religious celebrations and the delivery of sermons on the anniversary of the peace accords.
> 4. Public activities: inclusion of the Armed Forces in the celebrations of peace; naming "26 de octubre" of streets and plazas; sister-cities relations; issuing of stamps and medals to celebrate peace; institutionalizing of October 26 as a national holiday in both countries.

These and many other proposals were submitted in person by joint delegations of the Maryland Group to the foreign ministers in Quito and Lima.

There were also concrete proposals for business and development projects in the border areas. A member of the Group provided a detailed road map of the bi-national development plans in the border area. The Grupo Maryland established an inventory of existing and planned projects (at that time a total of 136 projects divided according to specific categories).[11]

Given that approximately 50 percent of peace agreements are neither partially nor fully implemented within the first five years, it was important to find ways to gain backing among the general public in both countries while at the same time supporting the inhabitants of regions in the disputed area, who were now able to engage in collaborative projects.

The Fourth Workshop (Cuenca, Ecuador): August 29-31, 2000

Background

Given the general political developments in the region, Grupo Maryland emphasized the importance of strengthening democracy. The notion that democracies do not wage war among themselves became particularly relevant as a result of the leaderships crises looming over the area. The fourth workshop focused, accordingly, on the consolidation of peace. For all practical purposes, its main thrust was the implementation and, particularly, securing funds for the border region's economic development. The event was reflexive in nature and centered on the scope of work accomplished to date, laying down a foundation to promote a culture of peace between both countries.

The benefits derived from training Ecuadorian and Peruvian "Partners" were applied by members of the Group to a significant number of rectors and deans who came from Universities located in southern Peru and northern Ecuador (members of AUSENP association). This meeting was held immediately following the Cuenca workshop and greatly contributed to consolidate this academic network. Similarly, the awarding of the first "Premio Pareja-Denegri" to Amb. Ayala Lasso, former Ecuadorian foreign minister and at the time his country ambassador to the Vatican, for being one of the architects of the peace accord, further enhanced the Group's standing and its role in both countries.

Track-Two Process

The fourth and final workshop focused on strengthening the planning and implementation of joint ventures between Peruvian and Ecuadorian institutions and people in the border regions, hence moving away from a consensus reached at the countries' capitals towards strengthening ties between the stakeholders themselves. According to the final document drafted by Grupo Maryland, the peace process between Ecuador and Peru was considered—regionally and worldwide—as a precedent for conflict resolution. Another point to be highlighted is that this process required no additional bilateral mechanisms other than the guarantor countries of the Rio de Janeiro Protocol.

Still, the international community and civil societies from Ecuador and Peru had not maintained the same level of interest in the consolidation of peace, according to Grupo Maryland. Therefore, it was considered imperative to initiate as soon as possible multiple steps that would seek to "broaden fraternization among different social sectors." The Group also believed that citizens should remain vigilant of resources that make up the peace fund destined for border development.

At the end of the workshop, Grupo Maryland proposed twelve themes for civil society in Ecuador and Peru:

1.   Promoting, through civil society and venues such as family, educational institutions, the press, trade unions, and popular organizations, the revitalization of citizenship understood as the quality and right of being a citizen.

2.   Demanding citizen participation in the oversight of public offices by establishing watchdog organizations that would guarantee the free exercise of human rights and accountability among those charged with protecting these rights.

3.   Creating, based on past experience, spaces on the Internet to comment on criteria for democracy and peace, as well as sharing experiences of citizenship.

4.   Promoting the creation of academic research and activity groups on civil society, democracy, and peace.

5.   Fomenting the horizontal, bi-national exchange of democratization experiences.

6.   Promoting the establishment of subsystems within protected areas along shared borders.

7.   Supporting sustainable development projects with local populations, using basins and microbasins in the region as a foundation.

8.   Creating healthy borders, involving governments and social sectors, by articulating official and traditional medicine and creating incentives for the participation of health agencies in the common zone.

9.   Facilitating the rapprochement of indigenous peoples, reconstruction of shared history, recognition of indigenous territories and participation on both sides of the border, given that these societies share a common identity.

10.   Periodically launching a business lobby in order to ensure respectful and responsible intervention with regards to environmental, social, economic norms and property rights in the border zones.

11.   Instigating governments to set up timelines for the realization of programs derived from the peace accords and strategies for the dissemination of information regarding citizenship.

12.   Suggesting that meetings be held between the Ecuadorian and Peruvian military on issues of common interest; specifically, among military academies of both countries.

Conclusions

The analysis of this case study concurs with the observation that "the participation of civil society in discussions on the conflict is fundamental, and when possible, the creation of lines of communication between official negotiations and nonofficial contacts is useful."[12]

The conflict between Ecuador and Peru can be read on three levels: military, political, and social. While on a military scale the conflict was real or instigated for institutional or personal purposes,[13] in terms of society the discord was negligible, despite political manipulation of public opinion. Moreover, both nations share nearly identical idiosyncrasies, a fact that improved the climate of the meetings from the start. In retrospect, in some ethnopolitical conflicts the general public tends to be more extremist than its representatives, whereas in our case the opposite proved to be true; hence, the advantage of citizens' diplomacy as a tool to consolidate peace from the bottom up.

Beginning with the first encounter, there was an attempt to build on what participants had in common; to this end, businesspeople, journalists, environmentalists and academics from both countries were brought together. In order to choose participants for the conferences, a videoconferencing screening process was used. Yet, "citizens' diplomacy" in the first workshop was confined to the selection of those "influentials" (Kelman, 2003) coming from the capitals of both countries. It was only for the second workshop that Shuar and Ashuar leaders from both countries were integrated. They had historical ties, but had been separated by decades of border conflict. The indigenous leaders underscored the fact that although they were directly affected by the dispute, they did not take an active role in it. In their view, the conflict had largely been prolonged by people lacking first-hand experience in the border area. This made the methods needed to advance conflict transformation different from those that had been adapted to other protracted communal conflicts, such as the case of Jerusalem. Having two indigenous leaders participate in the deliberations encouraged a greater focus on the border region. During an exercise of mutual understanding in which participants were to explore common interests, they formed a team and carried out a point-by-point analysis of the situation: "if it were up to us, the conflict would have been resolved long ago at a much lower cost." At any rate, this conflict fell into the category of *tractable* or manageable. To begin with, the conflict zone had few inhabitants. For those who lived in the Cenepa region, there were no *impasses*.

Using Rothman's methodology, the reflexive stage within the ARIA process revealed that in this kind of border conflict, belligerent attitudes are found within the Armed Forces for specific institutional reasons. Politicians have a more flexible attitude, perhaps to avoid being manipulated by opposition groups under the guise of patriotic flag waving. Diplomats experience tension between propagandistic attitudes and the professional challenge posed by conflict resolution. Civil society leaders in both countries are decidedly in favor of a commitment to end the conflict; with regional exceptions, this attitude prevails in public opinion as well. Clearly, in situations like that of Ecuador and Peru, the expectations of various sectors must be taken into account in order to realize, for example, that there are possible differences between civil society and the Armed Forces; between those who can be perceived as part of the solution and those who are part of the problem. Hence, the facilitating team adjusted the workshop program in keeping with specific needs. For example, we set aside "prejudice reduction" and "search for common vision" exercises because they were deemed unnecessary for this group.

The participation of two academics, one from Peru and one from Ecuador as co-facilitators was doubtless the right decision, not only because of their deep understanding of the issues, but because they allowed participants to mobilize towards designing specific results within the informal environment of the workshops. The fact that they belonged to countries in conflict was counterbalanced, likewise, by the coordination of two Argentinean-American academics in the facilitating team. The third-party team of four was thus characterized by both external impartiality and internal balance.

It is interesting to note that, despite the fact that this network of Peruvians and Ecuadorians had found many elements in common, they opted for the designation of "Grupo Maryland," because they wanted to give recognition to the origin of the network as well as a name and project already known in both countries that would set them apart from the efforts of other working groups, such as the Harvard Group.[14] Between the first and second workshops, an evolution came about that was not only parallel to the positive development of the peace process, but also important in terms of the degree of commitment of the participants. In this second case, the decision emerged among several participants to take on greater responsibilities for a more active follow-up. The enthusiasm of nearly all of the participants to continue in the "Grupo Maryland" was evident, and included those who in different ways joined official delegations to the negotiations, as well as the Mahuad administration in Ecuador. This interest was evident in the case of the Quito meeting through the presence and financial support of two university rectors who later went on to perform official duties.

It is noteworthy that a minimal rotation of participants took place as a result of their joining official positions or for personal reasons. New members received a half-day training in advance of the workshop in order to socialize them in the workshop process.

The confidentiality of the meetings was firmly stipulated. Yet while the "Partners" in the first workshop were unconcerned when one of them wanted to memorialize the event for his own records, they rejected the persistent request of one of the diplomats based in Washington, D.C. to participate. This differentiation between internal and external exposure became evident when, by mistake, an Ecuadorian television team wanted to film not only the opening act and the presentation of documents concluding the second workshop—events that were widely broadcast—but also part of the deliberations. In contrast, when one of the participants filmed much of the workshop proceedings, the remaining members were not bothered, showing the difference between a group that had come together quickly and possible outside interference.

The first workshop was funded in part by USIA (Washington, DC), with additional support from the University of Maryland. Its success led USIA offices in Ecuador and Peru to provide additional support, in conjunction with Ecuadorian universities, towards carrying out the second workshop. The lack of stable resources has made follow-up activities more difficult. But, paradoxically, this need motivated the facilitating team and Peruvian and Ecuadorian members of the Group to make substantial efforts in order to creatively develop the steps necessary for success.

In retrospect, the Group's role was specifically mentioned in the study conducted by the International Peace Academy. This recognition of the role performed by the "Partners" and its impact are especially noticeable in the incorporation of certain proposals to the deliberations of the Negotiations Commissions, as well as, on a more formal level, communiqués received from Ecuadorian Foreign Minister José Ayala Lasso. As previously noted, four of the original "partners" in the Maryland group were brought into the track-one official negotiation process, three on the Ecuadorian side and one on the Peruvian side.

While it is true that this type of track-two, or citizens' diplomacy, conflict resolution process is relatively new to the region, its reception has been extremely positive. It is possible to predict that it will serve an analogous purpose in other cases of latent border conflict, and that it could be used where there are internal ethnic tensions at levels that have not yet led to violence, as well as those cases in which violence does exist. Furthermore, it is also applicable in workshops with social sectors confronting the effects of economic and social policies; that is to say, the experience with the Ecuador-Peru conflict has allowed us to confirm the validity and usefulness of the method.

The high degree of civil society development in Latin America and the interest in alternate methods of resolving disputes in the areas of law, political science, psychology, sociology, and culture allow us to visualize the introduction of this methodology among study programs in many of our countries. In this vein, this observation no longer has to limit itself solely to training for the resolution of international conflicts, such as border disputes, but appeals to a proven methodology that can contribute towards the reduction of levels of domestic conflict.

An effective democracy not only defines itself or concludes with a government that represents the majority; it must also accept and promote the right to difference, plurality, and diversity. The methods to find and formulate consensus complement legitimate majority decisions and can become singularly important during times of crisis, on those occasions in which social pacts are relevant to a sustained and democratic development.

While many of the ideas originating in Grupo Maryland were incorporated by diplomats during the peace process, other projects remained unfinished. Once peace was signed, Grupo Maryland, at the Cuenca meeting, proposed its objectives be honed in order to develop a culture of peace between Ecuador and Peru. However, the political environment of both countries overshadowed the group's intentions. In 1999, Ecuador endured an unprecedented economic crisis, which triggered the fall of Jamil Mahuad's government in January 2000. Meanwhile, in

Peru, Alberto Fujimori was reelected as president in a dubious voting process. He resigned several months later in the midst of political scandal.

Moreover, a unique opportunity to obtain financing for the projects was lost when diplomats from both countries did not allow representatives of Grupo Maryland to accompany them on a diplomatic mission to Europe in 1998 aimed at garnering government funds to back up the economic development of the border region. Civil society representatives could not only have lent legitimacy to the request for funds, but simultaneously, during their visits to the European capitals, to the request for aid from large NGOs working to benefit children, education, development, etc.

Likewise, cultural projects such as the notion of creating a joint day of peace between Ecuador and Peru have not taken hold. Nonetheless, the door is open to greater bi-national cooperation. An example of this are recent economic figures: in 1995, trade between Ecuador and Peru reached $200 million. In 1998, despite losses caused by El Niño in both countries, trade doubled according to official data from the government of Ecuador.

Much of the contribution of the "Partners" was accomplished by advancing the set agenda individually or in bilateral personal cooperation, particularly according to professional affinity. In terms of individual effects, the participants gained a mutual sense of empowerment that they could positively influence the outcomes of the negotiations. The Group continues to exchange information and other messages through an Internet listserv, used mostly to share news about progress in regional developments as well as the activities of "Partners," some of whom now hold official positions. The facilitators continued to participate in this process as members of the Group, feeling very much a part of an emerging epistemic community. Whether this is to remain a permanent feature is hard to predict, but it seems plausible that if any future conflicts between Peru and Ecuador should ever emerge, these strong ties will be re-activated and the trust built will provide the "Partners" with an important relative advantage.

Notes

1. This chapter is based on a previous paper presented at the Latin American Studies Association 1998 meeting, prepared by the authors together with Dr. Bertha García of the Pontificia Universidad Católica de Ecuador (the Ecuadorian co-facilitator), and Oscar Schiappa Pietra, then lecturer at the Washington School of Law, American University (the Peruvian co-facilitator). Special thanks go to Juan Jaramillo of the Latin American Studies Center, College Park, for his research contribution to this chapter. We would also like to acknowledge with thanks the translation from Spanish and additional editorial assistance by Tanya Huntington, also from LASC.

2. See website of the Latin American Studies Center of the University of Maryland, College Park: www.umd.edu/LAS

3. A more detailed coverage of the "Grupo Maryland" Track Two can be found in the website of the Latin American Studies Center (http://www.inform.umd.edu/LAS).

4. For a succinct but clear background to the conflict see Mónica Herz and João Puentes Noguera, *Ecuador vs. Peru: Peacemaking Amid Rivalry* (Boulder, Lynne Rienner Publishers, International Peace Academy Occasional Paper Series, 2002).

5. At an early stage, when it was suggested that the participants adopt a name to identify the group, their clear preference was to call themselves by the name of the University that had brought them together and assisted them during the formative stages. The facilitators would have preferred a name relating to their national identities, but the "Partners" decision prevailed.

6. For a detailed description see John Davies and Edward (Edy) Kaufman, *Track II/Citizens Diplomacy: Concepts and Techniques of Conflict Transformation* (Lanham, Rowman and Littlefield, 2003). The book is dedicated to Edward Azar and includes a posthumous article with his writings.

7. This method consists of four stages: 1) *Adversarial*: allows participants to incorporate their own arguments and those of their adversaries through the advocacy of their countries' official position and then experimenting with reverse role playing and presenting each other's side. 2) *Reflexive*: both sides explore, within an environment of empathy and understanding, the most basic needs that led them to sustain their respective attitudes. In this stage, there is an attempt to progress from the question, "what is my initial position?" to "why this particular position?" 3) *Integrative*: attempts to find innovative shared solutions. Through a systematic process, separating the creation of ideas (brainstorming phase) from their critical review, classification and prioritization (re-formulation phase) and the search for common ground (consensus phase). And 4) *Reentry*: This final stage prepares the participants for a sustained effort implementing the agreed document through an action plan while anticipating the psychological, political and organizational difficulties involved in effecting it across the divide. For development of the model, see John Davies and Edward (Edy) Kaufman, *Track II/Citizens Diplomacy: Concepts and Techniques of Conflict Transformation*.

8. The indigenous peoples in the border area consist of homogenous populations across the divide with shared foundations: culture, territory and environment, aspects that favor the unity of these peoples and eliminate tensions. The Achuar and Shuar communities that live on both sides of the border collaborate and give mutual support to projects and actions related to health and education: the latter, through the support of intercultural bilingual schools. It is vital that the borders be permeable in order to facilitate joint work, above all in zones where the same ethnic groups live on both sides of the border. Thanks to European funds, over 150 runways have been constructed and there is now bilingual education via radio.

9. In fact, the final agreement between Ecuador and Peru established a bi-national park. This idea, generated by civil society from both countries, was taken up by the diplomatic proceedings. It is believed that a pacifying element could well be the creation of a bi-national park in the conflict zone in order to implement integrated development programs through the help of international organizations.

10. The subgroup dealing with the "citizens' role" showed more interest in the topic of constructing a climate of mutual trust from the perspective of citizens, proposing the following:

    a.   Providing incentives in civil society to generate and support a climate of trust between peoples, the search for lasting peace, and the acceptance of the benefits of the process through articles in the press, university debates, and other media. In this vein, there was talk of the need to generate awareness regarding the economic benefits that the establishment of a free port in Iquitos would bring. It was believed that this idea would not be accepted if the State promoted it, but that if it were done, civil society would certainly encounter support.

b.   Establishing "fraternal agreements" between like civil institutions to promote specific initiatives by public convocation and with financial resources. It was indicated that experiences of this kind already existed, such as, for example, a festival of choirs in the city of Piura in which groups from the city of Loja participated.

c.   Developing public audiences in zones near the border to discuss, technically and objectively, the potential economic and social impact of a peace accord, which would be carried out through goodwill missions. There was talk, likewise, of promoting meetings among special groups in ten key sectors. Upon concluding this experience, a plenary session would be held from which a project integrating these peoples would be derived.

d.   Doing an inventory of actions already taken in terms of projects for cooperation and cross-border relations. This issue could refer to:

1.   Citizens' initiatives. The project inventory would later be incorporated into the Grupo Maryland website: http://www.umd.edu/LAS/Projects/grupomaryland/Peace.htm

2.   Public projects. Unfinished works that are important to both countries, such as the Puyango-Túmbez hydroelectric project. Potential works that have not yet been proposed were also included, such as using a Peruvian oil pipeline that is not at full capacity to extract crude from Ecuador, for which it would only be necessary to construct a section linking the two.

e.   Promoting meetings between like existing groups (boy scouts, rotary clubs, border merchants, etc.) through an overall project.

f.   Promoting and consolidating "sister city" initiatives, such as the one already signed by Quito and Lima, with particular interest in the role of municipal areas.

g.   Promoting low-cost infrastructure projects with high or short-term impact. As an example, the construction of another bridge in the Huaquillas-Aguas Verdes border zone was mentioned, as well as the installation of a central telephone exchange circuited in the same zone so that merchants would be able to sustain direct communications.

h.   Promoting border city tourism projects as a "gateway" to the country. This would improve the image of these towns by highlighting aspects of basic infrastructure, tourist services, and urban development. For this activity, those who, through local works, contribute to consolidating the unity of peoples would be called on to collaborate through the creation of bi-national committees.

i.   Fomenting the interest in writing and publishing articles and essays on social or scientific topics with shared authorship between Ecuadorians and Peruvians in order to generate a public opinion favorable to peace. This activity requires no funds and can produce a high social impact.

j.   Requesting that official measures of mutual trust include the establishment of a special legal framework for arrests and detentions of civilians within the border zones.

k. Urging governments of both countries to subscribe to the Convention on the Prohibition of the Use, Stockpiling, Production and Transfer of Anti-Personnel Mines and on Their Destruction, requesting the adoption of specific agreements for the continued removal of said mines. This issue has taken on dramatic importance due to repeated cases of deaths and injuries in the border zone.

l. Requesting that official negotiators include in their documents the concept that peace accords should be carried out within a framework of human rights and sustainable, democratic development in both countries.

m. Committing to and reaffirming the Group's support of the official negotiations process carried out by both countries.

11. The Inventario de proyectos, iniciativas, acuerdos y convenios binacionales can be found in www.inform.umd.edu/EdRes/Colleges/ARHU/Deps/LAS/Projects

12. M. Herz and J. Pontes Nogueira, op. cit., 101. The analysis of the International Peace Academy team continues by specifically referring to the initiative of CIDCM that should be remembered: "Although the initiative was not directly connected to the mediation process itself, this contact among ten Ecuadorians and ten Peruvians, representing diverse sectors of their society, favored a new understanding of bilateral relations and focused attention on cooperative projects for these relations. In fact, many of the participants in the Maryland group became members of the negotiating commissions created to deal with four different areas of contention" (2002, pp. 87-88).

13. Recent revelations have demonstrated these elements of personal gain, corruption and prestige.

14. The so-called "Harvard Group" drew its name from the short-lived gathering of high Ecuadorian and Peruvian military officials who met at Harvard with the aim of achieving basic understandings following the end of military action.

Conclusion

Evidence for the Essential Contributions of Interactive Conflict Resolution

Ronald J. Fisher

Conceptual Base for the Comparative Analysis

In this chapter, the research method of comparative case analysis is applied to the nine cases of ICR intervention described in the preceding chapters. As indicated in the Introduction, this method is designed to examine comparable cases, in this instance of successful transfer effects from ICR interventions to official negotiations, in order to identify relationships among variables, and thereby build theory. The process is essentially an inductive one, and the identification of relationships among independent variables related to the intervention and dependent variables related to the effects of transfer provides some indication of whether and how such interventions are effective. Such indications can then serve as hypotheses for further research and also as interim guidelines for practice, if they are taken as tentative prescriptions to be carefully applied and assessed in each ensuing application. In this way, theory and practice can advance together toward better understanding and greater effectiveness—the dual Grail of applied social science.

The comparative method as outlined by George (1979) and others really has two important and related foci as operationalized here. In one instance, the analysis relates characteristics of the intervention (the independent variables) and conditions of the conflict (the intervening and contextual variables) to the transfer effects on negotiation processes and outcomes (the dependent variables). In this way, the method overcomes the oft-noted dilemma between describing the unique elements of a single case and finding generalizations that can be used to build theory. According to George (1979):

> The solution to this apparent impasse is to *formulate the idiosyncratic aspects of the explanation for each case in terms of general variables* [italics in the original]. In this way, the "uniqueness" of the explanation is recognized but it is described in more general terms, that is, as a particular value of a general variable that is part of a theoretical framework of independent, intervening, and dependent variables (p. 46-47).

In the second focus, the analysis goes further to relate differences in the independent variables and differences in the intervening variables to differences in the dependent variables. That is to say, variations in certain characteristics of the intervention and in the nature of the conflict are related to variations in the transfer effects. In this way, the analysis can tease out what elements or expressions in the intervention under what conditions appear to be related to differences in transfer outcomes. Again, George (1979) suggests that:

> The "uniqueness" of a single case be described not only in the specific terms that historians employ but also in the value of independent, intervening, and/or dependent variables. . . . Much depends upon the sensitivity and judgment of the investigator in choosing and conceptualizing his variables and also in deciding how best to describe the variance in each of his variables. It is particularly the latter task—the way in which variations for each variable are formulated— that may be critical for capturing the essential features of the "uniqueness." It is for this reason that investigators would do well to develop the categories for describing the variance in each of their variables not on an a priori basis but inductively, via detailed examination of how the value of a particular variable varies in many different cases (p. 47).

Thus, while the variables of interest are specified prior to the analysis of the cases, the categories of variation in the variables are discovered through the inductive process, much in the same way that content analysis is used to find commonalities in a set of qualitative data. At the same time, theoretical and practical sensitivity can direct the investigator to look in certain directions that are deemed to hold promise as important variations in variables. For the cluster of independent variables as a whole, that is, the characteristics of the intervention, variations that relate to the power or influence of the interventions would seem to hold particular promise. Therefore, the analysis was sensitized to look for variations related to the magnitude of the interventions, in terms of indicators such as number and duration of meetings, informality and neutrality of the setting, and connections of participants to decision makers. For the intervening or contextual variables, a number of theoretical propositions exist that bear on the most appropriate conditions or time to intervene. Therefore, variations that relate to the receptivity of the conflict were deemed important, such as stage of escalation, degree of intractability, existence of ripeness or readiness, and attitude of the parties to intervention. And for the dependent variables, the degree of transfer effects is of paramount concern, and therefore, variations such as in the number and nature of different effects were identified as important indicators.

The underlying general hypothesis guiding sensitivity in the inductive process is simply that more powerful interventions carried out under receptive or propitious conditions should result in more extensive transfer effects, all other things being equal of course. Whether the variations in the different variables entail large enough differences to allow for the emergence of any relationships among variables, is of course also an open question, and one that cannot be answered beforehand. However, because the cases have been initially chosen by their common nature as more or less successful ones, the possibility of finding such effects is attenuated. Hence, the emphasis remains on the first focus of the analysis, that is, looking for the common characteristics of relatively successful interventions across the nine cases.

The general questions to guide the development of the case descriptions were presented in the Introduction (see table I.1). These questions, which were provided to the authors of the cases, also reflect the theoretical framework that is applied in the comparative case analysis in terms of independent, intervening and dependent variables. For the comparative case analysis, the questions were elaborated through the development of a variable checklist, which identified the information to be gleaned from each case (table C.1).

Table C.1. The Variable Checklist

A. Nature of the Conflict	B. Nature of the Intervention	C. Nature of Transfer
1. Parties, Factions	1.Participants: Number per Party Identity Connections	1.Third-Party Rationale for Transfer
2. Parties' Goals	2. Meetings: Number Duration Frequency	2. Targets of Transfer: Leaders, Negotiators, Governmental Bureaucratic and Public-Political Constituencies
3. Brief History	3. Setting: Neutrality Informality Seclusion	3. Mechanisms of Transfer: Personal Contact, Briefings Writings, Speeches
4. Issues, Positions, Interests, Needs	4. Agenda/Topics	4. Objectives of Transfer

Continued

Table C.1—Continued

5. Power Relations Form of Interaction	5. Third-Party Team: Number Identity Knowledge Skills	5. Complementarity to Official Processes
6. Stage of Escalation: Discussion Polarization Segregation Destruction	6. Third-Party: Role Functions Relationship with Parties Relationship with participants	6. Transfer Effects: New realizations, attitudes, analyses, interpretations, language Creative ideas, directions, options, recommendations Principles, plans, frameworks, proposals Changed Relations: empathy, trust, cooperation Connections through new roles or structures
7. Indicators of Intractability: Persistence and Cycling Centrality of Issues Pervasiveness of Effects Lose-Lose Hopelessness Motive to Harm Other Resistance to Resolution	7. Objectives: Third Party Parties	7. Evaluation: Mechanisms Effects
8. Indicators of Stalemate: Intolerable deadlock Impending Catastrophe: Conditions worsening	8. Process of Meetings: Nature of discussions Necessary conditions	8. Conclusions of TP
9. Elements Affecting Appropriateness of Intervention	9. Outcomes of Meetings: Effects on partici- pants	

Continued

Table C.1—Continued

10. Cultural Differences: Among the Parties Parties and Third Party
11. Attitudes of Parties: Toward de-escalation Toward intervention
12. Appropriate Timing
13. Changes affecting Implementation

For some questions, the variable checklist simply requires the recording of the factual information, such as the identity of the parties or the conclusions of the third party on the nature and degree of transfer. For other questions, the variable checklist provided categories of response that could be used to code the answer to the question, such as stage of escalation or type of transfer effect. In many cases, the questions are based on theoretical notions about what manner of ICR intervention in what expression of conflict will result in what transfer effects.

The Nature of the Conflict

On the nature of the conflict, the first four questions and variables (A.1, A.2, A.3, and A.4) are simply descriptive, that is, ask for information that has become common fare in conflict analysis, such as the parties' goals and the issues in contention, expressed as positions, interests, and needs. Some of these elements may have particular importance in terms of the receptivity of the conflict to intervention and resolution. The nature of the goals, especially contentious goals, has implications for the course of the conflict. Kriesberg (2003) identifies two dimensions of contentious goals that can have important effects: the direction of change in terms of integration-separation, and the magnitude of change being sought in the relationship. Goals of an aggrieved party to achieve more life opportunities in education, employment and so on (integration) are likely more amenable to negotiation than goals that involve the expulsion of one party though ethnic cleansing or the independence of one through secession (separation). Similarly, minor changes in a relationship, such as a modification in existing policies, are likely to result in less conflict and be more manageable than major changes that radically redistribute overall power in the relationship. A second important distinction in conflict analysis is that between tangible interests, such as resources or access to desired opportunities, and basic human needs, defined as the essential requirements for human development, such as security and identity. Consensus in the field now appears to be that conflicts linked to needs, such as identity-based conflict, are much more resistant to resolution efforts than interest-based conflict (Rothman, 1997). Hence, the basic character of the cases must be examined in terms of what the parties aspire to achieve and what interests or needs are at stake or threatened in the conflict.

With regard to A.5, there is a general understanding that the power relations between the parties affect both the potential for third-party intervention and the nature of the outcome. Relatively equal power relations with some degree of power balance are generally seen as conducive to cooperative, accommodative processes and outcomes, whereas a severe power asymmetry is predicted to result in unilateral strategies and win-lose outcomes beneficial to the more powerful party. At the same time, such asymmetrical relationships are not regarded as conducive to third-party intervention, although unofficial approaches, which do not carry the connotation of recognition of the weaker party or an acknowledgment of its growing strength, may be more acceptable to a powerful party as compared to official methods. Nonetheless, early on in the development of the theory of ICR practice, I indicated that significant power imbalances were beyond the reach of the method (Fisher, 1972). Hence, the power relationship between the antagonists is an important variable to consider in the analysis.

The stage of conflict escalation (A.6) also carries some implications for the success of ICR interventions geared to transfer effects. A four-stage model of escalation was developed by Fisher and Keashly (1990) based on earlier theorizing, and was linked to third-party intervention through a contingency model, which specified the most propitious stage for intervention using different methods. ICR interventions are seen as most appropriate in the stages of polarization or segregation (following mediation or arbitration), rather than destruction, where more powerful, coercive interventions, such as peacekeeping, are necessary to control the violent interactions between the parties. Thus, the stage of conflict escalation in the case at hand may have implications for the applicability and success of ICR work.

ICR interventions have generally been directed toward violent, intractable conflicts, that is, those that endure over time with huge costs and appear to be resistant to management or resolution. Coleman (2000) presents a comprehensive treatment of the phenomenon of intractable conflict based in part on earlier theorizing, and provides a number of characteristics of intractability (A.7). Thus, it is possible to use these indicators to assess the degree of intractability in each of the cases, and to see if ICR interventions appear to be more effective in moderate versus severe cases of intractability, the quality being judged on a continuum rather than as a category.

Intractable conflicts are obviously deadlocked, but the nature of the deadlock and related characteristics of the situation have been postulated to affect the likelihood that the conflict will be addressed through cooperative action, such as negotiation. Zartman (1985) and others propose that parties are only willing to consider outside intervention and bilateral, rather than unilateral, action when their conflict has reached a mutually hurting stalemate, in which they are exhausted and see no possibilities for either decisive escalation or a graceful escape (Touval and Zartman, 1989). In addition, if both parties see that the situation will only get worse, as demonstrated by a recent or impending catastrophe, then they are more receptive to overtures of intervention. Thus, an unacceptable plateau and a threatening precipice combine to produce a state of ripeness or a ripe moment in Zartman's terms. In an extension of ripeness theory, Zartman (2000) contends that ripeness is a necessary but not sufficient condition for the start of negotiations, and also requires that parties perceive a way out of their intolerable situation. A third party can play a role in this process by persuading parties about the dangers of stalemate and the possibilities of finding a way out together. Pruitt (1997, 2002) has extended the notion of ripeness through the concept of readiness, which requires both motivation of the parties to settle their dispute and optimism that they can indeed reach a mutually acceptable agreement. Pruitt contends that optimism is a function of perceived common ground and working trust, both of these being components that ICR interventions work to induce. Thus, the analytical question is the degree to which these various conditions existed and were developed in the cases that were successfully addressed by unofficial third-party efforts.

With regard to item A.10 in the variable checklist, the role of cultural factors in conflict and conflict resolution has been gaining increasing attention in the field (e.g., Avruch, 1998). There is now a general understanding that each cultural group has its "culture of conflict" determining how conflict is defined, perceived, responded to and managed, and that when these beliefs and practices differ between groups, this can serve as a source or escalator of conflict. Thus, strong cultural differences can be an important element of intractable conflict, and it is incumbent upon third-party interveners to carry out a cultural analysis as part of their initial conflict analysis to assess the importance of cultural dimensions (Avruch and Black, 1993). The third party should also be sensitive to how differences between its own cultural base and those of the parties may affect the intervention process and outcomes. Thus, some comment in the case analysis is directed toward the element of cultural differences and the questions of whether and how these may have affected intervention success.

The remaining questions and variables on the nature of the conflict (A.11, A.12, and A.13) call for descriptive information from the case authors that may have relevance to the implementation and outcomes of the interventions. The attitudes of the parties toward de-escalation and intervention may link to considerations of the hurting stalemate and ripeness as discussed above, and may also provide further indications that the situation was receptive to intervention. Any reflections of the third party on the timing of the intervention might reveal assumptions and operating principles that relate to ripeness and readiness, and may also identify additional elements that created a green light for resolution efforts. Finally, the importance of changes in the situation must be acknowledged as potentially affecting the implementation and thereby ultimate success of the intervention. Sensitivity to all these elements in the case analyses should help assess the degree to which the conflict was amenable to outside efforts at that point in time.

The Nature of the Intervention

The questions on the nature of the intervention (B.1 to B.9) ask for mainly descriptive information, the focus of which is guided by the evolving theory of practice on ICR interventions as represented in the work of Azar (1990), Burton (1969, 1987), Davies and Kaufman (2002), Fisher (1997), Kelman (1992a), Mitchell (1981), Mitchell and Banks (1996), Saunders (1999b) and others. This body of practical theory specifies in a general way, with some variations, a number of the elements of ICR interventions, at least with respect to the implementation of workshops. The method is of course surrounded by a host of other characteristics and prescriptions that place the third party in the field of the conflict, but these aspects have been less discussed in the theoretical literature. With regard to workshops themselves, most prescriptive theorizing has focused on the characteristics of the physical and social setting, the participants who informally represent the parties, and the third party who organizes and facilitates the sessions.

Many of the important elements of ICR interventions are captured by a model of third party consultation that I developed based on the pioneering work of Burton and other scholar/practitioners (Fisher, 1972, 1976). A revised version of the original model is provided in figure C.1, which will be used to organize and guide the discussion of the questions on the nature of the intervention.

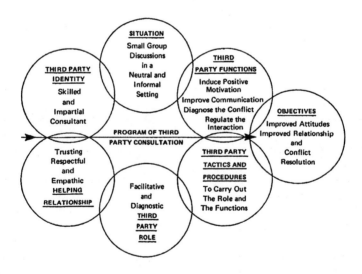

Copyright 1976 by the American Psychological Association,
Reprinted with my permission.

Figure C.1. A Model of Third Party Consultation

At the outset, it must be stressed that ICR is a small group approach, and the number of participants, usually only a few from each party, is thereby determined (B.1). The identity of the participants can vary from loyal members of their collectivities, to individuals who have influence in their communities, to highly placed individuals who have the ear of their leadership. In the kind of cases discussed here, which follow the focused definition of ICR and are selected for their apparent success in positive transfer, the participants are expected to be high-level influentials or officials who come to the meetings in a personal, unofficial capacity. This is important to note because the usual restrictions on official interactions are not in play, and participants are able to work openly with ideas in creative and flexible ways. The social identity of the participants is clearly linked to their group or country, but it is important to represent in the delegate group the diversity of that collectivity as well as the political spectrum that is relevant to the conflict. The connection of the participants to their leadership (i.e., decision makers) and to public-political constituencies is very important from a transfer point of view.

While there is no set standard, the evolving theory of practice of ICR prescribes that a series of workshops need to be held if transfer effects are to be a realistic objective. Thus, some number of sessions (B.2) over some period of time is predicted to be more effective in influencing policy and public opinion than a brief intervention of one or two meetings. The duration of the workshops is variable, but there appears to be some minimum in order to induce the analytical process and build adequate communicative relations among the participants. Typically, workshops last from three to seven days, and some involve separate pre-workshop meetings with participants from each side, such as in Kelman's Interactive Problem Solving model. The frequency of meetings is determined by many practical considerations, not the least of which is the changing conditions on the ground, but three to six meetings a year would seem necessary to maintain momentum and connect well with the evolving conflict.

Much has been said about the setting for workshops (B.3), and the consensus appears to be that a neutral and informal setting helps to support the impartiality of the initiative and to produce the relaxed yet focused atmosphere required for analytical, problem-solving discussions. An academic or retreat-style setting is seen as conducive to the flexible and informal analysis that is required, along the lines of a seminar discussion where ideas and options can be raised and explored without commitment or prejudice to other considerations. It follows that the discussions are off-the-record, and typically there is no transcription or recording, although the participants may agree to a summary or statement of some kind. The meetings are typical held quietly, but not usually in secrecy, as this may spark suspicions of back-channel negotiations, which are not the intent of workshops, and can also have negative repercussions if word gets out.

The agenda and topics for the workshops (B.4) are flexible, although the third party usually specifies a starting point and an overall flow. Workshops typically begin with each side being asked to make a statement on their perspective on the conflict or its current state, and this is followed by dialogue and analytical discussion induced by third-party queries and applications of concepts useful in conflict analysis. There is usually a motivation to get beyond surface positions on the issues and the standard rhetoric developed by each side to the underlying concerns in the form of interests, needs and values. Once conflict analysis has reached a point of some mutual satisfaction, options toward resolution begin to be explored in a problem-solving fashion, that is, the generation, integration, and selection of both single and joint activities that might help deescalate and resolve the conflict as appropriate to its current state of expression and with sensitivity to the many constraints and resistances that exist in the situation.

The characteristics of the third-party team or panel in workshops (B.5) are fundamental to the unique and effective implementation of ICR interventions. Usually a few to several members are engaged in order to cover the knowledge areas and skill sets required in general and in relation to any given conflict. The ideal identity of the third party is generally seen as an impartial one in national, ethnic, religious or cultural terms, but a team of balanced identities closer to the two sides of the conflict also has been postulated as being effective and as having some unique strengths, as for example, in the work of Kelman and his colleagues on the Israeli-Palestinian conflict. In any event, the third-party team must demonstrate impartiality in its attitudes and behavior to the two sides or difficulties will arise, particularly in conflicts of asymmetrical power where the weaker party may be more sensitive to potential bias. The set of conceptual and behavioral skills required to implement the third-party role is daunting, and speaks again to the necessity of working in teams to which the various members bring different competencies. Team members require general knowledge of conflict etiology and dynamics and all need a working knowledge to varying degrees of the history and expression of the conflict in question. Members should also have a good knowledge of international relations, which provides the context for ethnopolitical conflicts, and a good understanding of intergroup relations from the various social science disciplines. Elsewhere (Fisher, 2000), I have provided a list of qualities and skills that are relevant to facilitating productive confrontation between representatives of antagonists in workshop settings, that is, to assist them in directly addressing the emotional and substantive issues that define the conflict. Personal qualities, such as self-awareness and tolerance for ambiguity, need to be blended with interpersonal skills, such as empathic listening, with group skills, especially facilitative leadership and group problem solving, and with the capacity to manage interactions at the intergroup interface. Overall, the third-party role is one of professional consultation, with all of the diagnostic, facilitative and evaluative skills and ethical competencies which that role entails.

From the perspective of third-party intervention, the role of the ICR practitioner (B.6) is non-directive, non-judgmental and non-coercive, in comparison to more traditional roles such as mediation and arbitration. This facilitative and diagnostic approach is mainly carried out through a set of core strategies or functions, which entail inducing positive motivation for problem solving, improving the openness and accuracy of communication between the parties' representatives, helping to diagnose or analyze the conflict in concert with the participants, and regulating the interaction, as a moderator and at times as a referee, through the phases of the problem-solving process. Behavioral tactics, such as paraphrasing a comment, and additional procedures, such as an image-exchange exercise, are used as part of the work to carry out the functions. Successful implementation of this facilitative role requires establishing respectful and trusting relationships with the parties as well as the participants, so that empathic, genuine and constructive interactions occur within the workshop setting.

The objectives of the method (B.7) include the overarching one of a resolution of the conflict, meaning that understandings and agreements are reached in a mutually satisfactory manner so that the parties regulate their future behavior in jointly beneficial ways that are sustainable over time and in the face of changing conditions. These qualities of conflict resolution clearly distinguish the method and the objectives from those of conflict management, where the use of coercive inducements and ongoing surveillance is required to control violence and other destructive behaviors between hostile antagonists. Improving the relationship is an objective that distinguishes ICR interventions from processes of mere settlement, and challenges the method to transform relations between the parties toward greater understanding, trust and cooperation. In particular, a win-lose orientation demonstrated by unilateral coercive behaviors needs to be replaced by a win-win orientation, wherein the parties operate with both self and other interests, that is, mutual gain, in mind. Needless to say, these macro-level changes have to be initiated by micro-level improvements in intergroup attitudes in the participants and eventually in some large proportion of the two collectivities. Such improvements involve the reality or veracity of the beliefs that are held about the other party and the emotional or affective predispositions to respond to members of the other party. More accurate and positive attitudes replacing stereotypes and hostility are necessary to induce and support relationship improvement and the ultimate resolution of the conflict. The degree to which participants and parties share these objectives at the beginning of an ICR intervention is an open question, and may vary considerably over cases. In addition, the objectives which parties hold likely change during the course of a successful intervention, due to the intervention. Hopefully, in the beginning, parties, and even more the participants who represent them in problem-solving workshops, are looking for a way to reduce the costs of the conflict while still realizing some benefits related to their original goals. As the intervention progresses, the realization will hopefully grow that ultimate resolution requires changes in attitudes and in the relationship, and these objectives will then be similar to those of the third party.

The nature and process of meetings in ICR interventions (B.8) are thus markedly different from interactions in other venues or with other third-party methods. The challenge is to induce analytical and non-adversarial interaction that is full of honest exploration, wherein representatives of parties can come to better understand the causative and escalatory processes that have brought them to their present undesirable and intractable state, and can creatively explore options that will help them move toward de-escalation and resolution. In order for this to happen, the core functions of the third-party role need to establish related conditions that support the analysis and problem-solving processes. That is to say, increased problem-solving motivation, improved communication, deeper understanding of their conflict and their role in it, and more constructive interaction are all required to implement the approach. The third party takes a stimulating and facilitating role in this process, but the participants have to buy into and share the responsibility for this form of interaction or the intervention will fail. The roles of analyst and problem solver need to be widely shared as the workshop progresses in order for the process conditions to be established and movement toward the objectives to occur.

If the method is adequately implemented, there are immediate outcomes (B.9) that are expected, particularly in the minds and hearts of the participants in the first instance. New realizations about the nature of the conflict should be coupled with some of the positive attitude changes noted above. Thus, participants are able to see members of the other party in a new light, and interact with them in more open and trusting ways. They realize that both parties have contributed to the causation and escalation of their destructive conflict, not necessarily in equal amounts or at the same time, but both as perpetrators and as victims in some fashion. They can envisage a future together that does not entail controlling or eliminating the other, but working jointly to fashion mutually beneficial arrangements. These shifts in understanding, perspective and motivation are the personal changes that are the first step in positive transfer and need to be reinforced and supported for wider change in the relationship to occur. A successful ICR intervention will eventually create coalitions across the lines of the conflict, to use Herbert Kelman's phrase, and these coalitions need to work together to strengthen peace constituencies and to induce cooperation orientations in the political discourse and in policy making in both collectivities. This is the challenge of transfer.

The Nature of Transfer

The variables related to the analysis questions on transfer tend to be more descriptive in nature as opposed to flowing from theoretical notions, as was more the case with the nature of the conflict and the intervention. This is largely because there has been a limited amount of theorizing on the transfer process and effects as outlined in the Introduction. Thus, the content analysis here is more of an inductive process of building coding categories from the case information, rather than deriving these from previous theorizing. With regard to the third party's rationale for transfer (C.1), this is a matter of seeing in each case how the interveners believed the fruits of their work could be transferred to the official processes, such as negotiation.

On the targets of transfer (C.2), the schematic model offered in the Introduction (figure I.1) gives some direction for the analysis, in that two categories of individuals and two broad constituencies are identified as targets for potential transfer effects. In the original focused form of ICR defined by Burton and others, members of the leadership, who make policy and other decisions related to the conflict, are the individuals to whom the workshop participants are connected and to whom they report. In some cases, members of the leadership themselves may be involved in ICR interactions in an off-the-record, personal capacity. The second group of individuals who serve as targets of transfer are diplomats and other officials involved in negotiations with the other side. Thus, participants may provide briefings on workshop outcomes to negotiators or serve as their informal advisors. Again, in some forms of what is often called track one-and-a-half diplomacy, negotiators or advisors to negotiators may be directly involved in ICR interactions prior to or alongside official talks. In terms of constituencies, the model identifies two large social and organizational domains: the governmental-bureaucratic and the public-political. The former is composed of a vast array of governmental organizations, such as ministries of foreign affairs and defense, and nongovernmental organizations, such as think tanks or lobby groups, which affect policy making in situations of conflict. The latter consists of bodies and sectors in the public domain who also affect policy making, such as political parties, interest groups, academia and the media. Any of the elements in these constituencies can be targets for transfer effects with a view to influencing public opinion or policy making on the conflict. It is also possible that the analysis of the cases will identify other targets in general or within these categories.

Mechanisms of transfer (C.3) are not specified in the model, but have been commented on somewhat in the ICR literature. In terms of links to individual targets, personal contacts between participants and leaders or negotiators, or written statements provided by participants are likely common forms. In terms of constituencies, more public mechanisms, such as speeches, interviews or media statements, would be logical forms, particularly to influence public opinion. To communicate with the governmental-bureaucratic constituency, private briefings and confidential memos might be in order, and the research problem of documenting such mechanisms becomes apparent. Thus, the degree to which the ICR interveners actually know what mechanisms are used with what effect is an open question, and one on which very little direct research has been carried out.

The question on the objectives of transfer (C.4) is an open one on what the third party hoped to accomplish in this direction through the workshops. While one can speculate on objectives based on the ICR literature, for example, that an intervention intended to induce negotiations or to contribute to a negotiated settlement, it is better to leave the answers to the inductive process. Thus, it is a matter of seeing what objectives are specified in different cases and to develop categories for this variable accordingly. The same can be said of the complementarity between unofficial and official processes (C.5), as there is as yet no common set of possibilities specified in the literature.

However, on the nature or type of transfer effects (C.6) there has been some useful specification, for example, in the work of Kelman (1996a), Pearson

d'Estree and her colleagues (2001) and Rouhana (2000), all of this being produced in the context of how to evaluate ICR interventions. A distillation of these
and other sources produced the categories and subcategories of possible transfer
effects given in the variable checklist. At the level of the individual participants,
we can envisage new realizations, attitudes, orientations and other cognitive
changes that markedly affect how they see the other party. They may also gain a
new analysis or interpretation of the conflict and acquire in part a new language
to describe its causation, escalation, intractability and potential resolution. At the
conceptual level, workshops often produce creative ideas, directions, options or
recommendations that can enrich and redirect policy making, and also an array
of substantive products in the form of joint statements of principle, plans,
frameworks or proposals that are essential in the parties entering negotiations or
in moving talks forward. Participants themselves can experience changed relations with members of the adversary, and this outcome can be shared with compatriots in ways that begin to transform overall relations in terms of increased
empathy, trust and cooperation. Finally, participants may develop structural
connections with the other side through new roles, such as moving directly into
negotiations, or new social units, such as joint research institutes dedicated to
resolving the conflict. Thus, the literature has identified a myriad of ways that
effects from workshop participation can be diffused into the conflicting collectivities and their relationship and interaction. The problem in the field has been
that evaluation has been woefully inadequate to track such effects, and we must
rely primarily on the reports of ICR interveners and the odd participant to gain
some appreciation of these.

The question focusing on the evaluation of transfer mechanisms and effects
(C.7) will be addressed in an inductive manner. That is, the nature of the evaluation procedures will be identified for each case of intervention, but in line with
the above comment, will likely produce a limited yield of categories and occur-
rences. Typical methods include interviews of participants by third-party team
members or researchers and written documents produced by participants or
interveners. The final variable on the conclusions of the third party (C.8) is a
catch-all attempt to capture the interveners' overall sense of what the work accomplished in terms of transfer. This will be less direct in cases where the chapter author is a researcher as compared to cases where the author is also one of
the organizers of the workshops. Nonetheless, this question should produce
some useful information to complement other sources on the nature of transfer.

The Comparative Case Analysis

In order to carry out the comparative case analysis, the nine cases were reviewed
individually and were described in summary fashion on coding sheets developed
from the variable checklist. Thus, the main characteristics of each item were recorded as indicators of the variable in question across the nine cases. Then an
impressionistic, qualitative content analysis was carried out, and in some cases

was supplemented by numeric information, for example, the number of meetings. This analysis produced themes that provide an overall picture of the interventions, including exceptions to the norm, and an indication of how well theory holds up in practice, especially the theory of practice that can be used to guide ICR interventions. The analysis proceeds by describing: 1) the characteristics of these successful interventions, including some important differences that emerged, 2) the conditions of the conflicts with an emphasis on what influences their receptivity to intervention, and 3) the transfer effects that occurred.

Characteristics of Effective Interventions

This analysis generally follows the model of third party consultation (figure C.1) in identifying characteristics of the intervention deemed to be important, and in that way provides indications of the validity of the model and its precursors. Overall, the nine cases follow the classic approach of Burton quite well, including how it has been extended by Kelman. A small group of high-level or highly influential participants, with connections to their leaderships and/or publics, meet for a period of a few days in intense analytical, problem-solving and off-the-record discussions in a secluded, neutral and informal setting. The discussions are organized and facilitated by an impartial third-party team embodying a host of substantive and procedural skills with the objective of inducing change in the individuals resulting in behaviors that will influence decision making and public opinion regarding the conflict and how to approach it.

With regard to the third-party identity, scholar-practitioners from academic centers figure prominently in five of the nine cases (Indonesia-Malaysia, Israeli-Palestinian, Lebanon, Moldova, Peru-Ecuador), but not exclusively. The remaining four cases are a mixed bag of an international conference (Tajikistan), a religious NGO (Mozambique), a business corporation (South Africa), and a partnership of conflict resolution and humanitarian NGO's (Georgia-South Ossetia). However, in all but one of these cases (South Africa), academics were included on the third-party team for either substantive or process competencies of some kind. Therefore, it is clear that most third-party teams represented the full range of identified skills with the two exceptions being Mozambique and South Africa. However, in the former case, the human relations skills developed in the Community of Sant'Egidio were combined with knowledge of the case offered by two of the other team members, and in the latter case, it appears that the representatives of the parties brought forward both the substantive knowledge and many of the process skills to make the sessions work in the prescribed manner. In all cases, the third party was able to establish a positive consulting relationship with the parties and the participants.

The situation specified in the TPC model appears to have been closely followed in these ICR applications. Almost all meetings were held outside the intense field of the conflict, with one exception being the Peru-Ecuador case where meetings were held in both countries, but in a sequenced manner to approximate neutrality. All interventions but one were quiet but not confidential. The exception is South Africa, where the sensitivity of even meeting the other side was so high that the sessions were held in secret. The interventions exhibited a wide range with regard to the number of meetings, from two in the Lebanese case to now over thirty-five in the Tajikistan case. This, along with other indicators, tags the Lebanese intervention as potentially a "puny intervention," to introduce a term popular in program evaluation. The average number of meetings across cases is 8.5, with most being in a range of 4 to 7, which may provide a rough indicator of the requirement for a potentially effective intervention.

The implementation of the third-party role also follows the model closely, that is, being facilitative and diagnostic in helping the participants to probe the dynamics of the conflict and the relationship toward greater mutual understanding and realizations that can fuel change in how the parties see and approach the conflict. The facilitative aspect of the role was universal, although limited in the South African case, while the diagnostic aspect in terms of conflict analysis appears to be nonexistent in the South African and Mozambican cases. These two cases appear to be the outliers in terms of the model, in that discussions were directed toward achieving prenegotiation understandings and frameworks as opposed to building these elements on a prior and mutual analysis of the conflict. This conclusion holds true with regard to the third-party functions as well, in that inducing motivation for problem solving, improving communication and regulating the interaction held in all cases, whereas diagnosis was absent from these two cases. This raises the question as to whether the Mozambican and South African cases belong in the data set of successful ICR interventions, or whether they constitute a subset or a different form of intervention more akin to track one-and-a-half, back-channel negotiations, as epitomized by the Oslo process in the Israeli-Palestinian conflict. This issue will be considered below.

In all cases, it appears that the process conditions related to the third-party functions were established, for example, open and accurate communication. These conditions were in line with the agendas of the various interventions, which generally called for open and flexible discussion, and provided minimal guidance on topics including those of sharing perspectives, identifying common interests and concerns, and creating alternative scenarios. Thus, the process of the discussion typically moved from ventilation, to dialogue, analysis and problem-solving, which involved the generation and selection of options and action plans for implementation.

Two other exceptions to the rule occurred with regard to the agenda and the role of the third party: in the cases of Georgia-South Ossetia and Peru-Ecuador, the facilitators also became trainers, and training sessions on conflict analysis and resolution involving both conceptual and experiential components were added directly into the agenda. This goes beyond the tactic of injecting concepts or comparable cases into the discussion for diagnostic purposes, and even beyond the occasional use of training for one side or the other as occurred in the Tajikistan case. In Georgia-South Ossetia, the training drew on the forte of the Conflict Management Group in providing negotiation skill training that was directly relevant to the participants who were official negotiators. In the Peru-Ecuador case using the IPSW methodology, the training was broader in scope, covering both conflict resolution and facilitation skills, which were then used by two participants who became co-facilitators. In both cases, these enhancements are not so much a restriction of the TPC model as they are an extension of it, using training to enrich the experiential and practical elements of the workshops, in a manner envisaged by Diamond and Fisher (1995) in their discussion of the potential interplay between third party consultation and training.

One element of the original TPC model (Fisher, 1972) not noted in figure C.1 is the identity and role of the participants, which is critical to both successful implementation and transfer. Of the nine cases, four involved officials in their personal capacity (the Burton model), four involved highly influential individuals (the Kelman model), and one was a mix of the two (South Africa). These people are clearly very capable and well connected individuals who are directly linked to decision makers through their roles as advisors to the leaderships or as negotiators. Many could be regarded as second-level leaders, who are influential not only in the decision-making process, but also in affecting public opinion. In almost all the cases, there was considerable continuity of participation with some deletions (often to take on official roles) and additions (often to better represent the current reality of the conflict). The one exception is the case of Lebanon, where there was an almost complete turnover of representatives from the first to the second workshop (only two of eight attended both). While this may have enhanced the chances of transfer due to higher level representation, the lack of continuity may also have contributed to the limited influence of this intervention.

The immediate effects on participants are generally described as altered (i.e., more accurate) perceptions, changed (i.e., more positive) attitudes, useful insights and analyses relevant to the conflict, acknowledgment of the other party's legitimacy, new (i.e., more cooperative) orientations to dealing with the conflict, and in some cases, the development of good interpersonal relationships. In addition to these general effects, some interventions shifted the discussions toward negotiating frameworks and understandings (Indonesia-Malaysia, Mozambique, South Africa, Tajikistan, Moldova), thus providing the participants with ideas and tools directly relevant to peacemaking. In the Moldovan case, this approach was extended by an ongoing collaboration in the later workshops between the unofficial and the official (OSCE) third parties in a manner that may bode well for the future development of cooperative interventions.

Thus, the objectives of these nine cases generally are compatible with those specified in the TPC model. Many of the interventions focused more on prenegotiation or para-negotiation elements in trying to catalyze a cooperative orientation, while some deepened that focus to a more general concern with the overall relationship between the parties (Lebanon, Tajikistan and Peru-Ecuador). In all cases, the interventions were directed toward outcomes consonant with the basic values of conflict resolution in terms of voluntary, jointly determined and sustainable solutions to a mutual problem.

Characteristics of Receptive Conflicts

As noted in the Introduction, the nine cases of conflict evidence variety in their basic nature, for example, interstate versus intrastate, and yet the analysis indicates that all may be regarded as identity-based conflicts to some degree, that is, situations in which social groups with a common identity perceive themselves as a group to be under threat from an opposing identity group, whether it is constituted as a state, a competing faction or a rebel insurgency. Having said that, it must be noted that the modal conflict (five cases) is one where a government in power is being challenged by an opposition. Some of the identity lines are not as clear cut as others, for example, in Tajikistan, where a mixture of schisms in ideology, region and ethnic affiliation combine to produce a government-versus-opposition conflict, and in Moldova, where the distinctions between the center and the breakaway region are as much ideological as ethnic. Nonetheless, the common theme of identity-based conflict is compatible with the theory of practice in ICR, which singles out this type of conflict as most appropriate for intervention, partly because it appears to be impervious to traditional methods of conflict management.

In terms of goals, the parties are typically motivated to maintain or gain control of the government apparatus, or less so, territory and its resources. Thus, the acquisition and use of power is central to all these conflicts. In terms of contentious goals, most of the conflicts involve a potential major change in the situation that redistributes power significantly, with the exception of the two interstate conflicts (Indonesia-Malaysia and Peru-Ecuador) where the status quo is a not unacceptable fall-back position. The intrastate conflicts split almost evenly on the dimension of integration-segregation, and the interesting contrast is between those where the parties favor integration (Lebanon, Mozambique, South Africa, and Tajikistan) versus where at least one favors segregation (Israeli-Palestinian, Moldova, Georgia-South Ossetia). All of these conflicts may initially seem receptive to intervention, but the former have all achieved peace agreements, whereas none of the latter have been able to resolve the conflict at the present time.

The histories of the nine cases all demonstrate an inability or lack of motivation to manage the conflict constructively (i.e., cooperatively and nonviolently), as parties have engaged in unilateral coercive tactics to achieve their self-serving goals. The reciprocation of this approach has resulted in escalation to violent confrontations with varying degrees and types of costs. In a number of cases, the violence has been attenuated by the interposition of peacekeeping forces not always from a neutral party (for example, Russia in Moldova, Georgia-South Ossetia, and Tajikistan). Beneath the tangible interests of political control and territory are threatened basic needs for security, identity and its recognition, participation in decision making, and distributive justice. It would be fair to say that all the cases are needs-based in some fashion, in line with their primary identification as identity-based conflicts as opposed to interest-based ones.

In terms of power relations, the nine cases show variety, with power asymmetry being apparent in three (Israeli-Palestinian, South Africa, and Tajikistan) and a rough power balance in the other six (Indonesia-Malaysia, Lebanon, Mozambique, Moldova, Georgia-South Ossetia, and Peru-Ecuador). However, as noted above, the power balance in some cases is partly a result of the support of outside parties, which could be identified in a straight power analysis as a reason for the continuation of the conflict.

With regard to escalation, all of the conflicts appear at the time of intervention to be at or past the stage of segregation, involving indirect and threatening communication, a lack of trust and respect with good versus evil images predominating, frustration of basic needs, and a win-lose defensive competition between the parties. Some of the conflicts (Israeli-Palestinian, Lebanon, Mozambique) appear to have reached the maximum level of destruction—nonexistent communication with direct attacks, a sense of hopelessness with the other regarded as non-human, a threat not just to basic needs but the group's very survival (i.e., existential conflict)—and a lose-lose attitude where the goal is to wreak maximum destruction on the other side, even at great cost to one's self. Most of the cases appear to be in between levels three and four of escalation, and there appears to be no obvious relationship between level of escalation and eventual settlement. Also, most are at a higher level of escalation than proposed as the most propitious entry points for ICR interventions, which the contingency model identifies as level two (polarization) or level three (segregation) following successful mediation or arbitration to control the hostility, or level four (destruction) following peacekeeping to control the violence. Although some cases involved peacekeeping to control the violence, and some involved power mediation to achieve a cease-fire, the logic of some elements of the contingency model is thus brought into question by the analysis.

Intractability figures as a prominent element in each of the nine cases: all are coded as positive on at least some of the indicators of intractability. Thus, all cases demonstrated persistence and recycling to some degree, while many demonstrated centrality of issues, pervasiveness of effects, and resistance to resolution. Only three showed the deeper indicators of hopelessness and motivation to harm congruent with the highest level of escalation noted above (Israeli-Palestinian, Lebanon, Mozambique). The remainder demonstrated low to medium intractability (Malaysia-Indonesia, Moldova, Peru-Ecuador) or medium intractability (South Africa, Tajikistan, Georgia-South Ossetia). It must be stressed, however, that this categorization is based on a superficial analysis of the limited descriptions provided by the chapter authors augmented by the editor's general knowledge of the nine cases. A much fuller analysis by regional experts familiar with each of the cases would be required to produce definitive conclusions on the intractability of the conflicts. The best that can be said is that all of the conflicts evidenced some elements of intractability, and indeed it was this characteristic that in part occasioned interventions by ICR practitioners. In any case, there appears to be no relationship between level of intractability and resolution of the conflict, with the possible exception of the Israeli-Palestinian case.

Indicators of stalemate are also difficult to code without a more thoroughgoing assessment of each of the cases, but on the surface, it appears that most of the conflicts were not in a mutually intolerable hurting stalemate. While Mozambique, Israel-Palestine, Tajikistan, and South Africa could be placed here, it is evident that the costs of such conflicts usually fall more on the weaker party, thus attenuating the mutuality of the stalemate. The other five cases would seem not to constitute mutually hurting stalemates, although Lebanon certainly could be regarded as moving inexorably in that direction in 1984. Similarly, with regard to an impending or recent catastrophe, none of the nine cases would appear to fit this categorization, although the parties in Indonesia-Malaysia and South Africa might have harbored fears of a major conflagration. Overall then, the related concepts of a plateau and a precipice did not seem to have much applicability in the current analysis, and any relationships to successful interventions or outcomes are thereby precluded.

In terms of elements of the conflicts that may have affected the appropriateness of ICR interventions, a theme emerged of there being recent failures or stalemates in official interactions (Indonesia-Malaysia, Lebanon, Moldova, Georgia-South Ossetia, Peru-Ecuador) or of no official efforts underway (Israeli-Palestinian, Tajikistan, Mozambique, South Africa). Thus, it would appear that the parties may have been looking for an alternative track, specifically one that involved a low commitment, quiet and exploratory approach that had few costs and could be disavowed if necessary. This may not appear to be an earth-shattering conclusion, but it should be noted that these are cases of successful intervention. In comparison to cases of unsuccessful ICR interventions (a study yet to be done) it may very well be that this form of receptivity due to the failure of official efforts is contributive to success. A minor theme in this category is that one or both parties in the conflict were looking toward a future closer to the Western world in terms of its valued institutions and benefits. Thus, the cases of Mozambique, South Africa and to a lesser degree, Moldova, may have been influenced to move toward ICR intervention and eventual settlement because of the changing currents in world affairs at the end of the Cold War.

On the cultural dimension, the analysis is quite clear. All of the interveners came from a western and northern base (i.e., the United States and Europe), while the parties are predominantly non-Western and from many corners of the world. Of course, mainly Western institutions were practicing ICR during the period covered by these cases, as the theory of practice and the expertise resides in applied social science and the field of conflict resolution, which has only recently began an impressive dissemination throughout the world. Nonetheless, the situation can be interpreted as another indicator of cultural imperialism, and future practice and research is necessary to assess the cultural dynamics of ICR work. What is also clear from these cases is that there was no direct and systematic cultural analysis of the conflicts in question, even though cultural differences may be a hidden dynamic affecting both the conflict and the intervention. On the other hand, cultural differences between the parties did not appear to be a significant factor in the intervention, partly because the method demands the creation of a meta-culture into which the participants are quickly socialized through the functions of the third party.

On the question of timing, the point has already been made that mutually hurting stalemates were not predominant and that impending catastrophes were close to non-existent, thus precluding the existence of ripeness to any significant degree. However, in line with the absence or failure of concurrent official efforts, it does appear to be generally true that one or both parties in these conflicts were looking for a way out, although they may not have perceived one clearly. Thus, a degree of readiness may have existed in the absence of full ripeness that motivated the parties to seek an ICR intervention (e.g., Georgia-South Ossetia, Moldova) or respond positively to an invitation (e.g., Indonesia-Malaysia, Tajikistan).

In terms of changes affecting implementation of the ICR intervention, only three important instances were noted. In the Indonesia-Malaysia case, the power shifts in the Indonesian government that were occurring alongside the intervention and the coup d'etat that took Sukarno out of power clearly changed the motivation of that party to negotiate rather than confront. Thus, the intervention served as a source of useful realizations, new orientations and substantive ideas that were readily taken forward in an increasingly positive climate for settlement. In the second case, the initiation of official negotiations on the Israeli-Palestinian conflict under the wider umbrella of the Madrid talks allowed for direct connections with Kelman and Rouhana's continuing workshop, with a number of participants becoming negotiators or advisors. In the third instance, the signing of a peace agreement between Peru and Ecuador midway through the IPSW intervention by Kaufman and Sosnowski required a shift in focus from assisting negotiations to implementing the agreement and building public support for it. It appears that none of these changes affected the ICR process in a negative manner, although one can certainly envisage such things happening.

Transfer Effects of Successful Interventions

Given that each of the interventions described in the nine cases are generally regarded in the field as success stories to varying degrees, the analysis is designed to identify the common effects produced by such interventions. Thus, a content analysis was performed on each of the variables, guided in some cases by theory, but more often simply as an inductive process based on the information provided in the case descriptions.

On the third party's rationale for transfer, three categories emerged, although none in a very strong fashion. First, third parties talked about preparing the ground for negotiations or improving the current negotiating process. Second, interveners identified the creation of new ideas and insights, including options for solutions, to be fed into the political process. Finally, in one case, the third party took a system perspective and talked about transforming relationships among the parties at all levels. One tentative conclusion from this sparse treatment of rationale is that ICR practitioners may take it for granted, and operate on assumptions that are not always articulated.

The targets of transfer were identified in the model of transfer presented in the Introduction (figure I.1), and include leaders, negotiators, the governmental-bureaucratic constituency, and the public-political constituency. Very strongly in this analysis, the leaderships were the primary targets of transfer effects, with all nine cases making this identification. Next, five cases identified negotiators as a target for transfer, while four identified the public-political constituency, and three the governmental-bureaucratic one. Clearly, the interventions analyzed here are directed toward the elite level of societal decision making, as called for in the original approach defined by Burton and his colleagues. Only three interventions (Israeli-Palestinian, Tajikistan, and Peru-Ecuador) identified all four targets as being foci of transfer intentions and activities.

With regard to mechanisms of transfer, past theorizing presented a number of categories that were generally applicable to the present cases. The primary mechanism used in all cases was personal contact with the leadership and other decision makers including negotiators. Other mechanisms of transfer were mentioned sparingly, although there is always a concern that the case authors may not have provided all the available information on transfer, which in some cases is not even known to them. Nonetheless, only three cases (Israeli-Palestinian, Tajikistan, and Peru-Ecuador) identified three or more mechanisms of transfer, in line with their use of multiple targets noted above. It seems that these three ICR interveners took more of a multilevel, systems perspective in their work, seeking to influence a range of actors at different levels in the two societies toward a peaceful resolution.

The objectives of transfer are related to the rationale of the third party, and it therefore comes as no surprise that the most common objective of the interventions was to influence negotiations in a positive manner. Depending on whether negotiations were underway or not, interveners spoke of helping to start negotiations or removing obstacles to negotiation, or of supporting and improving negotiations. At a more general level, identified objectives included influencing public opinion and policy toward peace and improving relations between the parties.

Thus, it appears overall that these interventions were predominantly concerned with paving the way for track-one work. It therefore comes as no surprise that almost all the interventions were coded as high on the degree of complementarity with official processes. In most cases, the participants were high-level influentials, or officials with close links or direct connections to negotiations, and in some cases (Indonesia-Malaysia, Mozambique, South Africa, Tajikistan) the discussions transformed into a prenegotiation process that made very direct connections to official interactions. Only one case, that of Lebanon, was identified as restricted in complementarity, in part because the faction leaders who sent representatives were not the central crafters of the eventual agreement, and there was also a five-year lag between the workshops and the resolution.

A considerable range of transfer effects were specified as coding categories in the analysis based on theory, and on average the interventions demonstrated effects across this variety of indicators. Cognitive changes in term of new realizations, attitudes and so on were evident in all of the nine cases, while conceptual products, such as creative ideas or options, were identified in six of the cases. More substantive products such as frameworks or proposals were produced by eight of the interventions, for example, parts of a draft agreement in Indonesia-Malaysia, a joint communiqué in Mozambique, a statement of principles for Lebanon, a common state document in Moldova, and a proposal for a cross-border park in Peru-Ecuador. In terms of structural connections through roles or other social units, seven of the cases were coded positively, with the most common link being the movement of participants into official talks. Relationship changes, which are a more ambitious and amorphous outcome, were identified in six of the cases, although in some of these the indication was rather tentative or formative. This makes sense because changing the overall relationship between the parties is a very challenging agenda, although it does seem to have occurred at least in part due to some of the interventions, for example, Mozambique, South Africa and Tajikistan. Overall, the comparative case analysis is a very strong statement for the powerful effects that ICR interventions can bring to the negotiation and peace processes.

On a more sober note, the evaluation of transfer mechanisms and effects is in an anemic state, as judged by the dearth of systematic evaluation procedures used in this set of cases. The most common measure of success were positive comments by officials from the parties or third parties who maintained that the unofficial work had made a significant contribution to the peace process, whether or not it had culminated in a resolution at that time. Six cases identified these types of comments either verbally or in writing, while two interventions (Tajikistan, Peru-Ecuador) cited an external report on the work. Two interventions made use of debriefing sessions for evaluation (Indonesia-Malaysia, Mozambique), and two cases were of course based in part on interviews with participants (South Africa, Georgia-South Ossetia). Some cases, particularly Tajikistan, demonstrated multiple methods of documenting the work and gathering evaluative information, while others did very little. It is of course possible that the authors failed to include information on evaluation procedures, but overall the evaluative element of the work appears to be thin and in need of increased attention.

The conclusions of the third-party conveners are presaged by the variety and substance of the transfer effects noted above. All interveners believe that their work had positive outcomes, and in most cases this is supported by the resolution of the conflict. Third-party comments identify positive contributions to starting and/or assisting negotiations and to the overall peace process in line with the above analyses. In addition to tangible transfer effects, interveners also spoke of creating a sense of hope and of possibility, which could of course contribute to the necessary optimism identified by readiness theory. At the same time, there are three of the cases that have not achieved a peace agreement (Moldova, Israeli-Palestinian, Georgia-South Ossetia), and in such complex situations, it is not easy to identify the reasons. In the two former soviet republics, it may be that economic factors and internal domestic problems may be hampering the search for peace, and in the Israeli-Palestinian case, the two parties may have dug such a deep hole of intractability that positive movement requires highly engaged and extensive third-party involvement. However, the majority of six cases involve peaceful resolutions that required the alignment of many factors and the activities of numerous actors in order to be realized. The evidence presented here on transfer effects indicates that ICR interventions made important if not essential contributions to the achievement of peace.

The Essential Contributions of ICR:
Necessary but Not Sufficient

The first phase of the comparative case analysis has identified many of the characteristics of effective interventions, receptive conflicts and successful transfer effects. It has done so through identifying commonalities among cases from the same class of phenomena, but it has also provided some possibilities relevant to the second phase of the analysis, that is, a look at what differences in the interventions and in the conflicts might relate to differences in transfer effects and ultimately to the resolution of the conflict. Given the small number of cases and the vast array of identified and, even more so, unidentified variables, this limited, inductive approach must be regarded as highly speculative and tentative. Nonetheless, it can serve a useful purpose of generating hypotheses for more rigorous and detailed analysis of a larger number of cases.

For the second phase of the analysis, each of the nine cases was coded on variables in the variable checklist (figure C.1) that were determined to relate to: 1) the power or potential influence of the intervention, 2) the receptivity of the conflict to intervention at that point in time, and 3) the probability and degree of transfer. Thus, coding categories related to the intervention specified how the intervention should have been carried out in order to produce transfer effects as determined both by existing theory of practice and by the commonalities identified in the first phase of the analysis (given that these are generally regarded as successful cases). For example, positive codings on the power of the intervention were made if the participants were high-level officials or influentials with direct personal and structural connections to decision making, if an adequate number of meetings were held in a neutral, informal, secluded and quiet setting, if the third-party team possessed both process and substantive skills, and so on. Most of the divergences from the characteristics of effective interventions have already been noted in the above analysis, for example, the lack of the diagnostic function in the Mozambique and South African cases, which was seen as detracting from the power of those interventions. Based on the analysis, six of the interventions were coded overall as high on power or potential influence, the exceptions being Mozambique and South Africa, which were coded as medium power, and Lebanon, which was coded as low, due to the limited number of meetings and the turnover and lack of connection of participants to decision makers who eventually resolved the conflict.

The coding categories on the receptivity of the conflict attempted to capture how amenable the conflict was to intervention at the time the third-party became engaged, and covered most of the variables given in the checklist. For example, contentious goals involving integration were seen to render the conflict more receptive than goals that called for separation (i.e., elimination or secession); a power balance as opposed to power asymmetry was also seen in the same light. A higher stage of escalation and higher intractability were seen as reducing receptivity, even though that was the reality that some interveners faced. Although the existence and utility of the mutual hurting stalemate seemed unclear in the first phase of the analysis, based on ripeness theory the existence of such a condition was regarded as making the conflict more receptive to intervention. As a result of the analysis, four cases were categorized as high on receptivity (Indonesia-Malaysia, South Africa, Tajikistan, Peru-Ecuador), while two were judged as moderately receptive (Lebanon, Mozambique), and three as limited in receptivity (Israeli-Palestinian, Moldova, Georgia-South Ossetia).

With regard to transfer effects, it should come as no surprise that most cases were categorized as high or moderate on the probability and degree of such effects, given that all the cases are regarded as successes in the literature. On factors that increased the likelihood of transfer, such as a clear rationale and objectives, appropriate targets, and high complementarity, almost all the interventions, with the apparent exception of Lebanon, coded high. More useful distinctions were made on the degree or extent of transfer as determined over the five types of effects given in the variable checklist. However, a problem encountered here was that not all authors may have been as detailed and exhaustive as necessary in their description of transfer effects, and thus any differences in coding could be simply an artifact of that limitation. In any event, five cases were coded as high on transfer (Indonesia-Malaysia, South Africa, Tajikistan, Georgia-South Ossetia, Peru-Ecuador), three as moderate (Israeli-Palestinian, Mozambique, Moldova) and one as low (Lebanon).

The outcomes from the summative analysis provided by the second phase of comparison are presented in Table C.2, which plots the power of the intervention by the receptivity of the conflict. The degree of transfer effects is then shown by the typescript of the case name in the table: Limited in regular type, Moderate in italics, and Extensive in boldface. It is important to note that the distinctions among cases on the three variable dimensions are based on small differences, and so the labels such as limited, moderate and high are exaggerated. On the three dimensions, differences in one, two or three coding categories out of ten or eleven made the difference in how a case was categorized. The rationale was to stretch the distinctions among the cases in order to see if differences among cases appeared to be related in some fashion and if these relationships made any theoretical sense. As described below, it appears that there are some interesting and useful outcomes from the analysis and that some of these also relate to theory. Nonetheless, the small *n*, impressionistic nature of this enterprise must be acknowledged as being greater than it was in the first phase of the comparative analysis, and the reader is thereby forewarned to assess these results with considerable caution and with a view to alternative interpretations.

Table C.2. Comparative and Summative Analysis of the Cases

Receptivity of the Conflict	Power of the Intervention		
	Low	Moderate	High
Limited			*Israeli-Palestinian* *Moldova* **Georgia-South Ossetia**
Moderate	Lebanon	*Mozambique*	
High		**South Africa**	**Indonesia-Malaysia** **Tajikistan** **Peru-Ecuador**

Note: Degree of Transfer: Limited, *Moderate*, **Extensive**

In the table there is some indication that the combination of a powerful intervention and a receptive conflict result in both significant transfer effects and an eventual resolution of the conflict, as shown by the three cases of Indonesia-Malaysia, Tajikistan, and Peru-Ecuador. One other case of high receptivity combined with a moderately powerful intervention is related to extensive transfer effects (South Africa), and one case of high power and limited receptivity (Georgia-South Ossetia) also shows a high degree of transfer. Mozambique is moderate on both sets of indicator variables and shows moderate transfer. The anomalies in the analysis are the three cases in the upper right hand corner (Israeli-Palestinian, Moldova and Georgia-South Ossetia), which show limited receptivity and yet moderate to high degrees of transfer, due one assumes to effective interventions in the face of considerable resistance. On an examination of the codings, these three cases are singularly distinguished by goals of segregation rather than integration: Moldova and Georgia both being faced with break-away regions as their adversary, and the hard-line Israelis and Palestinians not wanting to share in a compromising manner enough of the land they both claim. In addition, these three cases are distinguished as approximating double minority problems, in that the dominant party in the bilateral conflict is threatened by powerful forces in the region that identify with and support the weaker party, Russia and the Arab states respectively. Thus, the bilateral relationship of power asymmetry is modified in a fashion that seems to perpetuate the conflict, as has occurred in similar situations such as Northern Ireland, Sri Lanka and Cyprus. It is instructive to note that of the nine cases, these three are the only ones that have not been resolved following both unofficial and official efforts of considerable magnitude and duration.

Concluding Comments

This work began with the thesis that unofficial problem-solving efforts with high-level influentials can have significant positive effects on the resolution of protracted and violent ethnopolitical conflicts. The nine cases presented are compatible with the focused definition of ICR and indeed follow most closely the original approach of Burton, which can be regarded as semi-official in nature given the identity of the ideal participants. The developing theory of practice in ICR offers a rationale for transfer as found in the work of a number of authors, which is captured in the model of transfer presented in the Introduction. The nine case descriptions provide valuable illustrations of this model in practice, and concentrate for the most part in preparing the way for negotiations or supporting negotiations once these are underway. Thus, most of the cases would be regarded as prenegotiation interventions, including two that do not conform as clearly to the theory of practice in ICR as summarized by the model of third party consultation.

Both the Mozambique and South African cases evidence a more restricted third-party role, particularly in terms of the diagnostic function, which has been a hallmark of the scholar-practitioner approach based in applied social science. Nonetheless, these interventions were clearly of an unofficial, prenegotiation character, as compared to the Oslo talks, which involved secret, back-channel negotiations by official emissaries on the political steps necessary to overcome the stalled Madrid negotiations. These interventions also engaged the third party in a more active facilitative role than in the Oslo process, and in the case of Mozambique, a relationship-building one as well. Without these contributions, it is doubtful that the parties would have achieved prenegotiation success on their own. Thus, the cases were included in the analysis even though they do not constitute a full implementation of ICR as commonly defined, and their inclusion can thus be legitimately questioned.

The overall conclusion from the comparative case analysis is that the interventions made important if not essential contributions to negotiations in eight of the nine cases (Lebanon being the exception) and to the ultimate resolution of the conflict in five cases (three cases still awaiting settlement). This conclusion is congruent with Herbert Kelman's comment that unofficial, problem-solving work is more than a side show to the main events of official diplomacy. In addition, the analysis has supported the existing theory of practice in ICR with respect to the character of the major components specified in the TPC model and related work. The characteristics of conflicts that may be more amenable to such interventions have also been somewhat illuminated, although the superficiality of this analysis must be stressed. The second phase of the analysis indicates that identity-based conflicts with important interests at stake are receptive to ICR intervention if they involve goals of integration rather than segregation, and if a power balance between the parties rather than a power asymmetry exists. Further, when a power asymmetry is augmented by a double minority situation, the resistance of the conflict to intervention and resolution appears to be increased. Obviously, much more research on the effectiveness of unofficial interventions as well as official ones in such situations is required to assess these hypotheses.

On the central question of transfer, the nine cases show clear intentions and targets, and provide for effects in a number of areas. Personal connections of participants to decision makers and to official roles appear to be important, and a mix of cognitive and substantive outcomes appear to be valued. Generally speaking, the conclusion is that more powerful interventions in more receptive conflicts produce greater transfer effects and make more of a contribution to eventual resolution. This appears to be an obvious point, but its significance lies in what constitutes powerful interventions and receptive conflicts. Not all interventions are equally powerful and not all conflicts are equally receptive. Thus, it is incumbent upon ICR practitioners to carefully design interventions with the identified characteristics in mind, and to systematically assess conflicts to gauge receptivity, given that the resources may not exist to address all existing and future conflicts. Thus, decisions to intervene can be based not only on important moral considerations, but also strategic ones, so that the chances of success can be maximized. That is the challenge that awaits the conflict resolution field as it moves into an uncertain and demanding future.

References

Abdullaev, Kamoludin, and Catherine Barnes. *Accord: Politics of Compromise: The Tajikistan Peace Process*. London, UK: Conciliation Resources, 2001.

Abrahamsson, Hans, and Anders Nilsson. *Mozambique: The Troubled Transition: From Socialist Construction to Free Market Capitalism*. London: Zed Books, 1995.

African National Congress (ANC). "Letter from Simon Makana to H. W. van der Merwe, 15 October 1984." University of Fort Hare, ANC Archive, 1984.

———. "Negotiations with the Enemy." Extract from Proposals to the ANC National Consultative Conference in Kabwe, Zambia, June 1985.

———. "Report of a Meeting Held in England on 1st and 2nd November 1987." 1987a.

———. "Notes on Meeting of 31-10-87 to 1-11-87." 1987b.

———. "Minutes of NWC 22nd February 1988." 1988.

———. "Special Meeting of the NWC Held on 13/10/89 at 09:00 Hours." 1989a.

———. "Minutes of an Extended President's Committee Meeting Held on 9 October 1989." 1989b.

———. "Minutes of a Meeting among ANC Leadership in Harare, Zimbabwe." August 26, 1989c.

———. English translation of "Prisons Service HQ 80668009." Letter received August 19, 1989d.

Alden, Christopher. *Mozambique and the Construction of the New African State: From Negotiations to Nation Building*. Basingstoke, UK: Palgrave, 2001.

Alpher, Joseph, and Khalil Shikaki (with other members of the Joint Working Group on Israeli-Palestinian Relations). "The Palestinian Refugee Problem and the Right of Return." Weatherhead Center for International Affairs Working Paper, no. 98-7. Cambridge, MA: Harvard University, 1998. (Reprinted in Middle East Policy 6, no. 3 [February 1999]: 167-189.)

American Task Force for Lebanon (ATFL). Working Paper: Conference on Lebanon, 1991.

Appleby, R. Scott. *The Ambivalence of the Sacred*. Oxford and Lanham, MD: Roman and Littlefield, 2000.

"The Ayalon-Nusseibeh Statement of Principles." *Israel Horizons* (fall/winter 2003): 9.

Avruch, Kevin. *Culture and Conflict Resolution*. Washington, DC: United States Institute of Peace, 1998.

Avruch, Kevin, and Peter Black. "Conflict Resolution in Intercultural Settings: Problems and Prospects." Pp. 131-145 in *Conflict Resolution Theory and Practice: Integration and Application*, edited by Dennis J. D. Sandole and Hugo van der Merwe. Manchester, UK: Manchester University Press, 1993.

Azar, Edward E. *Lessons from Lebanon: A Speech*. College Park, MD: Center for International Development, 1984.

————. *The Management of Protracted Social Conflict*. Hampshire, UK: Dartmouth Publishing, 1990.

Azar, Edward E., and John W. Burton, eds. *International Conflict Resolution: Theory and Practice*. Sussex, UK: Wheatsheaf Books, 1986.

Barnard, Niël. October 1994. Interview by Daniel Lieberfeld.

————. November 1994. Interview by Patti Waldmeir. Unpublished typescripts at the library archives, University of Cape Town.

Bartoli, Andrea. "Mediating Peace in Mozambique: The Role of the Community of Sant'Egidio." Pp. 245-273 in *Herding Cats: Multiparty Mediation in a Complex World*, edited by Pamela Aall, Chester A. Crocker, and Fen Osler Hampson. Washington, DC: United States Institute of Peace, 1999.

Birgerson, Susanne M. *After the Breakup of a Multi-Ethnic Empire: Russia, Successor States and Eurasian Security*. Westport, CT: Praeger, 2002.

Birmingham, David. *Frontline Nationalism in Angola and Mozambique*. London: James Currey, 1993.

Boykin, John. *Cursed is the Peacemaker: The American Diplomat Versus the Israeli General, Beirut 1982*. Belmont, CA: Applegate Press, 2002.

Bristol, Jeremy, and Jonathan Cohen, eds. *Conflict Resolution in the Former Soviet Union*. London: International Alert, 1995.

Bronner, Ethan. "Harvard Teacher Provided Early Middle East Forum." *The Boston Globe*, 30 September 1993.

Burton, John W. *Conflict and Communication: The Use of Controlled Communication in International Relations*. London: Macmillan, 1969.

————. *Deviance, Terrorism and War: The Process of Solving Unsolved Social and Political Problems*. New York: St. Martin's Press, 1979.

————. *Global Conflict: The Domestic Sources of International Crisis*. Brighton, Sussex: Wheatsheaf, 1984.

————. *Resolving Deep-Rooted Conflict: A Handbook*. Lanham, MD: University Press of America, 1987.

————. *Conflict: Resolution and Provention*. New York: St. Martin's Press, 1990.

————. "Negotiation to Prevent Escalation and Violence." Comments by John Burton on the Preventing Deadly Conflict Project of the Carnegie Commission. Canberra: Mimeo, 1998.

Cahen, Michel. *Mozambique: La Révolution Implosée—etudes sur 12 ans d'indépendence 1975-1987*. Paris: Editions l'Harmattan, 1987.

————. "Entrons dans la Nation: Notes pour une ƒtude du Discours Politique de la Marginalité: le cas de la RENAMO du Mozambique." *Politique Africaine*, no. 67, 1997.

Chan, Stephen, and Moisés Venâncio, eds. *War and Peace in Mozambique*. Basingstoke, UK: Macmillan, 1998.

Chataway, Cynthia J. "The Problem of Transfer from Confidential Interactive Problem-Solving: What Is the Role of the Facilitator?" *Political Psychology* 23, no. 1 (March 2002): 165-189.

Chufrin, Gennady, Ashurboi Imomov, and Harold H. Saunders, eds. *Memoranda and Appeals of the Inter-Tajik Dialogue within the Framework of the Dartmouth Con-*

ference (1993-1997). Moscow: Russian Center for Political and Strategic Studies and the Kettering Foundation, 1997.

Chufrin, Gennady, and Harold H. Saunders. "A Public Peace Process." *Negotiation Journal* 9, no. 2 (April 1993): 155-177.

Coast, John. *Recruit to Revolution: Adventure and Politics in Indonesia*. London: Christophers, 1952.

Cohen, Stephen P., Herbert C. Kelman, Frederick D. Miller, and Bruce L. Smith. "Evolving Intergroup Techniques for Conflict Resolution: An Israeli-Palestinian Pilot Workshop." *Journal of Social Issues* 33, no 1 (winter 1977): 165-189.

Coleman, Peter T. "Intractable Conflict." Pp. 428-450 in *The Handbook of Conflict Resolution: Theory and Practice*, edited by Morton Deutsch and Peter T. Coleman. San Francisco, CA: Jossey-Bass, 2000.

Coser, Lewis A. *The Functions of Social Conflict*. New York: The Free Press, 1956.

Crocker, Chester A., Fen O. Hampson, and Pamela Aall, eds. *Herding Cats: Multiparty Mediation in a Complex World*. Washington, DC: United States Institute of Peace, 1999.

"The Dakar Get-Together." *African Communist,* (September 1987): 9-11.

Davies, John, and Edward (Edy) Kaufman, eds. *Second Track/Citizens' Diplomacy: Concepts and Techniques for Conflict Transformation*. Lanham, MD: Rowman and Littlefield, 2002.

Dawisha, Adeed I. *Syria and the Lebanese Crisis*. New York, NY: St. Martin's Press, 1980.

De Bar, L. H. *Les Communautes Confessionelles du Liban*. Paris, France: Editions Recherches sur les Civilisations, 1983.

De Klerk, Willem. November 1994. Interview by Patti Waldmeir. Unpublished typescripts at the library archives, University of Cape Town.

———. July 1998. Interview by Daniel Lieberfeld, Johannesburg.

De Reuck, Anthony. "A Note on Techniques and Procedures." London: CIBA Foundation, Mimeo, May 1966.

De Villiers, Fleur. July 2002. Telephone Interview by Daniel Lieberfeld.

Diamond, Louise, and Ronald J. Fisher. "Integrating Conflict Resolution Training and Consultation: A Cyprus Example." *Negotiation Journal* 11, no. 3 (July 1995): 287-301.

Edis, Richard. "Mozambique's Successful Peace Process—An Insider's View." *Cambridge Review of International Affairs* 9, no. 2 (1995).

Egero, Bertil. *Mozambique: A Dream Undone. The Political Economy of Democracy 1975-84*. Uppsala, Sweden: Scandinavian Institute of African Studies, 1987.

Emery, Fred E. "The Rationalisation of Conflict: A Case Study." London: Tavistock Institute, Mimeo, June 1966.

Esterhuyse, Willie. November 1994. Interview by Patti Waldmeir. Unpublished typescripts at the library archives, University of Cape Town.

———. June 1998. Interview by Daniel Lieberfeld, Cape Town.

Faure, Andrew M. "Some Methodological Problems in Comparative Politics." *Journal of Theoretical Politics* 6, no. 3 (1994): 307-322.

Finnegan, William. *A Complicated War: The Harrowing of Mozambique*. Berkeley: University of California Press, 1992.

Fisher, Ronald J. "Third Party Consultation: A Method for the Study and Resolution of Conflict." *Journal of Conflict Resolution* 16, no. 1 (March 1972): 67-94.

———. "Third Party Consultation: A Skill for Professional Psychologists in Community Practice." *Professional Psychology* 7 (August, 1976): 344-351.

———. "Third Party Consultation as a Method of Intergroup Conflict Resolution: A Review of Studies." *Journal of Conflict Resolution* 27, no. 2 (June 1983): 301-334.

———. "Prenegotiation Problem-Solving Discussions: Enhancing the Potential for Successful Negotiation." Pp. 206-238 in *Getting to the Table: The Process of International Prenegotiation*, edited by Janice Gross Stein. Baltimore, MD: Johns Hopkins University Press, 1989.

———. *Interactive Conflict Resolution*. Syracuse, NY: Syracuse University Press, 1997a.

———, ed. "Conflict Resolution Training in Divided Societies." *International Negotiation* 2, no. 3 (December 1997b): 331-486.

———. "Intergroup Conflict." Pp. 166-184 in *The Handbook of Conflict Resolution: Theory and Practice*, edited by Morton Deutsch and Peter T. Coleman. San Francisco, CA: Jossey-Bass, 2000.

Fisher, Ronald J., and Loraleigh Keashly. "Third Party Consultation as a Method of Intergroup and International Conflict Resolution." Pp. 211-238 in *The Social Psychology of Intergroup and International Conflict Resolution*, edited by Ronald J. Fisher. New York: Springer-Verlag, 1990.

Flower, Ken. *Serving Secretly: Rhodesia into Zimbabwe 1964-81*. London: John Murray, 1987.

Geffray, Christian. *Le Cause des Armes au Mozambique: Anthropologie d'une Guerre Civile*. Paris: Editions Karthala, Paris, 1990.

"The Geneva Accord." *Tikkun* 19, no. 1 (January/February 2004): 34-45.

George, Alexander L. "Case Studies and Theory Development: The Method of Structured, Focused Comparison." Pp. 43-68 in *Diplomacy: New Approaches in History, Theory, and Policy*, edited by Paul G. Lauren. New York: The Free Press, 1979.

Gerner, Deborah J. *One Land, Two Peoples: The Conflict over Palestine*. Boulder, CO: Westview Press, 1991.

Gersony, Robert. *"Summary of Mozambican Refugee Accounts of Principally Conflict-Related Experience in Mozambique."* Report submitted to Ambassador Moore and Dr. Chester A. Crocker c/o Bureau for Refugee Programs, US Department of State, 1988.

Ginwala, Frene. September 1994. Interview by Daniel Lieberfeld, Cape Town.

Goryayev, Vladimir. "Architecture of International Involvement in the Tajik Peace Process," in *Accord: Politics of Compromise: The Tajikistan Peace Process*, edited by Kamoludin Abdullaev and Catherine Barnes. London, UK: Conciliation Resources, 2001.

Haley, Peter E., and Lewis W. Snider. *Lebanon in Crisis: Participants and Issues*. Syracuse, NY: Syracuse University Press, 1979.

Hall, Michael. *Conflict Resolution: The Missing Element in the Northern Ireland Peace Process*. Belfast: Island Pamphlets, 1999.

Halpern, Ben. *The Idea of a Jewish State* (2nd ed.). Cambridge, MA: Harvard University Press, 1969.

Harkabi, Yehoshafat. *Israel's Fateful Hour*. New York: Harper and Row, 1988.

Harvey, Robert. *The Fall of Apartheid: The Inside Story from Smuts to Mbeki*. London: Palgrave, 2001.

Henrikson, Thomas. *Revolution and Counter-Revolution: Mozambique's War of Inde-*

pendence 1964-74. Connecticut: Greenwood Press, 1983.

Hertzberg, Arthur. *The Zionist Idea*. New York: Atheneum, 1975.

Hill, William. "Moldova: Are the Russian Troops Really Leaving?" Speaking to the Commission on Security and Cooperation in Europe's CSCE Hearing, Washington, DC: Government Printing Office, 2001.

Hoile, David, ed. *Mozambique 1962-1993: A Political Chronology*. London: The Mozambique Institute, 1994.

Human Rights Watch. *Conspicuous Destruction: War, Famine and the Reform Process in Mozambique*. New York: Human Rights Watch, 1992.

Hume, Cameron. *Ending Mozambique's War: The Role of Mediation and Good Offices*. Washington, DC: United States Institute of Peace, 1994.

International Crisis Group. "Central Asia: Fault Lines on the New Security Map." *ICG Report*, no. 20, Brussels, 4 July 2001.

———. "Central Asia: Border Disputes and Conflict Potential." *ICG Report*, no. 33, Brussels, 4 April 2002.

———. "Moldova: No Quick Fix." *ICG Report*, no. 147, Brussels, 12 August 2003.

International Monetary Fund. "Republic of Mozambique: Poverty Reduction Strategy Paper Progress Report." Review of the Economic and Social Plan for 2003, 18 May 2004.

Irani, George E. *The Papacy and the Middle East: The Role of the Holy See in the Arab-Israeli Conflict, 1962-1984*. Notre Dame, IN: University of Notre Dame Press, 1989.

Johnston, Douglas, and Cynthia Sampson, eds. *Religion: The Missing Dimension of Statecraft*. New York and Oxford: Oxford University Press, 1994.

Joint Working Group on Israeli-Palestinian Relations. "General Principles for the Final Israeli-Palestinian Agreement." PICAR Working Paper, Cambridge, MA: Program on International Conflict Analysis and Resolution, Weatherhead Center for International Affairs, Harvard University, 1998. (Reprinted in *The Middle East Journal* 53, no. 1[February 1999]: 170-175).

———. "The Future Israeli-Palestinian Relationship." Weatherhead Center for International Affairs Working Paper No. 99-12. Cambridge, MA: Harvard University, 1999. (Reprinted in *Middle East Policy* 7, no. 2 [February 2000]: 90-112).

Kapeliouk, Amnon. *Sabra et Chatila: Enquete sur un Massacre*. Paris: Editions du Seuil, 1982.

Keashly, Loraleigh, and Ronald J. Fisher. "A Contingency Perspective on Conflict Interventions: Theoretical and Practical Considerations." Pp. 235-261 in *Resolving International Conflicts: The Theory and Practice of Mediation*, edited by Jacob Bercovitch. London: Lynne Rienner, 1996.

Keesings Contemporary Archives. 1964: 20182.

Kelman, Herbert C. "The Problem-Solving Workshop in Conflict Resolution." Pp. 168-204 in *Communication in International Politics*, edited by Robert L. Merritt. Urbana: University of Illinois Press, 1972.

———. "Israelis and Palestinians: Psychological Prerequisites for Mutual Acceptance." *International Security* 3, no. 1 (summer 1978): 162-186.

———. "An Interactional Approach to Conflict Resolution and Its Application to Israeli-Palestinian Relations." *International Interactions* 6, no. 2 (October 1979): 99-122.

———. "Creating the Conditions for Israeli-Palestinian Negotiations." *Journal of Conflict Resolution* 26, no. 1 (March 1982): 39-75.

———. "Talk with Arafat." *Foreign Policy*, no. 49 (winter 1982-83): 119-139.

———. "Interactive Problem-Solving: A Social-Psychological Approach to Conflict Resolution." Pp. 293-314 in *Dialogue toward Inter-Faith Understanding*, edited by William Klassen. Tantur/Jerusalem: Ecumenical Institute for Theological Research, 1986.

———. "The Political Psychology of the Israeli-Palestinian Conflict: How Can We Overcome the Barriers to a Negotiated Solution?" *Political Psychology* 8, no. 3 (September 1987): 347-363.

———. "The Palestinianization of the Arab-Israeli Conflict." *The Jerusalem Quarterly*, no. 46 (spring 1988): 3-15.

———. "Informal Mediation by the Scholar/Practitioner." Pp. 64-96 in *Mediation in International Relations: Multiple Approaches to Conflict Management*, edited by Jacob Bercovitch and Jeffrey Z. Rubin. New York: St. Martin's Press, 1992a.

———. "Acknowledging the Other's Nationhood: How to Create a Momentum for the Israeli-Palestinian Negotiations." *Journal of Palestine Studies* 22, no. 1 (autumn 1992b): 18-38.

———. "Coalitions across Conflict Lines: The Interplay of Conflicts within and between the Israeli and Palestinian Communities." Pp. 236-258 in *Conflict between People and Groups*, edited by Stephen Worchel and Jeffrey A. Simpson. Chicago: Nelson-Hall, 1993.

———. "Contributions of an Unofficial Conflict Resolution Effort to the Israeli-Palestinian Breakthrough." *Negotiation Journal* 11, no. 1 (January 1995): 19-27.

———. "The Contributions of Non-Governmental Organizations to the Resolution of Ethnonational Conflicts: An Approach to Evaluation." Paper presented at the Carnegie Corporation Conference on the Role of International NGOs in Ethnic and Nationalist Conflicts, New York, 15-16 November 1996a.

———. "Negotiation as Interactive Problem Solving," *International Negotiation* 1, no. 1. (1996b): 99-123.

———. "Social-Psychological Dimensions of International Conflict." Pp. 191-237 in *Peacemaking in International Conflict: Methods and Techniques*, edited by I. William Zartman and J. Lewis Rasmussen. Washington, DC: U.S. Institute of Peace Press, 1997a.

———. "Some Determinants of the Oslo Breakthrough." *International Negotiation* 2, no. 2 (1997b): 183-194.

———. "Social-Psychological Contributions to Peacemaking and Peacebuilding in the Middle East." *Applied Psychology: An International Review* 47, no. 1 (January 1998a): 5-28.

———. "Interactive Problem Solving: An Approach to Conflict Resolution and Its Application in the Middle East." *PS: Political Science and Politics* 31 (June 1998b): 190-198.

———. "Building a Sustainable Peace: The Limits of Pragmatism in the Israeli-Palestinian Negotiations." *Journal of Palestine Studies* 28, no. 1 (autumn 1998c): 36-50.

———. "Transforming the Relationship between Former Enemies: A Social-Psychological Analysis." Pp. 193-205 in *After the Peace: Resistance and Reconciliation*, edited by Robert L. Rothstein. Boulder, CO, and London: Lynne Rienner, 1999.

———. "Transcending the Balance of Power." *Middle East Insight* 15, no. 2 (March-April 2000): 51-53.

―――. "The Role of National Identity in Conflict Resolution: Experiences from Israeli-Palestinian Problem-Solving Workshops." Pp. 187-212 in *Social Identity, Intergroup Conflict, and Conflict Reduction*, edited by Richard D. Ashmore, Lee Jussim, and David Wilder. Oxford and New York: Oxford University Press, 2001.

―――. "Interactive Problem Solving: Informal Mediation by the Scholar-Practitioner." Pp. 167-193 in *Studies in International Mediation: Essays in Honor of Jeffrey Z. Rubin*, edited by Jacob Bercovitch. New York: Palgrave MacMillan, 2003.

Kelman, Herbert C., and Stephen P. Cohen. "The Problem-Solving Workshop: A Social-Psychological Contribution to the Resolution of International Conflict." *Journal of Peace Research* 8, no. 2 (1976): 79-90.

―――. "Resolution of International Conflict: An Interactional Approach." Pp. 323-342 in *Psychology of Intergroup Relations*, edited by Stephen Worchel and William G. Austin. Chicago, IL: Nelson-Hall, 1986.

Khalidi, Rashid. *Palestinian Identity: The Construction of a Modern National Consciousness*. New York: Columbia University Press, 1997.

Khalidi, Walid. "Thinking the Unthinkable: A Sovereign Palestinian State." *Foreign Affairs* 56, no. 4 (July 1978): 695-713.

―――. *Conflict and Violence in Lebanon: Confrontation in the Middle East*. Cambridge, MA: Harvard Center for International Affairs, 1979.

Khuwayri, Antoine. *Mawsuat al-Harb fi Lubnan, 1975-1981*. (The Encyclopedia of the War in Lebanon, 1975-1981). 12 volumes, 1975-1981.

King, Charles. "The Benefits of Ethnic War—Understanding Eurasia's Unrecognized States." *World Politics* 53, no. 4, (July 2001): 524-552.

Kriesberg, Louis. *Constructive Conflicts: From Escalation to Resolution* (2nd ed.). Lanham, MD: Rowman and Littlefield, 2003.

Kuzio, Taras. "Is Federalization the Right Option for Moldova?" RFE/RL *Newsline* 7, no. 45, Part II, 10 March 2003.

Lewicki, Roy J., Barbara Gray, and Michael Elliott, eds. *Making Sense of Intractable Environmental Conflicts: Frames and Cases*. Washington, DC: Island Press, 2003.

Lewin, Kurt. *Resolving Social Conflicts*. New York: Harper and Row, 1950.

Lieberfeld, Daniel. *Talking with the Enemy: Negotiation and Threat Perception in South Africa and Israel/Palestine*. Westport, CT: Praeger, 1999a.

―――. "Conflict 'Ripeness' Revisited: The South African and Israeli/Palestinian Cases," *Negotiation Journal* 15, no. 3 (July 1999b): 201-207.

―――. "Evaluating the Contributions of Unofficial Diplomacy to Conflict Termination in South Africa, 1984-1990," *Journal of Peace Research* 39, no. 3 (May 2002): 355-372.

Liphart, Arend. "Comparative Politics and the Comparative Method." *American Political Science Review* 65, no. 3 (September 1971): 682-693.

―――. "The Comparable Cases Strategy in Comparative Research." *Comparative Political Studies* 8, no. 2 (July 1975): 158-177.

Louw, Mike. May 1995. Interview by Patti Waldmeir. Unpublished typescripts at the library archives, University of Cape Town.

―――. June 1998. Interview by Daniel Lieberfeld, Pretoria.

Magaia, Lina. *Dumba Nengue: Run For Your Life. Peasant Tales of Tragedy in Mozambique*. Trenton, NJ: Africa World Press, 1988.

Ma'oz, Moshe. "Missed Opportunities for Peace? The Israeli-Palestinian Case." Presentation at the Middle East Seminar, Harvard University, March 2000.

Mbeki, Thabo, January 1995. Interview by Patti Waldmeir. Unpublished typescripts at the library archives, University of Cape Town.

Mendelsohn, Everett. *A Compassionate Peace: A Future for Israel, Palestine, and the Middle East* (rev. ed.). New York: Farrar, Straus and Giroux, 1989.

Middle East Council of Churches (MECC). "The Lebanese Conflict, 1975-1979: Dossier 2, Beirut." Lebanon: MECC Documentation, 1979.

Minter, William. "The Mozambican National Resistance (RENAMO) as described by Ex-Participants." *Development Dialogue*, no. 1, 1989.

———. *Apartheid's Contras and the Roots of War: An Inquiry in the Modern History of Southern Africa.* London: Zed Books, 1994.

Mitchell, Christopher R. *Peacemaking and the Consultant's Role.* Westmead, UK: Gower, 1981.

Mitchell, Christopher, and Michael Banks. *Handbook of Conflict Resolution: The Analytical Problem-Solving Approach.* New York and London: Pinter, 1996.

Morozzo della Rocca, Roberto. *Mozambico: Una Pace per l'Africa.* Milan: Leonardo International, 2003.

Msabaha, Ibrahim. "Negotiating an End to Mozambique's Murderous Rebellion." Pp. 204-230 in *Elusive Peace: Negotiating an End to Civil Wars,* edited by I. William Zartman. Washington, DC: The Brookings Institute, 1995.

Mukomel, Vladimir. "Voruzhonie Mezhnatsional'nie I regional'nie konflikti: ludskie poteri, ekonomicheskii usherb, I sotsial'nie posledstviia." In *Identichnost i Konflikt v Postsovietskih Gosudasrtvah.* Moscow: Carnegie Endowment for International Peace, 1997.

Muslih, Muhammad Y. *The Origins of Palestinian Nationalism.* New York: Columbia University Press, 1988.

Nan, Susan Allen. *Coordination and Complementarity of Multiple Conflict Resolution Efforts in the Conflicts over Abkhazia, South Ossetia, and Transdniestria.* Unpublished Dissertation. George Mason University. Fairfax, VA, 1999.

———. "Partnering for Peace: Conflict Management Group and the Norwegian Refugee Council Collaborating on the Georgia-South Ossetia Dialogue Process." Reflecting on Peace Practices Project, Collaborative for Development Action, 2000. *Confidential Case Study.*

———. "Intervention Coordination." Module of the Intractable Conflicts Knowledge Base. 2003. http://www.beyondintractability.org/m/intervention_coordination.jsp (22 May 2004).

———. "Track One and a Half Diplomacy: Searching for Political Agreement in the Caucasus." Pp. 57-75 in *NGOs at the Table: Strategies for Influencing Policies in Areas of Conflict,* edited by Mari Fitzduff and Cheyanne Church. Lanham, MD: Rowman and Littlefield, 2004.

Nan, Susan Allen, and Andrea Strimling. "Track One-Track Two Cooperation." Module of the Intractable Conflicts Knowledge Base. 2004. http://www.beyondintractability.org/m/track_1_2_cooperation.jsp. (4 June 2004).

Newitt, Malyn. *A History of Mozambique.* London: Hurst and Co., 1995.

Nordstrom, Carolyn. *A Different Kind of War Story.* Philadelphia: University of Pennsylvania Press, 1997.

Oppenheim, Abraham N. "Comments on Indonesia/Malaysia Meeting." London: London School of Economics, Mimeo, January 1966.

Ott, Marvin C. "Mediation as a Method of Conflict Resolution: Two Cases." *International Organisation* 26, no. 4 (autumn 1972): 575-618.

Pahad, Aziz. November 1994. Interview by Patti Waldmeir. Unpublished typescripts at the library archives, University of Cape Town.

———. Interview by Rupert Taylor. Unpublished typescript provided by Rupert Taylor, February 2000.

Pearson d'Estree, Tamra, Larissa A. Fast, Joshua N. Weiss, and Monica S. Jakobsen. "Changing the Debate about Success in Conflict Resolution Efforts." *Negotiation Journal* 17, no. 2 (April 2001): 101-113.

Picard, Elizabeth. "Role et evolution du Front Libanais dans la guerre civile." *Maghreb-Machrek,* 90 (Oct.-Dec. 1980): 16-39.

Pillar, Paul. "Ending Limited War: The Psychological Dynamics of the Termination Process," Pp. 252-263 in *Psychological Dimensions of War,* edited by Betty Glad. Newbury Park, CA: Sage, 1990.

Pruitt, Dean G. "Ripeness Theory and the Oslo Talks." *International Negotiation* 2, no. 2 (1997): 237-250.

———. "Mediator Behavior and Success in Mediation." Pp. 41-54 in *Studies in International Mediation: Essays in Honor of Jeffrey Z. Rubin,* edited by Jacob Bercovitch. New York: Palgrave Macmillan, 2002.

Rabbath, Edmond. *La formation historique du Liban politique et constitutionnel: Essai de synthese.* Beirut, Lebanon: Publications de l'Universite Libanaise, Librairie Orientale, 1973.

Riccardi, Andrea. *Il potere del papa.* Roma-Bari: Laterza, 1990.

———. *Sant'Egidio, Rome and the World.* London: St. Paulus, 1999.

Rothman, Jay. *Resolving Identity-Based Conflict in Nations, Organizations, and Communities.* San Francisco, CA: Jossey-Bass, 1997.

Rouhana, Nadim N. "Interactive Conflict Resolution: Issues in Theory, Methodology, and Evaluation." Pp. 294-337 in *International Conflict Resolution after the Cold War,* edited by Paul C. Stern and Daniel Druckman. Washington, DC: National Academy Press, 2000.

Rouhana, Nadim N., and Herbert C. Kelman. "Promoting Joint Thinking in International Conflict: An Israeli-Palestinian Continuing Workshop." *Journal of Social Issues* 50, no. 1 (spring 1994): 157-178.

Sarid, Yossi, and Walid Khalidi. "A Meeting of Minds on Middle East Peace" (adjoining op-ed articles). *New York Times,* 9 March 1984, p. A29.

Saunders, Harold H. "The Multilevel Peace Process in Tajikistan." Pp. 161-179 in *Herding Cats: Multiparty Mediation in a Complex World,* edited by Chester A. Crocker, Fen Osler Hampson, and Pamela Aall. Washington, DC: United States Institute of Peace Press, 1999a.

———. *A Public Peace Process: Sustained Dialogue to Transform Racial and Ethnic Conflicts.* New York: St. Martin's Press, 1999b.

———. "Prenegotiation and Circumnegotiation: Arenas of the Peace Process." Pp. 483-496 in *Turbulent Peace: The Challenges of Managing International Conflict,* edited by Chester A. Crocker, Fen O. Hampson, and Pamela Aall. Washington, DC: United States Institute of Peace, 2001.

Schiff, Zev, and Ehud Ya'ari. *Israel's Lebanon War.* New York, NY: Simon and Schuster, 1984.

Sengulane, Denis. *Vitória Sem Vencidos: A História do Processo de Paz para Mocambique do Ponto de Vista do Conselho Cristão de Mocambique.* Maputo: Bispo das Libombos, 1994.

Snider, Lewis W. "The Lebanese Forces: Wartime Origins and Political Significance." Pp. 117-161 in *The Emergence of a New Lebanon: Fantasy or Reality?*, edited by Edward E. Azar, et al. New York: Praeger, 1984.

Sparks, Allister. *Tomorrow Is Another Country.* New York: Hill and Wang, 1995.

Stedman, Stephen J., Donald Rothchild, and Elizabeth M. Cousens, eds. *Ending Civil Wars: The Implementation of Peace Agreements.* Boulder: Lynne Rienner, 2002.

Suleiman, Michael W. *Political Parties in Lebanon: The Challenge of a Fragmented Political Culture.* Ithaca, NY: Cornell University Press, 1967.

Synge, Richard. *"Mozambique: UN Peacekeeping in Action."* Washington, DC: United States Institute of Peace, 1997.

Tessler, Mark. *A History of the Israeli-Palestinian Conflict.* Bloomington and Indianapolis: Indiana University Press, 1994.

Touval, Saadia, and I. William Zartman. "Mediation in International Conflicts." Pp. 115-137 in *Mediation Research: The Process and Effectiveness of Third-Party Intervention,* edited by Kenneth Kressel and Dean Pruitt. San Francisco, CA: Jossey-Bass, 1989.

Ury, William. *The Third Side.* New York: Penguin Books, 2000.

Venâncio, Moisés. "Mediation by the Roman Catholic Church in Mozambique 1988-91." in *Mediation in Southern Africa,* edited by Stephen Chan and Vivienne Jabri. London: Macmillan, 1993.

Viljoen, Gerrit. October 1994. Interview by Daniel Lieberfeld, Pretoria.

Williams, Andrew. "The Centre for Conflict Analysis and Facilitation Workshops in the Context of the Moldovan Conflict, 1993-2002: Some Thoughts and Conclusions." Paper presented at a conference on Conducting Dialogues for Peace, United States Institute of Peace, Washington, DC, November, 2002.

Williams, Andrew. "States, Borders and the Idea of the 'Common State': The Case of Moldova, 1992-2002." *International Relations,* in press.

Young, Michael. October 2002. Interview by Daniel Lieberfeld, New York.

Zartman, I. William. *Ripe for Resolution: Conflict and Intervention in Africa.* New York: Oxford University Press, 1985.

———. "Prenegotiation: Phases and Functions." Pp. 1-17 in *Getting to the Table: The Processes of International Prenegotiation,* edited by Janice G. Stein. Baltimore: Johns Hopkins University Press, 1989.

———. "Explaining Oslo." *International Negotiation* 2, no. 2 (1997): 195-215.

———. "Ripeness: The Hurting Stalemate and Beyond." Pp. 225-250 in *International Conflict Resolution after the Cold War,* edited by Paul C. Stern and Daniel Druckman. Washington, DC: National Academies Press, 2000.

Zhibian, Sami. *Al-Haraka al-Wataniyya al-Lubnaniyya* (The Lebanese National Movement). Beirut, Lebanon: Dar al-Masirat, 1977.

Zook, David H. Jr. *Zarumilla-Marañon: The Ecuador-Peru Dispute.* New York: Bookman Associates, 1964.

Index

241

About the Contributors

Andrea Bartoli is Senior Research Scholar at the School of International and Public Affairs, Columbia University, where he is also the Founding Director of the Center for International Conflict Resolution and the Chair of the Columbia University Conflict Resolution Network. He has been engaged in conflict prevention and resolution work both academically and through the Community of Sant'Egidio, of which he has been a member since 1970. Through the Community, he participated in the peace processes in Mozambique, Algeria, Guatemala, Kosovo, and Burundi, and through his academic work has been involved in Burma, Iraq, Colombia and Timor Leste. His primary interest focuses on the emergence of peace and its sustainability, through both preventive and systemic approaches. Dr. Bartoli's publications include *Somalia, Rwanda and Beyond* (ed., 1994), "Mediating Peace in Mozambique: The Role of the Community of Sant'Egidio" in *Herding Cats: Multiparty Mediation in a Complex World* (C.A. Crocker, F.O. Hampson and P. Aall, eds., 1999), and "Christianity and Peacebuilding" in *Religion and Peacebuilding* (H. Coward and G. Smith, eds., 2004). He holds a *laurea* from the Universita` degli Studi di Roma and a *dottorato di ricerca* from the Universita` degli Studi di Milano.

Ronald J. Fisher is Professor of International Peace and Conflict Resolution in the School of International Service at American University in Washington, DC, and was previously the Founding Coordinator of the Applied Social Psychology Graduate Program at the University of Saskatchewan, Saskatoon, Canada. His primary interest focuses on interactive conflict resolution, which involves informal third party interventions in protracted and violent ethnopolitical conflict. Dr. Fisher's publications include *Social Psychology: An Applied Approach* (1982), *The Social Psychology of Intergroup and International Conflict Resolution* (1990), *Interactive Conflict Resolution* (1997), and numerous articles in interdisciplinary journals in the field of peace and conflict resolution. In 2003, Dr. Fisher received the Morton Deutsch Conflict Resolution Award from the Society for the Study of Peace, Conflict and Violence, which is a Division of the American Psychological Association. He holds a B.A. (Hon.) and an M.A. in psychology from the University of Saskatchewan and a Ph.D. in social psychology from the University of Michigan.

George Emile Irani is Professor in the Peace and Conflict Studies Division at Royal Roads University in Victoria, Canada. Prior to that, he was senior policy analyst with the U.S. Commission on International Religious Freedom. In 1997-1998, Dr. Irani was Jennings Randolph Senior Fellow at the United States Institute of Peace (USIP) where he conducted research on rituals as methods of conflict control and reduction in the Middle East. Between 1993 and 1997, Irani was an Assistant Professor in political science at the Lebanese American University in Beirut. Dr. Irani is the author of *The Papacy and the Middle East: The Role of the Holy See in the Arab-Israeli Conflict* (1989), which has been translated into French, Italian, Arabic, and Portuguese. Together with his wife, Dr. Laurie King-Irani, he co-edited *Acknowledgment, Forgiveness and Reconciliation: Lessons from Lebanon* (1996), and with Vamik Volkan and Judy Carter, he is currently completing a *Workbook on Ethnopolitical Conflicts*. He holds a *laurea* in political science from the Universita Cattolica del Sacro Cuore (Milano, Italy) and an M.A. and Ph.D. in international relations from the University of Southern California

Edward (Edy) Kaufman has served as the Executive Director of the Harry S. Truman Research Institute for the Advancement of Peace at the Hebrew University of Jerusalem since 1983. He is also Senior Research Associate at the Center for International Development and Conflict Management at the University of Maryland, and was Director from 1994 to 1996. Dr. Kaufman has concentrated on applied research and the teaching and training of conflict resolution and human rights in Israel and worldwide. At the global level, he has served as a member of the International Executive Committee of Amnesty International and the Advisory Board of Human Rights Watch/Middle East. His current research and advocacy interests are in merging the paradigms of human rights and conflict resolution. He has authored and co-authored eleven books (the latest co-edited with John Davies is *Second Track/Citizen Diplomacy: Concepts and Techniques of Conflict Transformation*) and more than sixty academic articles in the general area of international relations, with an emphasis on human rights and conflict resolution and a regional specialization on Latin America and the Middle East. Dr. Kaufman holds B.A. and M.A. degrees in political science, international relations and sociology from the Hebrew University of Jerusalem, a doctorate from the University of Paris (Sorbonne), and conducted post-doctoral studies at the Univerisity of Michigan.

Herbert C. Kelman is the Richard Clarke Cabot Professor of Social Ethics, Emeritus at Harvard University and was (from 1993 to 2003) Director of the Program on International Conflict Analysis and Resolution at the Weatherhead Center for International Affairs. He is past president of the International Studies Association, the International Society of Political Psychology, the Interamerican

Society of Psychology, and several other professional associations. He has been engaged for many years in the development of interactive problem solving, an unofficial third party approach to the resolution of international and intercommunal conflicts, and in its application to the Arab-Israeli conflict, with special emphasis on its Israeli-Palestinian component. His major publications include *International Behavior: A Social-Psychological Analysis* (ed., 1965), *A Time to Speak: On Human Values and Social Research* (1968), and *Crimes of Obedience: Toward a Social Psychology of Authority and Responsibility* (with V. Lee Hamilton, 1989). He is a recipient of many awards, including the Socio-Psychological Prize of the American Association for the Advancement of Science (1956), the Kurt Lewin Memorial award (1973), the American Psychological Association's Award for Distinguished Contributions to Psychology in the Public Interest (1981), the Grawemeyer Award for Ideas Improving World Order (1997), and the Austrian Medal of Honor for Science and Art First Class (1998). He received his Ph.D. in social psychology from Yale University in 1951.

Daniel Lieberfeld is Assistant Professor in the Peace Studies and Conflict Resolution Program at Duquesne University's Graduate Center for Social and Public Policy. His research interests concern the question of why adversaries in protracted conflicts decide to initiate negotiation. Dr. Lieberfeld's publications include *Talking With the Enemy: Negotiation and Threat Perception in South Africa and Israel/Palestine* (1999) and articles on South African politics and society in journals including *The Journal of Peace Research, Negotiation Journal, Politikon: South African Journal of Political Studies, Peace Review,* and *The Drama Review.* His research on South Africa was funded by the United States Institute of Peace and Harvard Law School's Program on Negotiation. He holds an M.A.L.D. and a Ph.D. in international relations from the Fletcher School of Law and Diplomacy at Tufts University.

Christopher Mitchell is the Drucie French Cumbie Professor of Conflict Analysis and Resolution in the Institute for Conflict Analysis and Resolution at George Mason University, where he has been on faculty since 1988, serving as Director from 1991 to 1994. He has held research and teaching appointments at the Centre for the Analysis of Conflict, University College, London, the London School of Economics, the Universities of Surrey and Southampton, and City University, London, where he became Professor of International Relations in 1985. His main interests include international mediation and peacemaking processes, particularly the practical development of problem-solving approaches to protracted conflicts, the causes, dynamics and resolution of major ethno-nationalist conflicts, especially those that become internationalized, and the termination of protracted conflicts, with particular reference to those in Africa and Latin America. As a consultant and facilitator he has worked on conflicts in Northern Ireland, Spain, Cyprus,

Columbia, the Middle East and Africa. Dr. Mitchell's publications include *The Structure of International Conflict* (1981), *Peacemaking and the Consultant's Role* (1981), *Handbook of Conflict Resolution: The Analytical Problem-Solving Approach* (with M. Banks, 1996), and *Gestures of Conciliation* (2000). He also edited *International Relations Theory* (with A.J.R. Groom, 1978), *In the Aftermath: Anglo Argentine Relations Since 1982* (with W. Little, 1988), and *New Approaches to International Mediation* (with K. Webb, 1988). He received his undergraduate and post-graduate education at University College, London and his Ph.D. from the University of London in 1972.

Susan Allen Nan is an Assistant Professor in the School of International Service at American University in Washington, DC, where she teaches primarily in the International Peace and Conflict Resolution Division. Previously, Dr. Nan served as Director of the Alliance for Conflict Transformation in Fairfax, Virginia, and as Senior Program Associate for Conflict Resolution at The Carter Center in Atlanta, Georgia. Her primary interests focus on the complementarity and coordination of multiple conflict resolution efforts, particularly involving the interaction of official (track one) and unofficial (track two) approaches. Dr. Nan has published journal articles in *Peace Review, Peace and Change, Group Decision and Negotiation,* and *Accord,* and chapters in several edited collections on conflict resolution. She holds a B.A. (distinction) in political and social thought from the University of Virginia, and an M.S. and a Ph.D. in conflict analysis and resolution from George Mason University.

Harold H. Saunders is Director of International Affairs at the Kettering Foundation and President of the International Institute for Sustained Dialogue. He is a former staff member of the National Security Council and Assistant Secretary of State for Near Eastern and South Asian Affairs. Following the Arab-Israeli war in 1973 he flew on the Kissinger shuttles and in 1978-1979 he worked with President Carter in drafting the Camp David accords and the peace treaty between Israel and Egypt. In his current position, Dr. Saunders helps establish and conduct sustained dialogues in deep-rooted conflict in the United States and abroad. His publications include *The Other Walls: The Politics of the Arab-Israeli Peace Process* (1985), *American Hostages in Iran: The Conduct of a Crisis* (1985), and *A Public Peace Process: Sustained Dialogue to Transform Racial and Ethnic Conflicts* (1999). Dr. Saunders is a recipient of the President's Award for Distinguished Federal Civilian Service and the State Department's Distinguished Honor Award. He holds an A.B. from Princeton University and a Ph.D. from Yale University.

Saúl Sosnowski is Professor of Latin American Literature and Culture, Founding Director of the Latin American Studies Center, and Director of International

Programs at the University of Maryland. In 1995 he launched the project "A Culture for Democracy in Latin America," and he has also coordinated "New Leadership for a Democratic Society," a project he started in Buenos Aires in 2000. His main interests have centered on issues of civil education, democracy and conflict management with a focus on Latin America. Dr. Sosnowski's publications include *Una cultura para la democracia en América Latina* (ed. with R. Patiño, 1999), *Economía de la cultura: Mecenazgo* (1999), and three volumes that resulted from the joint University of Maryland-Ministerio da Cultura, Brazil project, "A Culture for Democracy in Brazil", *Cultura e Democracia* (2001-2002, ed. with J. A. Moisés). Dr. Sosnowski is the founder and Director of the journal *Hispamérica*, author of numerous chapters and journal articles, and serves on the editorial boards of five scholarly journals. He holds a Ph.D. in Latin American Literature from the University of Virginia.

Andrew Williams is Professor of International Relations at the University of Kent at Canterbury, United Kingdom. His main research interests include international conflict resolution, international history, and international organization. Dr. Williams' publications include *Failed Imagination? New World Orders of the Twentieth Century* (1998) and *Liberalism and War: The Victors and the Vanquished* (forthcoming). He has published a variety of journal articles in his fields of interest, including "Reconstruction Before the Marshall Plan" in the *Review of International Studies* (2005), "States, Borders and Conflicts in Europe: The Case of Moldova, 1992-2002" in *International Relations* (2004), and "Sir John Bradbury and the Reparations Commission, 1920-1925" in *Diplomacy and Statecraft* (2002). He holds degrees from the University of Keele and the University of Geneva.